Debrett's
Correct Form

HER MAJESTY THE QUEEN

Debrett's Correct Form

Compiled and Edited by

PATRICK MONTAGUE-SMITH

Editor of Debrett

Published by

KELLY'S DIRECTORIES
NEVILLE HOUSE, EDEN STREET
KINGSTON UPON THAMES, SURREY

PRICE £2. 15. 0 (£2·75)

Printed in England by
Chapel River Press, Andover, Hants.
S.B.N. 610 00165 5

CONTENTS

NOTE

As many varied subjects are covered, and several border upon others, the index should be consulted for the appropriate reference. A few remarks upon certain offices are included, such as the various departments which comprise the Royal Household and their functions; but where information is readily available from other sources it has been omitted.

In many instances forms of address are in a transitional state from elaborate formality to considerable informality. Some have been simplified, such as for clergy of the Church of England, resulting from a diocesan conference held in 1968 under the guidance of the Archbishop of Canterbury. Others, such as those which concern the peerage, have remained virtually unchanged from last century, apart from the simplification of elaborate endings to letters. New forms have either been laid down or adopted when women have been appointed to certain offices for the first time, such as a female High Court Judge and Diocesan Chancellor.

In the main I have given two styles for the written form, and sometimes also for the spoken form, which I have labelled 'formal' and 'social'. The latter is usually adopted when the writer knows his correspondent. Most of the examples given are of fictitious titles and names, but actual instances are shown where they are considered to be appropriate.

In Part V, detailed information will be found concerning invitations and functions, both official and private, including table plans, guest lists, admission cards, place cards, and speeches.

ACKNOWLEDGEMENTS

I am deeply grateful to the following who have given me much help and advice:

Sir Anthony R. Wagner, K.C.V.O., D.Litt., Garter Principal King of Arms

W. J. G. Verco Esq., C.V.O., Chester Herald of Arms

Sir Iain Moncreiffe of that Ilk, Bt., Albany Herald of Arms

Major Francis Jones, C.V.O., T.D., Wales Herald of Arms Extraordinary

Captain Geoffrey Bennett, D.S.C., F.R.Hist.S., R.N., Hon. Secretary, The London Mayors Association

The Reverend Stanley B-R. Poole, M.A.

E. Grey-Turner Esq., M.C., T.D., M.A., M.R.C.S., L.R.C.P., Deputy Secretary, British Medical Association

Church Information Office, The Church of England

The Editors of the Commonwealth Universities Yearbook (published by The Association of Commonwealth Universities)

and many others, including Embassies and Government Departments, who were kind enough to answer my questions.

I also thank Mrs. E. M. Nottage for typing my manuscript.

OCCURRENCE DURING PRINTING

In November 1970 it was announced that women are to be admitted to the Order of the Bath. They will be known as Dame Grand Cross (G.C.B.), Dame Commander (D.C.B.) and Companion (C.B.).

INTRODUCTION

By Sir Iain Moncreiffe of that Ilk
Bt., D.L., Ph.D., F.S.A.

Like most of you, I'm a keen reader of gossip columns. The only thing is, it's hard really to believe the latest rumour about one's friends' private lives when the gossip writer evidently knows them so little as to be unable to get their names right. Anybody who refers to Lady Mary de Vere as 'Lady de Vere' or to Lady Bohun as 'Lady Mary Bohun' can't know much about them really. So all columnists *must* get their bosses to buy this book for them: so that they can add verisimilitude to otherwise bald and unconvincing stories.

New titles are more fun than they would be in an entirely non-hereditary system like that of the American senators, because they equate the new to the old in a continuous flow of history. A new snobbery is being encouraged whereby some peers' eldest sons think themselves so grand that they won't use their courtesy titles (this is a friendly dig at Lord Silchester). It's different when a real function is involved, like the peerages of Sir Alec Douglas-Home or Sir Max Aitken, where they choose to remain free of the Upper House. My late cousin, who shared this house with me, used to call himself normally Lord James Stewart Murray and only be Duke of Atholl when functioning as such, for he said to be Duke of Atholl and live at Easter Moncreiffe would be like being King of Bulgaria and living at Nice.

The world would be a duller place if we lost the Knight of Kerry, the Master of Polwarth, or The McGillycuddy of the Reeks. Last year I was interviewed by successive telephone calls on the American wireless. Questioner after questioner asked,

'What does *Sir* Moncreiffe think about . . . ?' until the studio bell rang and a voice said, 'Mr. Moncreiffe, I do call you *Mr.* don't I?' I thought 'less of that' and caught him out with the reply: 'Well, you could call me Mr. as I'm a Master of Arts, but you can call me *Dr.* if you prefer.' The other side of the coin turned up at a Press Conference in Denmark. An intelligent journalist said, 'I see you are a Doctor of Philosophy. Why do you prefer to be called *Sir* Iain?' The reply then was: 'Because as a baronet I am a living memorial to a greater man than myself, while having earned the doctorate myself I would only be swanking if I pretended it bettered his life-work.' How sad it would be if we had no such living memorials as the Duke of Wellington or Earl Lloyd George, to cite far more historic examples.

The custom of putting letters after people's names has only arisen in comparatively modern times, but has proliferated as our enormous increase of population—and the rewarding of service to the economy and not just service to the State—has led to a great expansion of our Orders of Chivalry and higher honours, together with the multiplication of degrees and appointments. Since these letters are but abbreviations, we can write them as we please. However, custom has evolved certain standard abbreviations, and most people seek guidance about present conventions. Officially, and in business, it's polite to get all that lettering right: for what's the use of earning all those gongs if the poor fellow can't use them?

In this invaluable guide to usage Mr. Patrick Montague-Smith combines a sense of historic names and styles with a helpful understanding of the practical need of courteous people to find a guide to present-day usage through our fascinating Hampton Court maze of precedence, lettering, and modes of address. But it's hardly necessary to introduce the Editor of *Debrett* as an obvious authority on the subjects dealt with in this book.

EASTER MONCREIFFE, PERTHSHIRE
26th October, 1970   IAIN MONCREIFFE OF THAT ILK

GENERAL INSTRUCTIONS

HEADED LETTERS

It is of considerable assistance to correspondents when all letters, except those which are purely social, include the sender's name and appropriate letters at the top, e.g.:

'From Air Marshal Sir John Donne, K.C.B., O.B.E., M.C.'

A reply is often wrongly addressed because the writer has no knowledge of the correct letters, or sometimes the rank. Even when this information can be obtained (such as by access to a reference book), this usually takes a considerable amount of time and trouble.

When the writer is a woman, this practice gives the recipient the advantage of knowing whether she should be styled with a title (e.g. Lady Blank) or, much more often, Mrs. or Miss Blank. One also knows that the correct form of address is Mrs. Henry Johnson, instead of, according to her signature, Mrs. Lillian Johnson or Mrs. L. J. Johnson.

The inclusion of this information on correspondence does not infringe the bounds of modesty; in fact it is thoughtful. As an exception, because it sounds pretentious, 'Esq.' or 'Mr.' may be omitted, e.g. 'From John Brown M.V.O.' The addition of Esq. presents no difficulty to those who reply.

This system has many advantages over typing the name under the signature, which only facilitates deciphering handwriting, because it is not customary to include the letters after the name here, and seldom a title.

BEGINNING A LETTER

The writer has to decide whether to adopt the formal or social form of address. A letter to a complete stranger should be written in the formal style. When a reply is received in the social style, this should normally be followed in further correspondence. The individual beginning is to be found in each section throughout this book. If a very formal style is adopted, 'Sir' or 'Madam' takes the place of 'Dear Sir' or 'Dear Madam'. The very formal styles adopted in ending a letter are given on p. 3.

SOCIAL STYLE

The more friendly style of inserting 'My' before 'Dear ——', may be adopted when warranted, but this is not included in the examples to keep them as simple as possible.

The style 'Dear Jones' is often adopted when male correspondents know each other and they are either both equal in age and importance, or when writing to a younger man in a more junior position.

The American system of including both the christian and surname is growing in Britain. This is frequently adopted as half-way between the use of the surname or the christian name, e.g. 'Dear John Robinson'. Many do not like this form, but others, especially the younger generation, consider it to be useful in the business world, where informality is on the increase.

ENDING A LETTER

The various stereotyped very formal styles of ending letters have now become almost obsolete, except for the following:

1. Letters to The Queen and members of the Royal Family.
2. Official and formal letters to Ambassadors, High Commissioners, Governors, and similar senior officials.
3. Official or formal letters within the Armed Forces.

The following endings of letters are now generally used, but the very formal style which is given in the next section may occasionally be preferred.

FORMAL

(a) I remain (or *I am*),

Your Grace, Most Reverend Sir, Right Reverend Sir, Your Excellency, My Lord, My Lord Mayor, Mr. Mayor, Mr. President, Mr. Chairman, Sir, Madam, etc.

Yours faithfully (*or* Yours truly)

(b) or more simply, Yours faithfully (*or* Yours truly).

It is usually considered that there is a distinction between *faithfully* and *truly* (sometimes *very truly*), but the former is more widely used.

> *Faithfully* is used on a matter of business
> *Truly* (or *very truly*) is used when one does not know the recipient, but the subject is not a matter of business. This is slightly less distant than *yours faithfully*.

SOCIAL

> Yours sincerely (*or* Yours very sincerely),

VERY FORMAL STYLES FOR ENDING A LETTER

Although the following styles are now seldom used, they are included for those who may prefer them.

Even so, they are a simplified version of what was once in vogue, when there was an elaborate scale of '*Most devoted and most obedient*', '*Most obedient*', '*Most humble and devoted*', '*Most humble and obedient*' etc., and other styles with '*Most*' omitted.

When the conclusion '*I have the honour to be*' or '*remain*' is used, the second line of '*My Lord Duke*', '*My Lord*', '*Sir*', or '*Madam*' is frequently omitted.

Dukes and Duchesses

> I have the honour to be (*or* to remain),
>> My Lord Duke (Madam),
>>> Your Grace's obedient servant,

Other Peers, and those with the style of Lord

> I have the honour to be (*or* to remain),
>> My Lord,
>>> Your Lordship's obedient servant,

Other Peeresses and those with the style of Lady

> I have the honour to be (*or* to remain),
>> Madam,
>>> Your Ladyship's obedient servant,

Baronets, Knights and Esquires (including Privy Counsellors and Ministers of the Crown)

> I have the honour to be (*or* to remain),
>> Sir,
>>> Your obedient servant,

Untitled Ladies

> I have the honour to be (*or* to remain),
>   Madam,
>   Your obedient servant,

Archbishops

As for a *Duke,* with the substitution of *Your Grace* or *My Lord Archbishop* in the second line.

Bishops

As for *Other Peers* (above), with the alternative style of *My Lord Bishop* in the second line.

Other Appointments

As for *Baronets, Knights and Esquires* or *Untitled Ladies* (above), with the appropriate appointment in the second line, i.e. Mr. President, Madam President, Mr. Chairman, Madam Chairman, Very Reverend Sir (or Mr. Dean), Reverend Sir, etc.

> *Joint Forms of Address*—see Part V.
> *Christmas Cards*—see Part V.

FORM OF ADDRESS OF MEMBERS OF THE FAMILY BETWEEN THE DEATH
AND FUNERAL OF A PEER OR BARONET

When a peer, peeress in her own right or baronet dies, it is customary for letters written to members of his (or her) family to be addressed by the titles or styles by which they were previously known until after the funeral has taken place.

Consequently a letter of sympathy to the eldest son of the late Lord Rugeley, written before his father's funeral, should be addressed to The Hon. John Rugeley, even though he has succeeded his father as Lord Rugeley.

For this reason, members of the family are described at the funeral as they were previously known, whereas at a memorial service some days later they are referred to by their new titles and styles.

This custom is followed by courtesy even when the successor to the title is only remotely related to the deceased, and the two families may have had little or no contact with each other.

CORRESPONDENCE WITH FIRMS

Whenever possible, correspondence is addressed to an individual member of a firm, either by his, or her name or appointment, such as The Chairman, The Managing Director, The Secretary, or The Manager.

When a firm writes to another firm, 'Gentlemen' sometimes takes the place of the usual 'Dear Sirs'. This form is also occasionally adopted by a private individual when writing to an organization or group.

The term 'Mesdames', the feminine equivalent of 'Sirs', is not normally used in business circles, either in the commencement of the letter or on the envelope. It may be avoided by writing: 'Dear Madam' or 'Dear Mrs. Jones'.

Use of Messrs

The use of the prefix 'Messrs' (a contraction of the French Messieurs), for the plural of 'Mr.', is becoming archaic in Britain, Australia and New Zealand for commercial firms, but is still generally used by the professions, especially the law. It is not generally used in Canada or in the United States.

For those who prefer to use the term 'Messrs', this is restricted to firms with personal names, e.g.

Messrs Berkeley, Stratton & Co.
Messrs Ethelred Smith & Sons
Messrs John & Henry Whitegate

It is never used in the following instances:

(a) Limited Companies
(b) Firms which do not trade under a surname, or the surname does not form the complete name, e.g.

The Devon Mechanical Toy Co.
Anglo-Icelandic Travel Services
John Baker's School of Motoring
The Maurice Wainwright Scholastic Agency.

(c) Firms whose name includes a title, e.g. Sir John Jones & Partners.
(d) Firms which bear a lady's name, e.g. Josephine Taylor & Associates. (See use of 'Mesdames' above.)

MULTIPLE SURNAMES

Usually, but not invariably, those with double-barrelled names use both names for everyday purposes, and those with triple-barrelled names the final name only, e.g. the Douglas-Homes use both names, whereas the Twisleton-Wykeham-Fiennes are often generally known as Fiennes, and the Montagu-Douglas-Scotts as Scott.

There are exceptions, for some with two names often use only the second. One remembers that Sir Winston Churchill did not use 'Spencer', though his surname was Spencer-Churchill, and some Fitzalan-Howards are generally known as Howard. The Earl of Minto's surname is Elliot-Murray-Kynynmound (but not his collaterals); his family is usually known by the first name of Elliot. Others prefer to use all three names, such as some of the Cave-Browne-Caves.

A few families have four or more surnames. Sometimes the final two are used for everyday purposes, e.g. the Hovell-Thurlow-Cumming-Bruce family as 'Cumming-Bruce', and the Stirling Home Drummond Morays as 'Drummond Morays'.

Practice varies according to the individual's wishes. Sometimes all the surnames are restricted to formal occasions such as in wedding announcements and legal documents: it is more usual for all surnames to be placed on the envelope. *If the practice is not known, it is not wrong to use all the surnames.*

A multiple surname was often acquired by Royal Licence from the eighteenth century onwards. When a member of a family marries an heiress who bears arms, and he (or a descendant) desires to commemorate her surname in addition to his own, the Sovereign's permission for such a change is necessary. By common law a change of name in itself is not regulated in the United Kingdom, in which respect we differ from many other countries and states. One's surname is that by which one is commonly known; but a deed poll is usually required as legal proof of identity and this officially records the change of name. A deed poll may be registered in the College of Arms in any appropriate case. In Scotland a change of name and arms is recognized by Lyon Court, and in other cases the Lord Lyon King at Arms issues a certificate of a change of name.

In recent years it has become fashionable in England to dispense with hyphens, a practice which probably originated in Scotland in order to place the emphasis on the final name, though a few families never adopted them.[1] Without a hyphen it is sometimes difficult to know whether an individual has one surname or two, especially if the signature includes an initial, e.g. J. Leslie Thomas. Is he Mr. John Leslie Thomas, or Mr. Leslie Thomas who prefers

---

[1] In Scotland the majority of those with multiple names did not use hyphens.

to use his second christian name? Accordingly, should one start a letter 'Dear Mr. Leslie Thomas', or 'Dear Mr. Thomas'? There is a distinction between a surname and a family name. In England the latter is often added to the surname to show the identity of a particular family or a branch. For example, should the surname be Browning, and in one branch most or all children are christened Scott, they are known collectively as the 'Scott Brownings'. Due to the fluid system of names in England it often happens that some members of this family adopt Scott as an additional surname, with the result that their children no longer have Scott included as their final christian name.

In Wales, as surnames usually evolved from male line christian names, there are a great number of people with such surnames as Jones, Powell, Evans, Davies, Morgan and Price. This has resulted in the frequent use of an additional name for identification purposes. Sometimes this becomes a surname, and sometimes not.

Also, for the same reason, in England and elsewhere those with a common surname, such as Smith or Brown, often acquire an additional name. This sometimes arises by tacking on a second christian name, especially if derived from a surname, accelerated by the practice of using this second christian name in the signature, e.g. John Berkeley Brown is known by the christian name of Berkeley, and he signs 'J. Berkeley Brown'. People therefore call him and his wife Mr. and Mrs. Berkeley Brown, instead of Mr. and Mrs. Brown as they do for his brother Mr. George Brown. In course of time his children become known by the double name of Berkeley-Brown.

LEGAL DOCUMENTS

Peers and Peeresses are accorded their full formal styles with their christian names, *but with no surname*, viz.:

> The Most Noble Charles John Duke of Blank
> The Most Noble Anne Frances Duchess of Blank
> The Most Honourable Charles John Marquess (of) Blank
> The Most Honourable Anne Frances Marchioness (of) Blank
> The Right Honourable Charles John Earl (of), Viscount, *or* Baron Blank
> The Right Honourable Anne Frances Countess (of), Viscountess *or* Baroness Blank.[1]

---

[1] Though the term Baroness is sometimes restricted to a peeress in her own right, and wives of Barons are described as 'Lady' in lieu, there is no good reason for this distinction.

Those territorial designations of Viscounts and Barons which do not form an integral part of the title, and which are not ordinarily used, may be added if desired (see p. 24).

'Lord' before Marquess and Viscount is now considered to be archaic.

Peers by courtesy and their wives are not accorded the prefix 'Most Honourable' or 'Right Honourable' (unless they are members of the Privy Council). The full description would be 'The Honourable John Smith commonly called Viscount Hammersmith', but the use of the courtesy title only, e.g. Viscount Hammersmith, is generally considered to be sufficient.

Membership, etc., of Orders of Chivalry are either spelt in full (with or without the honorific prefix of the Order, e.g. Knight Commander of the *Most Excellent* Order of the British Empire), or by the recognized abbreviations, e.g. K.B.E.

Baronets are accorded 'Baronet' after the name. Knights Bachelor are accorded 'Knight Bachelor' or 'Knight' after the name.

Wives and widows of Baronets and Knights are formally described as 'Dame Frances Elizabeth Smith' or as 'Mary Elizabeth Lady Smith'. It is incorrect to place 'Lady' *before* the christian name, as this signifies that she is the daughter of a Duke, Marquess, or Earl.

For further information on the above, and styles for others in legal documents see *Encyclopaedia of Forms and Precedents*, Butterworth & Co., 4th edition, 1970, Vol. XV, pp. 802–825.

SHARE CERTIFICATES

As above, with the recognized abbreviations, but it is not usual to include territorial designations for Viscounts and Barons which are not ordinarily used. Dukes and Duchesses may be described by the slightly less formal 'His (Her) Grace'.

As many firms prepare certificates and plates for addresses by the same process, it is recommended that wives of baronets and knights should be described as 'Mary Elizabeth Lady Blank', *not* 'Lady Mary Elizabeth Blank', which is incorrect.

Part I

THE ROYAL FAMILY

The Sovereign

The Queen Mother and other Members of the Royal Family

Mistress of the Robes and Ladies in Waiting

Her Majesty's and other Royal Households

THE ROYAL FAMILY

The Sovereign

Except from personal friends, all communications should be addressed to 'The Private Secretary to Her Majesty The Queen'. These letters should ask 'if Her Majesty's attention may be directed to . . .', or 'it may interest Her Majesty to know that . . .', etc.

Such a letter should be addressed to the holder of the office and not by name, but subsequent correspondence should be sent to the actual writer of the reply.

The letter is a straightforward one, commencing 'Dear Sir', but the first reference to The Queen should be written 'Her Majesty', and thereafter 'The Queen'. The phrase 'Her Majesty' should be substituted for 'She' and 'Her Majesty's' for 'Her'.

For those who wish to communicate direct with The Queen, the following is the style used. Letters in the third person are now obsolete.

BEGINNING OF LETTER
> Madam,
> With my humble duty,

(In the body of the letter 'Your Majesty' should be substituted for 'You' and 'Your Majesty's' for 'Your'.)

ENDING OF LETTER
> I have the honour to remain (*or* to be),
>> Madam,
>>> Your Majesty's most humble and obedient servant,

ENVELOPE

Her Majesty The Queen.

VERBAL ADDRESS

'Your Majesty' for the first time. Subsequently 'Ma'am'. This should always rhyme with Pam. Pronunciation to rhyme with Palm is never used, nor has this been so for some generations. See also *Introduction to The Queen* (below).

DESCRIPTION IN CONVERSATION

Her Majesty, *or* The Queen, as applicable.

INTRODUCTION TO THE QUEEN

On introduction, and on leaving, a bow or curtsey is made.

In conversations with The Queen, the rules mentioned under *Verbal Address* apply. 'Your Majesty' should be substituted for 'You'. References to other members of The Royal Family are made to 'His/Her Royal Highness' or the appropriate title (e.g. The Duke of Edinburgh, The Prince of Wales). When introducing another person to The Queen it is only necessary to state the name of the person to be introduced, i.e. 'May I present . . . , Your Majesty?'

OFFICIAL SPEECHES

At official functions a speech should start 'May it please Your Majesty'. The term 'Ma'am' is not used.

Queen Elizabeth The Queen Mother

The same instructions as for The Sovereign apply, with 'Queen Elizabeth The Queen Mother' substituted for 'The Queen'.

Other Members of The Royal Family

Unless the writer is personally known to the Prince, Princess, Duke, etc., concerned, it is the usual practice to write to the Equerry, Private Secretary, or Lady in Waiting of the particular member of the Royal Family.

These letters should be addressed to the holder of the office and not by name, but subsequent correspondence should be sent to the actual writer of the reply.

The letter is a straightforward one, commencing '(Dear) Sir' or '(Dear) Madam' but reference for the first time to the particular member of the Royal Family should be written 'His (Her) Royal Highness', and subsequently to 'The Duke of . . .' 'Prince . . .' or 'Princess . . .' as applicable. The phrase 'His (Her) Royal Highness' should be substituted for 'He (She)', as far as possible, without peppering the letter with these formal descriptions as was done in the past.

For those who wish to communicate directly with a member of the Royal Family with the prefix His (or Her) Royal Highness, the style given below is used. Orders of Chivalry are now accorded to members of the Royal Family, with the exception of The Queen and Queen Elizabeth The Queen Mother.

BEGINNING OF LETTER

Sir, (Madam,)
In the body of the letter 'Your Royal Highness' should be substituted for 'you' and 'Your Royal Highness's' for 'your'.

FNDING OF LETTER

I have the honour to remain (or 'to be'),
Sir (Madam),
Your Royal Highness's most humble and obedient servant,

ENVELOPE

'His (Her) Royal Highness', followed on the next line by the name, e.g.:

The Duke of Gloucester
The Princess Anne
Princess Alexandra, The Hon. Mrs. Angus Ogilvy

Children of a Sovereign are given 'The' before Prince or Princess.

Members of the Royal Family, apart from the Sovereign's children, who are not peers are addressed according to their particular branch of the Royal Family, e.g.:

'His Royal Highness
Prince William of Gloucester.'

The 'of Gloucester' is included in all written forms, viz. envelopes, invitations, etc.

VERBAL ADDRESS

'Your Royal Highness' for the first time. Subsequently 'Sir' (or 'Ma'am'). Pronunciation should be an ordinary 'Sir', or 'Ma'am' to rhyme with 'Pam'. Sire, or Ma'am to rhyme with Palm are never used, nor has this been so for some generations.

INTRODUCTION TO A MEMBER OF THE ROYAL FAMILY

On introduction, and on leaving, a bow or curtsey is made. The method ranges from the formal to the more informal. The formal system was the invariable practice in the past, and should follow that described in *Introduction to the Queen*, with, of course, the substitution of 'Your Royal Highness' for 'Your Majesty' and subsequently 'Sir or Ma'am' (to rhyme with Pam).

The more informal method is preferred by some members of the Royal Family, particularly those of the younger generation.

If there is any doubt concerning which degree of formality is preferred by a particular Prince or Princess etc. reference should be made to the respective Private Secretary, Equerry[1], or Lady in Waiting.

Even when the more informal method is adopted, a member of the Royal Family should always be addressed in conversation as 'Your Royal Highness' for the first time, and subsequently as 'Sir or Ma'am' and references to other members of the Royal Family, as Her Majesty, or His/Her Royal Highness, or more informally by their title, e.g. The Duke of Kent or Prince Michael.

When introducing another person to a member of the Royal Family, it is only necessary to state the name of the person to be introduced, e.g. 'May I present . . ., Your Royal Highness?'

OFFICIAL SPEECHES

At official functions a speech should start, 'Your Royal Highness(es)'. The terms 'Sir or Ma'am' are not used.

MISTRESS OF THE ROBES AND LADIES IN WAITING

The Queen Regnant and The Queen Dowager each appoint a Mistress of the Robes, Ladies of the Bedchamber, and Women of the Bedchamber. The last named take consecutive turns of

---

[1] Pronounced Eq-*uerry*.

duty, and are generally known as 'Ladies in Waiting'. This duty is usually of a fortnight's duration. On commencing a tour of duty it is notified in the Court Circular in 'The Times' and 'Daily Telegraph' that . . . has succeeded . . . as Lady in Waiting.

By custom, the Mistress of the Robes is a peeress, and until recently a Duchess. The present Mistress of the Robes to The Queen is the Countess of Euston whose husband is heir to a Dukedom, and to the Queen Mother, the Duchess of Abercorn.

The Mistress of the Robes and Ladies of the Bedchamber normally accompany The Queen or The Queen Mother only on State or other important occasions.

Ladies in Waiting are appointed to Lady members of the Royal Family who are Royal Highnesses.

All these Ladies are members of Her Majesty's or other Royal Households.

Forms of address are according to the rank of the lady concerned.

HER MAJESTY'S HOUSEHOLD

The Queen's Household is headed by three Great Officers, the Lord Chamberlain, the Lord Steward, and the Master of the Horse, and is organized into separate departments, which are briefly mentioned below.

The Lord Chamberlain is Head of The Queen's Household, and supervises all royal ceremonial, except such State functions as a Coronation, Opening of Parliament, or a State Funeral, which are arranged by the Earl Marshal, and a State Banquet by the Lord Steward. The Lord Chamberlain supervises all The Queen's functions except those of a domestic category. Consequently, on Her Majesty's behalf he organizes and sends out invitations to such functions as a Garden Party. He also administers the Ecclesiastical and Medical Households, and makes such appointments as The Librarian of Windsor Castle, Keeper of the Jewel House or the Tower of London, The Master of the Queen's Music (formerly spelt 'Musick') and the Poet Laureate.

The Lord Steward is in technical control of all The Queen's domestic arrangements, and personally is in charge of *State* Banquets, for which he sends invitations on Her Majesty's behalf, supervises the function and presents the guests. Day to day arrangements are exercised by the Master of the Household. He sends other invitations on Her Majesty's behalf, apart from those issued by the Lord Chamberlain.

The Master of the Horse is responsible for The Queen's safety. At ceremonial occasions, such as The Queen's Birthday Parade, often known as 'Trooping the Colour', he rides immediately behind the Sovereign. In a procession such as the State Opening of Parliament, his carriage immediately follows The Queen's. His day to day functions are exercised by the Crown Equerry.

The Departments of the Royal Household are as follows:

1. The Private Secretary's Office, which includes the Press Secretary's Office and the Royal Archives (at Windsor Castle).
2. The Privy Purse and Treasurer's Office, which includes the Royal Almony.
3. The Lord Chamberlain's Office (at St. James's Palace) which includes:

    (a) The Surveyor of Pictures and Works of Art;
    (b) The Marshal of the Diplomatic Corps;
    (c) The Central Chancery of the Orders of Knighthood (8 Buckingham Gate, S.W.1).

4. The Master of the Household's Office.
5. The Royal Mews.

Her Majesty has a separate Household in Scotland.

———

The Keeper of the Privy Purse and Treasurer to The Queen deals with all financial matters.

The Master of the Household supervises The Queen's domestic household not only at Buckingham Palace but wherever Her Majesty is resident at the time.

The Crown Equerry is the senior member of the Royal Household in the Royal Mews Department (after the Master of the Horse), and is responsible for all The Queen's travelling arrangements.

The Vice-Chamberlain is a political appointment, and is appointed on the advice of the Prime Minister. He is a Member of Parliament and serves as a Government Whip. He submits to The Queen a daily summary of the proceedings in Parliament.

The Treasurer and *Comptroller of the Household* are also political appointments in the Household. In the House of Commons they act as Whips, and assist Her Majesty at the State Opening of Parliament.

The Captain of the Corps of Gentleman of Arms and the *Captain of the Yeoman of the Guard* are also political appointments and are Government Whips in the House of Lords. *The Lords-in-Waiting* are members of the House of Lords. Ladies are known as Baronesses-in-Waiting. At present there are six, one of whom (Lord Nugent) is a Permanent Lord-in-Waiting. Of the remaining five, who take their turn for duty a month at a time, three hold political appointments in the House of Lords. Lords-in-Waiting perform duties for The Sovereign such as to accompany or represent her at various ceremonies, including the arrival and departure of important persons.

The forms of address to members of Her Majesty's Household are according to the rank of the member concerned.

OTHER ROYAL HOUSEHOLDS

Queen Elizabeth The Queen Mother has her own Household at Clarence House, with her Lord Chamberlain, Comptroller, Treasurer, Private Secretary, and Equerries.

The Duke of Edinburgh's Household at Buckingham Palace includes his Treasurer and Private Secretary, and his Equerries.

The Prince of Wales, Princess Margaret, The Dukes of Gloucester and Kent, and Princess Alexandra all maintain small Households. Correspondence with these members of the Royal Family is dealt with by the Private Secretary concerned or, in the case of Princess Alexandra, by her Lady in Waiting.

The forms of address to a member of these Households are according to the rank of the person concerned.

INVITATIONS

For invitations from and to Her Majesty The Queen and other members of the Royal Family see *Royal Invitations, Part V*.

Part II

THE PEERAGE

The Peerage

Duke, his wife, widow and former wife

Peer, other than a Duke

Life Peer and Life Peeress

Peeress in her own right

Wife of a Peer, other than a Duke, his widow and former wife

Widow of one who would have succeeded to a Peerage had he survived

Children of a Peer

Peerage titles by courtesy

Wife of a Peer by courtesy, his widow and former wife

THE PEERAGE

TITLES AND STYLES OF THE PEERAGE

The most complicated series of titles and styles concern the Peerage. They are summarized on p. 59 and consist of the following groups:

1. *Peer* (of five grades, viz. Duke, Marquess, Earl, Viscount, and Baron).
2. *Peeress* (Duchess, Marchioness, Countess, Viscountess, and Baroness; either in her own right,[1] or the wife, widow, or former wife[2] of a peer).
3. *Courtesy Lord* (Son and heir apparent of a Duke, Marquess and Earl and eldest son of the heir apparent).
4. *Wife, Widow and Former wife[2] of a courtesy Lord.*
5. *The other sons of a Peer*—with the courtesy style of 'Lord' or 'The Honourable' before the christian name, i.e.,

   (a) Younger sons of a Duke and Marquess (Lord John Brown);
   (b) Younger sons of an Earl, and *all* sons of a Viscount and Baron (The Honourable John Brown, abbreviated to The Hon. John Brown or the more old-fashioned style of 'The Honble John Brown').

6. *Sons of a Courtesy Lord.* They have courtesy styles which follow the same system mentioned in group 5.
7. *Wives of sons of a Peer or Courtesy Lord*—mentioned in group 5 (Lady John Brown, or The Hon. Mrs. John Brown).

---

[1] At the present time all peeresses in their own right are Countesses or Baronesses.
[2] Strictly speaking the former wife of a peer is not a peeress, but details are placed here for convenience.

8. *Daughters of a Peer—*

  (a) Daughter of a Duke, Marquess and Earl (Lady Mary
      Brown);
  (b) Daughter of a Viscount and Baron (The Hon. Mary
      Brown, if unmarried, or, The Hon. Mrs. Brown if
      married).

9. *Daughters of a Courtesy Lord.* They follow the same
   system mentioned in group 8.

PEER

There are five grades of the Peerage:

DUKE
MARQUESS
EARL
VISCOUNT
BARON (or *Lord of Parliament* in the Peerage of Scotland, see
  below)

The son and heir apparent of a Duke, Marquess, or Earl, may
by courtesy use and be known by the title of one of his father's
peerage dignities of lower grade than that by which his father is
known. See *Children of a Peer* (p. 41).

Similarly, the eldest son of a courtesy lord of the grade of
Marquess or Earl may by courtesy also use and be known by the
title of one of his grandfather's peerage dignities, provided
that it is of a lower grade than that used by the father. See *Bearers
of Peerage Titles by Courtesy* (p. 42).

The Peerage, so far as oral and written forms of address are
concerned, falls into two sections, each with different rules:

  1. DUKE—see *Duke* (p. 25).
  2. OTHER PEERS—see *Peer Other Than a Duke* (p. 31).

Though popularly known collectively as 'the Peerage', it is
technically divided into five separate Peerages, viz. the Peerage
of England, of Scotland, of Ireland, of Great Britain, and of the
United Kingdom.

The separate Peerages of *England* and *Scotland* continued until
1707, when the two Kingdoms combined under the Act of Union.
The Peerages were then united and styled the Peerage of *Great
Britain*. From that year the Peerage of Great Britain and the

separate Peerage of *Ireland* existed until 1801, when Great Britain and Ireland were combined under a second Act of Union. Since 1801 the Peerage has been styled the Peerage of the *United Kingdom.*

The *Peerage of Ireland* was not entirely discontinued at the Union of 1801. Creations have occasionally since been made as a means of reward but they do not carry the right to sit in the House of Lords (e.g. Lord Curzon of Kedleston in 1898).

It is important that the description Peerages of Scotland and Ireland are used only in the technical sense of creation and do not imply that a peer is a Scotsman or Irishman, e.g. Lord Fairfax of Cameron in the Peerage of Scotland, and Viscount Gage in the Peerage of Ireland both belong to English families.

THE PEERAGE OF SCOTLAND

The term MASTER is used by the heir apparent, the heir presumptive and, as a courtesy title, by the heir of a courtesy lord, see *Scottish Title of Master* (p. 56).

In the Peerage of Scotland there is no rank of Baron, since in Scotland this term concerns a Barony of land. The equivalent rank of Baron in the Peerage of Scotland is Lord of Parliament, abbreviated to 'Lord'.

THE PEERAGE OF IRELAND

If an Irish peer holds a peerage dignity of a lower grade which enables him to sit in the House of Lords, he is introduced there by the peerage which enables him to sit, e.g. the *Earl of Lucan* sits in the House as *Baron Bingham.* For all other purposes he is known by his higher title, e.g. as *Earl of Lucan.*

With but few exceptions, peers are known by the senior peerage which they possess; such exceptions include the Earl Brooke and of Warwick who is known as the Earl of Warwick, and Lord Leconfield and Egremont who is known as Lord Egremont. For those who have several peerages of the same grade, the choice of style rests with the peer himself, e.g. the Duke of Richmond, Lennox and Gordon is generally known as the *Duke of Richmond and Gordon.*

TITLE OF A PEER

Every Viscount and Baron is described in his Letters Patent of creation as being of a place in the United Kingdom, followed by the appropriate county, e.g. BARON REDMAYNE, of Rushcliffe in the county of Nottingham. The place may be his residence, domicile, former constituency, or some location with which he has a connection. Such description is called the territorial designation and is *not* used except in very formal documents.

A few peers have two territorial designations of which one at least must be of a place in the United Kingdom (e.g. Viscount Allenby, of Megiddo and of Felixstowe in the county of Suffolk; Baron Keyes, of Zeebrugge and of Dover in the county of Kent; Baron Wilson, of Libya and of Stowlangtoft in the county of Suffolk).

Some peers have a territorial or place name which actually forms part of their title, such as Baron Ritchie of Dundee, Baron Russell of Liverpool, and Baron Brassey of Apethorpe. Such titles must always be used in full. They are so printed in the heading of the article concerned in DEBRETT, and are so given in the Roll of the House of Lords.

This territorial part of the peerage title may be granted for two main reasons:

    (a) *as a special honour*, e.g.

        Earl Alexander of Tunis
        Earl Mountbatten of Burma
        Viscount Montgomery of Alamein

    (b) *as a method of differentiation from the title of another peer*, e.g.

        Baron Erroll of Hale, to distinguish him from the holder of the Earldom of Erroll.

        This is particularly prevalent now that surnames are so often adopted as peerage titles.
        Differentiation may also be necessary if the first part of the title chosen sounds like another existing peerage, even though the spelling may vary, e.g. Baron Hylton and Baron Hilton of Upton, Baron Layton and Baron Leighton of St. Mellons.

A territorial or place name which forms part of a peerage title has not always been that of a place in the United Kingdom (e.g.

Earl of Ypres). War leaders frequently embody the name of their battles or campaigns in their titles.

Duke

(*For summary see p.* 59.)

BEGINNING OF LETTER

Formal	My Lord Duke
Social	Dear Duke
	Dear Duke of Hamilton may be used if the acquaintanceship is slight

ENDING OF LETTER

Formal	Yours faithfully (see also p. 2)
Social	Yours sincerely

ENVELOPE

Formal	His Grace the Duke of Hamilton[1]
Social	The Duke of Hamilton

Note: A few Dukes prefer to be styled 'His Grace' even in social correspondence.

VERBAL ADDRESS

Formal	Your Grace
Social	Duke
Employee Status	Your Grace

DESCRIPTION IN CONVERSATION

A Duke is always so described (unlike the four lower grades of the peerage, viz. Marquess, Earl, Viscount, and Baron, who in speech are all called 'Lord', e.g. Lord Bath).

If reference is only made to one Duke, he may be called 'the Duke'. If distinction is necessary, or on introduction, he should be referred to as 'the Duke of Ramsgate'. Employee Status, 'His Grace'.

LIST OF DIRECTORS AND PATRONS

It is optional whether the formal style (His Grace the Duke of Ramsgate) or the social style (The Duke of Ramsgate) is adopted,

---

[1] When preceded by other word(s), 'The' or 'the' may be used as preferred, though the Royal Family use the former.

so long as the same style is followed for all other patrons, etc., in a list. It is *recommended* that the social style should be used.

FORMAL STYLE

The formal style of 'The Most Noble' has given place to the more informal 'His Grace', but the former is still used occasionally in official announcements, documents and on monuments.

MEMBERSHIP OF THE PRIVY COUNCIL

If a Duke be a Privy Counsellor, the letters P.C. should be included after his title, since it would not be otherwise apparent that he holds that office. The letters P.C. follow any orders and decorations he may hold, e.g. '(His Grace) the Duke of Dover, K.C.V.O., C.B.E., P.C.'. See *Privy Counsellor* (p. 78).

WITH ECCLESIASTICAL, AMBASSADORIAL, OR SERVICE RANK

These precede ducal rank, i.e.

> The Very Reverend the Duke of Ramsgate
> His Excellency the Duke of Ramsgate
> Major the Duke of Ramsgate

SIGNATURE

By title only, e.g. Ramsgate.

STYLE FROM SOURCES OTHER THAN THE CROWN

See p. 33.

Wife of a Duke

(*For summary see p. 59.*)

BEGINNING OF LETTER

Formal	Madam *or* Dear Madam[1]
Social	Dear Duchess
	Dear Duchess of Somerset may be used if the acquaintanceship is slight.

---

[1] Strictly speaking the commencement of 'Madam' is the very formal style, for which the corresponding conclusion is given on p. 3. As this form of conclusion is now seldom used, 'Madam', instead of the more usual 'Dear Madam', is sometimes adopted in a very formal or official letter.

ENDING OF LETTER

Formal	Yours faithfully (see also p. 2)
Social	Yours sincerely

ENVELOPE

Formal	Her Grace the Duchess of Norfolk
Social	The Duchess of Norfolk

VERBAL ADDRESS

Formal	Your Grace
Social	Duchess
Employee Status	Your Grace

DESCRIPTION IN CONVERSATION

A Duchess is *always* so described, unlike the four lower grades of the peerage, who in speech are called Lady Blank.

If reference be only made to one Duchess, she may be called 'the Duchess'. If distinction is necessary, or on introduction she should be referred to as 'the Duchess of Norfolk'. Employee Status, 'Her Grace'.

LIST OF DIRECTORS AND PATRONS

It is optional whether the formal style (Her Grace the Duchess of Ramsgate) or the social style (The Duchess of Ramsgate) is adopted, so long as the same style is followed for all other patrons, etc. in a list. It is *recommended* that the social style should be used.

FORMAL STYLE

The formal style of 'The Most Noble' has given place to the more informal 'Her Grace' but the former is still used occasionally in official announcements, documents and on monuments. See *Legal Documents* (p. 7) and *Share Certificates* (p. 8).

SIGNATURE

Christian name and title, e.g. Helen Middlesex.

Widow of a Duke

Officially the widow of a Duke is known as 'The Dowager Duchess of Southampton', unless there is already a Dowager Duchess in that family still living. In the latter event, the widow of the senior Duke retains this title for life, and the widow of the junior Duke is known by her christian name, e.g. 'Mary, Duchess of Southampton'.

Socially many prefer to use their christian name in preference to 'The Dowager Duchess of Southampton'. An announcement is often made in the Press. Otherwise it will be necessary to discover her wishes. If in doubt I *recommend* the use of the christian name.

If the present holder of the Dukedom is unmarried, *socially* the widow of the previous Duke does not use the term of either 'The Dowager Duchess of Southampton' or 'Mary, Duchess of Southampton' but continues to be known as 'The Duchess of Southampton'.

Should the present Duke marry, it is usual for the widowed Duchess then to announce the style she wishes to adopt.

BEGINNING OF LETTER

Formal	(Dear) Madam[1]
Social	Dear Duchess
	Dear Duchess of Middlesex may be used if the acquaintanceship is slight

ENDING OF LETTER

Formal	Yours faithfully (see also p. 2)
Social	Yours sincerely

ENVELOPE

Formal	Her Grace the Dowager Duchess of Middlesex *or*
	Her Grace Mary, Duchess of Middlesex (as applicable)
Social	The Dowager Duchess of Middlesex *or*
	Mary, Duchess of Middlesex (as applicable)

VERBAL ADDRESS

As for the wife of a Duke.

DESCRIPTION IN CONVERSATION

As for a Duchess. If distinction from the wife of the present Duke is necessary, or on introduction, she should be described as 'The

---

[1] See p. 26, note [1].

Dowager Duchess of Middlesex' or 'Mary, Duchess of Middlesex' as applicable. Employee Status, 'Her Grace'.

LIST OF DIRECTORS AND PATRONS

Formal	Her Grace the Dowager Duchess of Southampton *or*
	Her Grace Mary, Duchess of Southampton
Social	The Dowager Duchess of Southampton *or* Mary, Duchess of Southampton

For the choice of formal or social style, see wife of a Duke.

FORMAL STYLE

As for wife of a Duke.

SIGNATURE

As for wife of a Duke.

Former Wife of a Duke

If a marriage to a Duke has been dissolved, his former wife continues to use her title as a Duke's wife, preceded by her christian name.

The continuance of her title henceforward is regarded as a name rather than the retention of the attributes and status of the wife of a peer. Accordingly she is not entitled to the prefix of 'Her Grace'.

In Scotland, due to the difference of laws for divorce, a former wife is legally equivalent to a widow in England. On marriage, as well as adopting her husband's surname, she also retains her maiden name as an alias. Should her marriage to a Duke be dissolved and she marries again, she also retains her first husband's title as an alias.

Socially, former wives of Dukes in Scotland are usually treated as former wives of Dukes in general, unless any specific ruling is announced by Lyon King of Arms.

BEGINNING OF LETTER

As for the wife of a Duke.

ENDING OF LETTER

As for the wife of a Duke.

ENVELOPE

Formal and Social   Mary, Duchess of Wiltshire

VERBAL ADDRESS

Formal   Madam
Social   Duchess
Employee Status   Your Grace[1]

DESCRIPTION IN CONVERSATION

Duchess of Blankshire. If some distinction from the wife of the present Duke is necessary, she should be described as Mary, Duchess of Blankshire.

LIST OF DIRECTORS AND PATRONS

Mary, Duchess of Wiltshire.

REMARRIAGE

She adopts her style from her present husband: e.g. Mary, Duchess of Blankshire marries Mr. Cuthbert Jones and becomes Mrs. Cuthbert Jones.

If she has a courtesy style from her father, she will revert to this on remarriage, e.g. Lady Mary Brown marries first the Duke of Blankshire and secondly Mr. John Green. Upon her second marriage she is known as Lady Mary Green.

Similarly, if the Hon. Mary Brown marries first the Duke of Blankshire and secondly Mr. John Green, she becomes the Hon. Mrs. Green.

---

[1] Although officially she is no longer entitled to the prefix of 'Her Grace' since she is no longer a peeress, by custom this rank continues to be given to her verbally. As former wives of other peers are referred to as 'My Lady' or 'Your Ladyship' (Employee Status p. 40), there is no other alternative by which she could be known. It is *recommended* therefore that she should be referred to as 'Her Grace'.

Peer, Other than a Duke—
Viz. Marquess, Earl, Viscount, and Baron

(For summary of titles see p. 59.)

Peers of the grades of Marquess[1], Earl, Viscount, and Baron are all referred to in conversation as Lord Washington. The use of their exact rank is socially incorrect, unless for some reason it has to be specifically mentioned. It is, however, used on envelopes, visiting cards and invitations.

The only exception to the above general rule is at a formal function. The exact title of a peer may then be given at the first mention of a peer, but he is usually subsequently referred to, or invited to speak, as 'Lord Washington'.

The fifth grade of the peerage, a Baron, is never referred to by this title, except in legal or formal documents (see p. 7), but always as Lord Gretton, both verbally and in correspondence. In the Peerage of Scotland, the term 'Lord' is the legal term of the fifth grade in the peerage.

The use of Baron is restricted to a foreign title, and is never translated to '*Lord* Braun' for any purpose. See *Foreign Titles* (p. 103).

BEGINNING OF LETTER

Formal	My Lord
Social	Dear Lord Tweeddale

ENDING OF LETTER

Formal	Yours faithfully (see also p. 2)
Social	Yours sincerely

ENVELOPE

Formal (see p. 36, note [2])	The Most Hon. the Marquess of Tweeddale[2]
	The Rt. Hon. the Earl of Gainsborough[2]
	The Rt. Hon. the Viscount Falkland[3]
	The Rt. Hon. the Lord Gretton[4]

[1] The official spelling of this title is 'Marquess', and this is adopted in the Roll of the House of Lords. Some newspapers, not 'The Times', spell the word 'Marquis', as for the title in France. In the past, when spelling was not standardized, both forms were adopted in Britain. Some Scottish Marquesses, in memory of the 'Auld Alliance' with France, have used the shorter spelling.
[2] There are some Marquessates and Earldoms whose titles do not include the word 'of', e.g. The Marquess Conyngham, The Earl Sondes.
[3] All Viscounts in the Peerage of Scotland were created '*of*' somewhere, but only The Viscount of Arbuthnott normally uses it.
[4] The only Baron who sometimes uses '*of*' is Baron of Dunsany, but he is usually known as 'Lord Dunsany'.

Social	The Marquess of Tweeddale
	The Earl of Gainsborough
	The Viscount Falkland
	The Lord Gretton

DESCRIPTION OF A PEER WITHIN A LETTER, ARTICLE, CAPTION, ETC.

The first formal reference to a peer is usually made to his exact rank. Subsequent references to a peer of all these four grades may be made to Lord Tweeddale, Lord Falkland, etc.

References to these peers in social letters usually do not quote the exact rank but give the style of Lord, viz. Lord Tweeddale, not Marquess of Tweeddale.

VERBAL ADDRESS

Formal	My Lord
Social	Lord Tweeddale
Employee Status	My Lord *or* Your Lordship[1]

DESCRIPTION IN CONVERSATION

Lord Gainsborough—this style applies to all four grades of the Peerage.

Employee Status	His Lordship

LIST OF DIRECTORS AND PATRONS

It is optional whether one adopts the formal style, viz.:

> The Most Hon. the Marquess of Findon
> The Rt. Hon. the Earl of Storrington
> The Rt. Hon. the Viscount Washington
> The Rt. Hon. the Lord Ashington

or in the social style, viz.:

> The Marquess of Findon
> The Earl of Storrington
> The Viscount Washington
> The Lord Ashington

so long as the same style is followed for all other patrons, etc., in the list. It is *recommended* that the social style should be used.

MEMBERSHIP OF THE PRIVY COUNCIL

If a peer be a Privy Counsellor, the letters P.C. should be included after his name, orders, and decorations, since it would not otherwise be apparent that he holds that office.

---

[1] The difference is purely grammatical, e.g. 'Yes, my Lord'; 'Will your Lordship come this way?'.

A Marquess still has the prefix or formal style of Most Hon., and an Earl, Viscount, and Baron all have the prefix or formal style of Rt. Hon., which is also the attribute of a Privy Counsellor. See *Privy Counsellor* (p. 78).

WITH ECCLESIASTICAL, AMBASSADORIAL OR SERVICE RANK

These precede a peer's rank in correspondence, e.g.:

His Excellency the Earl of Storrington
The Rev. Canon the Viscount Washington
Major the Lord Ashington.

SIGNATURE

By title only, e.g., Washington.

STYLE FROM SOURCES OTHER THAN THE CROWN

It is not customary in *formal* usage to combine the style emanating from other sources with titles conferred by the Sovereign. 'Alderman the Lord Jones' and 'Professor the Lord Smith' are solecisms. In *social* usage this is not uncommon, though deprecated by purists.

Life Peer and Life Peeress

A life peer or peeress has exactly the same style and attributes as an hereditary peer.

Children of life peers or peeresses have the same courtesy styles as the children of an hereditary peer. They continue to bear these for life. For the son of a Baron see p. 50 and the daughter of a Baron, p. 53.

Peeress in Her Own Right

(*For summary see p.* 60.)

At present all peeresses in their own right are either Countesses or Baronesses.

All peeresses in their own right, whether their peerage is hereditary or for life, are addressed as for the wife of a peer of the applicable grade, but a Baroness has the option of two alternative styles.

The use of the continental style of 'Baroness' for social purposes is of fairly recent origin. It is believed that the first to term themselves 'Baroness' were Baroness Zouche (who styled herself Baroness de la Zouche) and Baroness Burdett-Coutts. As several Life Baronesses have been created since the Peerage Act 1963, its use has now become widespread. It is *recommended* that the personal wishes of the lady concerned should be ascertained as to which form of address should be used, 'Baroness' or 'Lady'.

A husband derives no title or style from his wife.

BEGINNING OF LETTER

As for the wife of a peer, other than a Duke, though a Baroness may prefer the style of 'Baroness' instead of 'Lady'. In this case, socially, she should be addressed:

Dear Baroness Green

Most Baronesses in their own right prefer the style Dear Lady Green.

Note: 'Baroness' should not be used on its own, as is sometimes done. One would not address a peeress just as 'Lady'. The style is, however, correct for a continental Baroness, see *Foreign Titles* (p. 103).

ENDING OF LETTER

Formal	Yours faithfully (see also p. 2)
Social	Yours sincerely.

ENVELOPE

As for the wife of a peer, other than a Duke (p.35), but if a Baroness prefers the style of 'Baroness' she should be addressed:

Formal	The Rt. Hon. the Baroness Green
Social	The Baroness Green.

WRITTEN DESCRIPTION

See wife of a peer, other than a Duke (p. 35).

VERBAL ADDRESS

As for the wife of a peer, other than a Duke, with the option, for Baronesses, of the style 'Baroness Green' instead of 'Lady Green' if preferred. 'Lady Green' is the style usually adopted.

Note: 'Baroness' should not be used on its own. See *Beginning of Letter* above.

DESCRIPTION IN CONVERSATION

Formal and Social   Lady Teddington *or* Baroness Teddington
Employee Status   Her Ladyship.

LIST OF DIRECTORS AND PATRONS

It is optional whether one adopts the formal or the social method so long as the same style is followed for all other patrons, etc., in the list. It is *recommended* that the social style should be used.

SIGNATURE

Teddington (as for a peer).

CHILDREN

The children of a peeress adopt the same courtesy titles and styles as do the children of a peer, e.g. the Countess of Sutherland's son and heir is Lord Strathnaver: Baroness Spencer-Churchill's daughter is the Hon. Mrs. Soames.

Wife of a Peer, Other than a Duke

(*For summary see p.* 59.)

> The wife of a Marquess is a Marchioness
> The wife of an Earl is a Countess
> The wife of a Viscount is a Viscountess
> The wife of a Baron is a Baroness

The last named title is not used, except in formal documents, the usual style being Lady Blank. The exception is that a Baroness in her own right has the option of using it in place of Lady Blank.

The term 'Baroness' is used for continental titles, and is never translated, see *Foreign Titles*, p. 109).

For nearly all purposes a peeress of all these four grades of the peerage is referred to in conversation as 'Lady Blank'. The use of the exact rank in speech (e.g. Viscountess Blank) is socially incorrect, unless for some reason it needs to be specifically mentioned, but it is always used on envelopes and visiting cards. An exception may occasionally be made at a formal function, such as in the introduction of a speaker who is a peeress, when normally her exact rank is mentioned for the first time only, e.g. 'We are very happy to have the Countess of Hallamshire here tonight. Lady Hallamshire, as you know . . .'

BEGINNING OF LETTER

Formal	(Dear) Madam[1]
	Dear Lady Angmering (irrespective of which of the four grades of peerage is applicable)

ENDING OF LETTER

Formal	Yours faithfully (see also p. 2)
Social	Yours sincerely

ENVELOPE

Formal[2]	The Most Hon. the Marchioness of Bath
	The Rt. Hon. the Countess of Derby
	The Rt. Hon. the Viscountess Kemsley
	The Rt. Hon. the Lady Poole
Social	The Marchioness of Bath
	The Countess of Derby
	The Viscountess Kemsley
	The Lady Poole

WRITTEN DESCRIPTION

Where a Viscountess or Baroness is referred to in the body of a formal letter, article, caption, etc., she may be described as Viscountess Molesey or Lady Surbiton without the prefix 'the'. Any subsequent reference to such a peeress can be made to Lady Molesey, without regard to her exact rank in the peerage.

Informal letters again do not usually refer to the exact rank at all, but as Lady Molesey throughout.

The second and subsequent reference to a Marchioness or a Countess can be made to Lady Bath, without regard to her exact rank. Informal letters do not usually refer to her exact rank at all, but as Lady Bath throughout.

VERBAL ADDRESS

Formal	Madam (*not* My Lady[1])
Social	Lady Poole
Employee Status	My Lady *or* Your Ladyship[3]

[1] See p. 26, note [1]. The term 'My Lady' is not used as the feminine equivalent of 'My Lord' but is restricted to Employee Status.
[2] There is no definite rule concerning the use of the word 'The' before these styles. As some consider that the double use of 'The' is superfluous 'Most Hon. the Marchioness of Bath' may, if desired, be used. This practice is not, however, recommended.
[3] The difference is purely grammatical, e.g. 'Yes, my Lady'; 'Will your Ladyship come this way?'. These forms are now only used by those of Employee Status.

DESCRIPTION IN CONVERSATION

Formal and Social   Lady Poole
Employee Status   Her Ladyship

LIST OF DIRECTORS AND PATRONS

It is optional whether one adopts the formal or the social method so long as the same style is followed for all other patrons, etc., in the list. It is *recommended* that the social style should be used.

SIGNATURE

By christian name and title, e.g., Helen Middlesex.

Widow of a Peer, Other than a Duke

Officially the widow of a peer of the above-mentioned grades is known as 'The Dowager Marchioness of Reading', 'The Dowager Countess of Pembroke', etc., unless there is already a dowager peeress of the family still living. In the latter event, the widow of the senior peer of the family retains the title of Dowager for life, and the widow of the junior peer in that family is known by her christian name, e.g. 'Mary, Marchioness of Hammersmith', until she becomes the senior widow.

Many dowager peeresses prefer the use of their christian name in preference to the word 'Dowager'. An announcement is often made in the press. Otherwise it is necessary to discover the wishes of the lady concerned. If in doubt, I recommend the style of 'Mary, Lady Blank' (or appropriate rank), as the majority of peers' widows do not like the style of dowager.

When the present peer is unmarried, *by custom* the widow of the late peer continues to call herself as she did when her husband was living, i.e. without the prefix of (a) dowager, or (b) her christian name. Should the present peer marry, it is usual for the widowed peeress to announce the style by which she wishes to be known in future, i.e. 'The Dowager Lady (or appropriate rank) Lancing' or 'Mary, Lady Lancing'.

BEGINNING OF LETTER

Formal   (Dear) Madam[1]
Social   Dear Lady Lancing

[1] See p. 26, note [1].

ENDING OF LETTER

Formal	Yours faithfully (see also p. 2)
Social	Yours sincerely

ENVELOPE

Formal (see p. 36, note [2])	The Most Hon. the Dowager Marchioness of Hammersmith The Rt. Hon. the Dowager Countess of Flintshire The Rt. Hon. the Dowager Viscountess Angmering The Rt. Hon. the Dowager Lady Lancing *or* The Most Hon. Mary, Marchioness of Hammersmith (or applicable title)
Social	The Dowager Marchioness of Hammersmith The Dowager Countess of Flintshire The Dowager Viscountess Angmering The Dowager Lady Lancing *or* Mary, Marchioness of Hammersmith (or applicable title)

VERBAL ADDRESS

Formal	Madam
Social	Lady Hammersmith
Employee Status	My Lady *or* Your Ladyship[1]

DESCRIPTION IN CONVERSATION

Lady Hammersmith. If distinction is necessary or on introduction she should be described as 'the Dowager Lady Hammersmith' or 'Mary, Lady Hammersmith'. Employee Status, 'Her Ladyship'.

LIST OF DIRECTORS AND PATRONS

It is optional whether one adopts the formal or the social method so long as the same style is followed for all other patrons, etc., in the list. It is *recommended* that the social style should be used.

SIGNATURE

By christian name and title, e.g. Helen Hammersmith.

[1] See p. 36, note [3].

REMARRIAGE

If the widow of a peer remarries, she adopts her style from her present husband, e.g. 'The Dowager Lady Green' having married Mr. Edward Brown would be known as Mrs. Edward Brown.

If a peer's widow who has a courtesy style as a peer's daughter marries again, she reverts to the use of the courtesy style derived from her father, e.g. if Lady Mary White (daughter of the Earl of Ditton) marries first the Marquess of Surbiton and secondly Mr. Thomas Jones, she will be known as Lady Mary Jones. If the Hon. Mary Smith (daughter of Viscount Twickenham) marries first Lord White and secondly Mr. Robert Green she will be known as the Hon. Mrs. Green.

Former Wife of a Peer, Other than a Duke

If a former wife of a Marquess, Earl, Viscount, and Baron does not marry again, she may continue to use the title as she did when she was married to the peer, with the prefix of her christian name. *She no longer uses the formal style of a peeress,* viz.:

The Most Hon. for a Marchioness
The Rt. Hon. for a Countess, Viscountess and Baroness

On remarriage, she takes her style from her present husband.

In Scotland, due to the difference in divorce laws, a former wife is legally equivalent to a widow in England. On marriage, as well as adopting her husband's surname, she also retains her maiden name as an alias. Should her marriage to a peer be dissolved, and she marries again, she also retains her first husband's title as an alias.

Socially, former wives of peers in Scotland are usually treated as are former wives of peers in general, unless any specific ruling is announced by Lyon King or Arms.

BEGINNING OF LETTER

Formal	(Dear) Madam[1]
Social	Dear Lady Surbiton

ENDING OF LETTER

Formal	Yours faithfully (see also p. 2)
Social	Yours sincerely

[1] See p. 26, note [1].

ENVELOPE

Formal and Social   Mary, Countess of Surbiton

VERBAL ADDRESS

Formal   Madam
Social   Lady Surbiton
Employee Status   My Lady *or* Your Ladyship[1]

DESCRIPTION IN CONVERSATION

Lady Surbiton. If distinction from the wife of the present peer is necessary, or on introduction, she should be described as 'Mary, Lady Surbiton'. Employee Status, 'Her Ladyship'.

LIST OF DIRECTORS AND PATRONS

Mary, Countess of Surbiton.

SIGNATURE

Christian name and title, e.g. Mary Surbiton.

REMARRIAGE

On remarriage she adopts her style from her present husband, e.g. the former wife of the Earl of Surbiton marries Mr. John Brown: she is known as Mrs. John Brown. If she has a courtesy style derived from her father she will revert to this on remarriage, e.g. (a) Lady Mary Green marries first the Viscount Ferring and secondly Mr. John Smith: she becomes Lady Mary Smith; (b) The Hon. Mary Smith marries first the Lord White and secondly Mr. John Brown: she becomes the Hon. Mrs. Brown.

Widow of One who would have succeeded to a Peerage had He survived

The Queen may issue a Royal Warrant conferring on the lady concerned the title, rank, place, pre-eminence, and procedure which would have been hers if her late husband had survived and succeeded to the title.

This privilege has been granted in certain instances when the lady's husband died on active service.

[1] See p. 36, note [3].

Example

The Hon. Roger Mortimer, son and heir of Viscount March, is killed in action. On the Peer's death, Roger's widow may be accorded by Royal Warrant the title of the *Viscountess March*, as if her husband had survived and succeeded to the peerage.

Children of a Peer

The children of a peer use either:

    (a) a peerage title by courtesy, *or*
    (b) a courtesy style.

A courtesy title indicates and reflects a legal right of precedence, unless in particular cases they are confirmed or recognized by the Sovereign.

The son and heir apparent[1] of a Duke, Marquess, or Earl may use one of his father's peerage titles by courtesy providing it is of a lesser grade than that used by his father. If the Duke, Marquess or Earl is of the Peerage of Scotland, see *Scottish Title of Master*, p. 56.

The younger sons of a Duke or Marquess have the courtesy style of 'Lord' before christian name and surname.

The younger sons of an Earl, and *all* sons of a Viscount or Baron have the courtesy style of 'The Hon.' before christian name and surname.

The daughters of a Duke, Marquess, or Earl have the courtesy style of 'Lady' before christian name and surname.

The daughters of a Viscount or Baron have the courtesy style of 'The Hon.' before christian name and surname.

A peer's sons and daughters who are legitimated under the Legitimacy Act 1926, as amended by the Act of 1959, are now under an Earl Marshal's Warrant accorded the same courtesy styles as the legitimate younger children of peers, though they have no right of succession to the peerage or precedence from it.

---

[1] The heir apparent to a dignity is either the eldest son, the eldest surviving son (where a deceased elder brother has left no heir apparent) or the only son of the holder of a dignity. When the heir apparent is deceased, *his* heir apparent succeeds him in this respect. A woman can only be an heiress apparent when she is the eldest child (without surviving brothers with issue) or the only child of a deceased heir apparent. Legally the holder of a dignity, so long as he lives, may have a son. Thus Queen Elizabeth II was never heiress apparent to the Crown since she could have been displaced by the birth of a brother.

The heir presumptive to a dignity is the next in line, but who could be displaced in succession by the birth of an heir apparent. Thus a relative of a peer is only his heir presumptive until such time as the peer has a son and heir apparent. Alternatively, when a dignity may pass in the female line, the holder's daughter is heiress presumptive until such time as a son is born. If there be more than one daughter, but no son, they are co-heirs to an English Barony created by writ of summons. This falls into abeyance between them or their representatives.

Although 'heir' is used loosely for the heir apparent or heir presumptive, legally it means the person in occupation of the title, estate, etc.

Courtesy styles may continue to be borne by the children of peers who have disclaimed their peerages if desired. See *Children of a Disclaimed Peer* (p. 55).

A few children of peers or courtesy lords prefer not to use their courtesy titles or styles, and this fact is noted in their fathers' respective paragraph in DEBRETT.

The children of the younger sons of a peer have no titles or special styles.

Children who are or have been adopted by a peer do not acquire any titles, styles and precedence as a result of such adoption.

Bearers of Peerage Titles by Courtesy

Though the bearer of a peerage title by courtesy enjoys none of the privileges of a peer he is addressed as such a peer with the following exceptions:

1. A Marquess by Courtesy is not given the formal style of 'The Most Hon.', e.g. Marquess of Tavistock.[1]
2. An Earl, Viscount or Baron by Courtesy is not given the formal style of 'The Rt. Hon.' e.g. Earl of Burford,[1] Viscount Savernake or Lord Porchester.
3. A peer by courtesy is not addressed as 'The' in correspondence. This is restricted to actual peers.[2]

Normally he is called Lord Blank as a peer, but if there is a special reason for a Marquess or Earl by Courtesy to be referred to by his courtesy title, he is called verbally, 'the Marquess of Blandford' or 'the Earl of Burford', this being the usual colloquial form of reference. The definite article is never given to courtesy Viscounts and Barons.

The eldest (or only) son and heir apparent of a Duke, Marquess or Earl may by courtesy use a title in the peerage of a rank junior to his father. This is usually, but not invariably, the second senior peerage borne by the peer (e.g. the son and heir apparent of the Duke of Rutland is known as the Marquess of Granby). The question is discussed in the *Complete Peerage*, Vol. IV, App. E, and by Valentine Heywood in his *British Titles*, 1951.

[1] Some Marquessates and Earldoms used as courtesy titles do not contain the word 'of' in their title, e.g. Marquess Douro and Earl Grosvenor.
[2] Some hold that the prefix of 'The' is an abbreviation for The Most Noble, The Most Hon. and The Rt. Hon.

Second Heir to a Peerage

When a Marquess or Earl by courtesy has an eldest (or only) son (who consequently is the second heir apparent to the peer), he, too, may use a courtesy title in the peerage, provided that it is junior in rank to that by which his father is known, e.g. Lord Eskdaill is the son of the Earl of Dalkeith, who is son and heir of the Duke of Buccleuch.

For the eldest son of an Earl by courtesy in the Peerage of Scotland, see *Scottish Title of Master* (p. 56).

Grandson who is Heir Apparent of a Peer

When the heir apparent of a Duke, Marquess or Earl is deceased, but has left a son (who then becomes the heir apparent to the peer), he is allowed to use the courtesy title borne by his father. In 1955, Viscount Swinton was created Earl of Swinton. His son and heir, the Hon. John Cunliffe-Lister had died of wounds in 1943, leaving male issue. On the creation of the Earldom, the elder of these sons became heir apparent to his grandfather and known by courtesy as Lord Masham.

If the eldest son of a Viscount or Baron predeceases his father, his children do not use the courtesy style of 'The Honourable' in the same way that a courtesy title may pass to a grandson.

Thus the present Lord Kingsale, who succeeded his grandfather, did not have the style of 'The Honourable' when his grandfather was the peer.

EXAMPLES OF PEERAGE TITLES BORNE BY COURTESY

There is no hard and fast rule about which title borne by the peer is selected for use by his eldest son as a peer by courtesy, though in most families custom is followed. If the Marquess of Lansdowne has a son, his heir is usually known as Earl of Kerry or Earl of Shelburne in alternate generations. When the Marquess of Ailesbury died, he was succeeded in that dignity by his eldest son, known by courtesy as Earl of Cardigan. The latter's son, however, preferred to retain the use of his courtesy title of Viscount Savernake and was not known as Earl of Cardigan. See for this the *Complete Peerage*, Vol. IV, App. E.

All courtesy titles used are shown in DEBRETT under the heading of the peer concerned.

The following examples of (1) the peer, (2) his son and heir apparent, and (3) the heir's eldest son, are included to show how the system varies according to the particular peerage. Each example given consists of a different sequence of rank in the courtesy titles. Where a rank has been omitted, this is usually because the peer does not possess a peerage dignity of that grade (e.g. the Marquess of Bath is not also an Earl, but he is also the Viscount Weymouth, and by courtesy his eldest son is styled Viscount Weymouth).

The third heir in line of succession has not been included in the examples, but if a courtesy Earl is the second heir, *and he has sons*, the eldest would also use a courtesy title, a Viscountcy or Barony, as applicable.

1. The Duke of Wellington
2. Marquess Douro
3. Earl of Mornington

1. The Duke of Abercorn
2. Marquess of Hamilton
3. Viscount Strabane

1. The Duke of Bedford
2. Marquess of Tavistock
3. Lord Howland

1. The Duke of Grafton
2. Earl of Euston
3. Viscount Ipswich

1. The Duke of Richmond and Gordon
2. Earl of March and Kinrara
3. Lord Settrington

1. The Duke of Manchester
2. Viscount Mandeville

1. The Duke of Somerset
2. Lord Seymour

1. The Marquess Camden
2. Earl of Brecknock
3. Viscount Bayham

1. The Marquess of Zetland
2. Earl of Ronaldshay
3. Lord Dundas

1. The Marquess of Bath
2. Viscount Weymouth

1. The Earl of Verulam
2. Viscount Grimston

1. The Earl of Westmorland
2. Lord Burghersh

Peers by courtesy are eligible to sit in the House of Commons, e.g. Earl of Dalkeith, M.P.

Wife of a Peer by courtesy

The wife of a peer by courtesy is addressed as the wife of a peer of the same rank, but with the following exceptions (also mentioned under a peer by courtesy):

1. The wife of a Marquess by Courtesy is *not* given the formal style of 'The Most Hon.', e.g. Marchioness of Blandford.
2. The wife of an Earl, Viscount and Baron by Courtesy is *not* given the formal style of 'The Rt. Hon', e.g. Countess of Euston.
3. The wife of a peer by courtesy is *not* given the prefix 'The' in correspondence.

Widow of a Peer by courtesy

The widow of a peer by courtesy is addressed as the widow of a peer of the identical rank, with the following exceptions, also mentioned under the wife of a peer by courtesy:

1. Without the prefix of 'The Most Hon' (Marchionesses) or 'The Rt. Hon' (Peeresses of lower grades).
2. Without the prefix 'The' before the title.

If the courtesy title has passed to her late husband's brother or other relation, she would prefix her title by her christian name. If it has passed to her son or stepson, she would prefix the title by her christian name when he marries.

Former Wife of a Peer by courtesy

She is styled as the former wife of a peer, other than a Duke (see p. 39).

Younger Sons of a Duke or Marquess

The younger sons of a Duke or Marquess are known by the courtesy style of Lord, followed by their christian name and surname, e.g. Lord Edward FitzGerald.

BEGINNING OF LETTER

Formal	My Lord
Social	Dear Lord Edward
	The surname may be added if the acquaintanceship is slight

ENDING OF LETTER

Formal	Yours faithfully (see also p. 2)
Social	Yours sincerely

ENVELOPE

Formal and Social	Lord Edward FitzGerald

VERBAL ADDRESS

Formal	My Lord
Social	Lord Edward
Employee Status	My Lord *or* Your Lordship[1]

DESCRIPTION IN CONVERSATION

Lord Edward. If distinction is necessary, or on introduction, he is described as Lord Edward FitzGerald. *He should never be described as Lord FitzGerald*, and there is no authority for the prefix of 'The' before his name.

LIST OF DIRECTORS AND PATRONS

Lord Edward FitzGerald

MEMBERSHIP OF THE PRIVY COUNCIL

Precede his style with 'The Rt. Hon.', e.g.:

The Rt. Hon. Lord Edward FitzGerald (see *Privy Counsellor*, p. 78)

WITH ECCLESIASTICAL, AMBASSADORIAL, OR SERVICE RANK

These should precede his rank, e.g.:

His Excellency Lord Edward FitzGerald

Rear Admiral Lord Edward FitzGerald

[1] See p. 36, note [3].

SIGNATURE

Edward FitzGerald

Wife of a Younger Son of a Duke or Marquess

The wife of a younger son of a Duke or Marquess is known as *Lady*, followed by his Christian and surname, e.g. the wife of Lord Edward FitzGerald is known as Lady Edward FitzGerald. This style is identical for the wife of a younger son of a courtesy Marquess.

If she derives senior precedence as the daughter of a Duke or Marquess from that which she acquired on marriage, she may continue to use *her* prefix instead of *his*, e.g. Lady Mary Jones, married to Lord Edward Brown, may if she wishes, be known as Lady *Mary* Brown instead of Lady *Edward* Brown, but this is seldom done today. This form should only be used if it is known that it is preferred. This alternative style, however, is generally used by ladies whose marriage has been dissolved.

BEGINNING OF LETTER

Formal	(Dear) Madam[1]
Social	Dear Lady Edward
	The surname may be added if the acquaintanceship is slight e.g. Dear Lady Edward FitzGerald

ENDING OF LETTER

Formal	Yours faithfully (see also p. 2)
Social	Yours sincerely

ENVELOPE

Formal and Social	Lady Edward FitzGerald

VERBAL ADDRESS

Formal	Madam
Social	Lady Edward
Employee Status	My Lady *or* Your Ladyship[2]

[1] See p. 26, note [1].
[2] See p. 36, note [3].

DESCRIPTION IN CONVERSATION

Lady Edward. If distinction is necessary, or on introduction, she should be described as Lady Edward FitzGerald.

She should not be described as Lady FitzGerald, and would only be described as Lady Mary FitzGerald if she were senior in precedence to her husband, and she prefers to use her own style. Employee Status, 'Her Ladyship'.

LIST OF DIRECTORS AND PATRONS

Lady Edward FitzGerald

Widow of a Younger Son of a Duke or Marquess

Her style in widowhood does not change, except on remarriage, when she adopts her style from her husband. See *Wife of a younger son of a Duke or Marquess* (p. 47).

Former Wife of a Younger Son of a Duke or Marquess

She continues to be known by the same title she held on marriage, e.g. the former wife of Lord George Jones is still known as Lady George Jones.

If she has a courtesy style derived from her father, it is probable that she will revert to its use on dissolution of her marriage, e.g. Lady Mary Green formerly married to Lord George Black, will probably be known as Lady Mary Black.

Younger Son of an Earl

The style of 'The Honourable' is only used on the envelope in correspondence, in written descriptions or in formal documents. It is never used in conversation or on invitations and visiting cards, when the correct style is 'Mr.' or his ecclesiastical, Service rank, etc.

The more usual abbreviation is 'The Hon'. but the more old-fashioned form 'The Honble.' is sometimes used.

Sons of Earls by Courtesy also have the same style as sons of Earls.

BEGINNING OF LETTER

Formal   (Dear) Sir[1]

Social   Dear Mr. Brown

ENDING OF LETTER

Formal   Yours faithfully (see also p. 2)
Social   Yours sincerely

ENVELOPE

Formal and Social   The Hon. John Brown

VERBAL ADDRESS

Mr. Brown (or appropriate rank, e.g. Major Brown).

DESCRIPTION IN CONVERSATION

Mr. Brown

WITH ECCLESIASTICAL, AMBASSADORIAL, OR SERVICE RANK

These should precede his rank in correspondence, e.g.:
The Reverend the Hon. John Brown
His Excellency the Hon. John Brown
Major the Hon. John Brown

Wife of a Younger Son of an Earl

The wife of a gentleman with the courtesy style of 'The Honourable' is known by her husband's christian name and surname, with the addition of 'Mrs'. as a prefix. Thus, the wife of 'The Hon. John Brown' is 'The Hon. Mrs. John Brown'.

If she is the daughter of a Duke, Marquess, or Earl, with the style of 'Lady' followed by her christian name, she continues to use this style with her husband's surname, i.e. Lady Mary Brown.

If she is the daughter of a Viscount or Baron, with the style of 'The Hon.', she does not use her husband's christian name, e.g. 'The Hon. Jane White' marries 'The Hon. John Brown', she is known as 'The Hon. Mrs. Brown'. There is no difference in her style if her husband also has the style of 'The Honourable'.

[1] Strictly speaking the commencement of 'Sir' is the very formal style, for which the corresponding conclusion is given on p. 3. As this form of conclusion is now seldom used, 'Sir' instead of the more usual 'Dear Sir' is sometimes adopted in a very formal or official letter.

'The Honourable' is *never* used in conversation, invitations, and visiting cards.

BEGINNING OF LETTER

Formal   (Dear) Madam
Social   Dear Mrs. Brown

ENDING OF LETTER

Formal   Yours faithfully (see also p. 2)
Social   Yours sincerely

ENVELOPE

Formal and Social   The Hon. Mrs. John Brown

VERBAL ADDRESS

Mrs. Brown

DESCRIPTION IN CONVERSATION

Mrs. Brown

Widow of a Younger Son of an Earl

There is no difference in the forms of address in widowhood. Should she remarry, she adopts her style from her husband. See *Wife of a Younger Son of an Earl* (p. 49).

Former Wife of a Younger Son of an Earl

There is no difference in the forms of address on the dissolution of her marriage, but should she remarry, she adopts her style from her husband. See *Wife of a Younger Son of an Earl* (p. 49).

Son of a Viscount or Baron

All the sons of a Viscount or Baron, and of those who by courtesy enjoy the style and title of Viscount or Baron, have the courtesy style of 'The Honourable'.

In all respects the forms of address are identical with those accorded to a *Younger Son of an Earl* (p. 48).

For the elder son of a Viscount or Baron, in the Peerage of Scotland, see *Scottish Title of Master* (p. 56).

Wife of a Son of a Viscount or Baron

There is no difference in the forms of address from those of the wife of a younger son of an Earl. See *Wife of a Younger Son of an Earl* (p. 49).

Widow of a Son of a Viscount or Baron

There is no difference in her form of address as a widow from when her husband was alive, provided that she does not remarry. In this case she adopts her style from her husband. See *Wife of a Younger Son of an Earl* (p. 49).

Former Wife of a Son of a Viscount or Baron

There is no difference in the forms of address on the dissolution of her marriage, provided that she does not remarry. In this case, she adopts her style from her husband. See *Wife of a Younger Son of an Earl* (p. 49).

Daughter of a Duke, Marquess or Earl

A daughter of a Duke, Marquess or Earl has the style of 'Lady' before her Christian name and surname: e.g. the eldest daughter of the Duke of Norfolk is Lady Anne Fitzalan-Howard.

A daughter of those who by courtesy enjoy the title of a Marquess or Earl, has the identical style or 'Lady'.

On marriage she continues to use the same style, with her husband's surname, i.e. Lady Mary Brown marries Mr. John Black: she becomes Lady Mary Black. In no case does she drop from 'Lady Mary Brown' to 'The Hon. Mrs. Brown', even though her husband has this prefix.

Should she marry a peer she adopts his title, e.g. if 'Lady Mary Brown' marries the Earl of Flintshire, she becomes 'The Countess of Flintshire'.

If she marries a courtesy lord, and the precedence she derives from this is lower than that she derives from her father, she has the option of:

(a) adopting the usual style of the wife of a courtesy lord, e.g. Viscountess Molesey, *or*

(b) continuing her own style followed by the courtesy title, e.g. Lady Mary Molesey.

In practice very few ladies now adopt course (b) unless the marriage has been dissolved, as it is difficult therefrom to determine the relative degree of precedence. It was generally used a generation ago.

If she marries the younger son of a Duke or Marquess, who has the courtesy style of Lord John Jones, again she has the option of:

(a) adopting the usual style of the wife of a younger son of a Duke or Marquess, e.g. Lady John Jones, *or*

(b) continuing her own style followed by her surname, e.g. Lady Mary Jones.

In practice very few ladies now adopt style (b) unless the marriage has been dissolved, as it is difficult therefrom to determine the relative degree of precedence. It was generally used a generation ago.

BEGINNING OF LETTER

Formal	(Dear) Madam[1]
Social	Dear Lady Mary
	The surname may be added if the acquaintanceship is slight, e.g. Dear Lady Mary Jones

ENDING OF LETTER

Formal	Yours faithfully (see also p. 2)
Social	Yours sincerely

ENVELOPE

Formal and Social	Lady Mary Smith

VERBAL ADDRESS

Social	Lady Mary
Employee Status	My Lady *or* Your Ladyship[2]

[1] See p. 26, note [1].
[2] See p. 36, note [3].

DESCRIPTION IN CONVERSATION

Lady Mary.

If distinction is necessary, or on introduction, she is described as Lady Mary Smith. Employee Status, 'Her Ladyship'.

LIST OF DIRECTORS AND PATRONS

Lady Mary Smith.

Daughter of a Viscount or Baron

A daughter of a Viscount or Baron, or of those who by courtesy use the style and title of a Viscount or Baron, bears the courtesy style of 'The Honourable'.

When she is unmarried this style is followed by her christian name (e.g. The Hon. Mary Brown[1]). After marriage she drops the use of her christian name and uses her surname only, following Mrs. (e.g. the Hon. Mrs. Smith). The style of 'The Honourable' is not used before 'Miss'.

The style of 'The Hon.' is only used on an envelope, in written descriptions (usually on only the first mention) and in formal documents. It is never used in conversation, or on invitations or visiting cards when the correct style is 'Miss' or 'Mrs.'

A husband does not derive any style or title from his wife.

BEGINNING OF LETTER

Formal	(Dear) Madam[2]
Social	Dear Miss Brown *or*
	Dear Mrs. Brown (as applicable)

ENDING OF LETTER

Formal	Yours faithfully (see also p. 2)
Social	Yours sincerely

ENVELOPE

Formal and Social	The Hon. Mary Brown
	(unmarried ladies only)
	The Hon. Mrs. Brown

[1] The alternative abbreviation of 'The Honble', now regarded as old-fashioned, may be used if preferred.
[2] See p. 26, note 1.

VERBAL ADDRESS
VERBAL ADDRESS
Miss Brown or Mrs. Brown (as applicable)

DESCRIPTION IN CONVERSATION
Miss Brown or Mrs. Brown (as applicable)

LIST OF DIRECTORS AND PATRONS
The Hon. Mary Brown (unmarried ladies only)
The Hon. Mrs. Brown

Brothers and Sisters of a Peer, whose Father did not live to succeed to a Peerage

The Queen may issue a Royal Warrant conferring on the brothers and/or sisters of a Peer the style and precedence of the sons or daughters of a peer which would have been theirs had their father lived and succeeded to the peerage in question.

Disclaimed Peer

Under the Peerage Act of 1963, it is possible to disclaim a peerage of England, Scotland, Great Britain or the United Kingdom for life. The disclaimer is irrevocable, and operates from the date by which an instrument of disclaimer is delivered to the Lord Chancellor.

When a peerage has been disclaimed, no other *hereditary* peerage shall be conferred. An example of this occurred in 1970. The second Viscount Hailsham disclaimed his hereditary peerages for life in 1963, in order to sit in the House of Commons. As the Rt. Hon. Quintin Hogg, he was elected as Member for St. Marylebone. In 1970 he was appointed Lord Chancellor and received the customary life peerage, becoming Lord Hailsham of St. Marylebone.

The principal provisions of the Peerage Act are summarized in DEBRETT.

As soon as a peer has disclaimed his peerage he reverts to the status held before he inherited the peerage, and he is not accorded any courtesy title or style which he previously possessed deriving from that peerage.

Even if he disclaims the peerage within a few days after succession he must first have succeeded as a peer immediately on his predecessor's death, and will figure in the numbering in works of reference, e.g. 12th Earl of Flintshire.

Should he also be a baronet or knight, these dignities and appropriate styles are retained, being unaffected by his disclaiming the peerage.

EXAMPLES

> The Rt. Hon. Sir Alexander Douglas-Home, K.T., M.P.
>   (previously the Earl of Home)
> Victor E. P. Montagu, Esq.
>   (previously the Earl of Sandwich)
> Sir Max Aitken, Bt., D.S.O., D.F.C.
>   (previously the Lord Beaverbrook)

Wife of a Disclaimed Peer

Immediately her husband disclaims his peerage she reverts to the same style as her husband, e.g. if he becomes Mr. John Jones she becomes Mrs. John Jones.

If her husband is also a baronet or has been knighted, she will use the title of 'Lady Jones'.

If she inherited any courtesy style from her father she may revert to its use, e.g. Lady Mary White marries Lord Blank who disclaims his peerage, and thereby becomes Mr. Blank. His wife may then revert to the style of Lady Mary Blank. The Hon. Mary White who marries Lord Blank similarly reverts to The Hon. Mrs. Blank.

Children of a Disclaimed Peer

The children of a disclaimed peer retain their precedence as the children of a peer, and any courtesy titles and styles borne while their father was a peer. It is open to any child of a disclaiming peer to say that he or she no longer wishes to be known by these styles, e.g. the children of Sir Max Aitken (previously the Lord Beaverbrook) and Mr. Victor Montagu (previously the Earl of Sandwich) have retained such styles, but those of Sir Alec Douglas-Home (previously the Earl of Home) and Mr. Anthony Wedgwood Benn (previously the Viscount Stansgate) have decided not to use them.

Scottish Title of Master

There are three kinds of Master, all of which are connected with the Peerage of Scotland, see p. 22.

They are:

1. The heir apparent (usually the eldest son) of a peer, or peeress in her own right.[1]

2. The heir presumptive of a peer, or a peeress in her own right.[1]

3. The son and heir of an heir apparent (as in 1 above), who bears a peerage by courtesy.

1. *Heir Apparent*

He bears the title of Master, which is a legal dignity in its own right. As such he was ineligible to sit in the old Scottish Parliament, or for a Scottish seat in the House of Commons at Westminster, but only for an English seat, until the law was amended in the late eighteenth century.

Generally the Master's designation is the same as the peerage title, having evolved to show whose heir he was, e.g. the son of Lady Sempill is the Master of Sempill. If the peer is known by more than one peerage or designation, e.g. Lord Belhaven and Stenton, his son and heir is known by the first designation, the Master of Belhaven. See also *Titles Borne by Scottish Peers and Masters* (p. 58).

As the eldest sons of the first three grades of peers (Dukes, Marquesses, and Earls) use courtesy titles, heirs apparent fall into two categories.

(a) *Heir Apparent of a Duke, Marquess, Earl or a Countess in her own right*[2]—Though socially he is generally known by his courtesy title in the peerage, he is referred to by his substantive title of Master in all legal documents, commissions or proceedings in court, e.g. the son and heir of the Marquess of Lothian is referred to as Michael, Master of Lothian, commonly called Earl of Ancram.

(b) *Heir Apparent of a Viscount, Lord or Lady of Parliament*[3]—The title of Master is borne both legally and socially.

---

[1] For the meanings of heirs apparent and presumptive, see p. 41, note [1].
[2] There is no Duchess or Marchioness in her own right in the Peerage of Scotland.
[3] There is no Viscountess in her own right in the Peerage of Scotland.

2. *Heir Presumptive*

The heir presumptive of a peer of Scotland may bear the title of Master, which he gives up when he ceases to be heir to the peerage. One historic case was the heir presumptive to Lord Glamis. For two periods Sir Thomas Lyon was designated Master of Glamis, but he first gave up the title on the birth of his nephew. Later he became heir presumptive for eighteen years and was again Master of Glamis until his great-nephew was born.

If the heir presumptive is not a close relation of the peer, it will be necessary for the Lord Lyon to approve his use of the title.

See also *Titles Borne by Scottish Peers and Masters* (p. 58).

3. *Son and heir of the Heir Apparent who has a Peerage by Courtesy*

The grandson of a peer of Scotland bears *by courtesy* the title of Master. In practice this usage is limited to an Earl's grandson, since a grandson of a Duke or Marquess is generally known by a courtesy title.

The Master's designation is usually the same as his father's courtesy title, since the title evolved to show whose heir he was. Thus when the Earl of Strathmore has a son and grandson, the son and heir is Lord Glamis, and the latter's son and heir is the Master of Glamis. If the designation does not follow the usual practice it is by family arrangement, and by the decision of the Lord Lyon. The following are exceptions to the general custom:

The Earl of Crawford (Chief of the Lindsays) is father of Lord Balniel, whose son and heir is Master of Lindsay. In the lifetime of the Countess of Seafield, her son and heir was Viscount Reidhaven, and the latter's son and heir was the Master of Deskford.

See also *Titles Borne by Scottish Peers and Masters* (p. 58).

BEGINNING OF LETTER

If he is a peer by courtesy (see p. 42), otherwise as follows:

Formal	(Dear) Sir[1]
Social	Dear Master of Glamis

ENDING OF LETTER

Formal	Yours faithfully (see also p. 2)
Social	Yours sincerely

ENVELOPE

The Master of Glamis
Major the Master of Glamis

[1] See p. 49 , note [1].

VERBAL ADDRESS

Formal
Social } Master
Employee Status

DESCRIPTION IN CONVERSATION

The Master
If distinction is necessary, or on introduction:
The Master of Glamis

SIGNATURE

Thomas, Master of Glamis

MISTRESS

When the Mastership is held by a woman the official designation is 'Mistress of Blank' (e.g. Mistress of Mar). For obvious reasons the style is not much in favour among ladies nowadays, and is seldom used.

TITLES BORNE BY SCOTTISH PEERS AND MASTERS

The Scots Parliament ruled that a peer who belonged to a cadet branch of a family must not use his *surname only* for his peerage, as this is restricted to the chief of the whole name, consequently he must be Lord Blank 'of' somewhere to distinguish him. There are several examples in the peerage, e.g. Lord Hay of Yester, a title of the Marquess of Tweeddale, or Lord Forrester of Corstorphine, a title of the Earl of Verulam. Today this rule still applies for United Kingdom peerages. Even though the chief is not a peer, someone else of his name cannot use the undifferenced name for his title. Thus when Lord Mackintosh of Halifax was created a peer in 1948, he could not be styled Lord Mackintosh alone, as he was not Chief of Clan Mackintosh.

Masters who belong to cadet (younger) branches may not use only that part of their father's titles which is identical to the surname. In this category is Lord Balfour of Burleigh, who is not the Chief of the Balfours. (In fact he is not a Balfour at all, as the peerage passed through the female line.) Consequently his heir is the *Master of Burleigh* and not the *Master of Balfour*.

During the seventeenth century, the Earl of Roxburghe (forebear of the Duke) and then Chief of the Kers, obtained a pronouncement in Parliament that his heir apparent alone was to be known as Lord Ker. The Earl of Lothian's heir, a Ker cadet, was to be known in distinction as Lord Ker of Newbottle. (Subsequently the Marquess of Lothian succeeded as Chief of the Kers, the Dukes of Roxburghe having become Chiefs of the Innes family.)

These lengthy titles became abbreviated for ordinary purposes, and the peer came only to use the latter part of his title. Thus Lord Ker of Newbottle became known as Lord Newbottle. Today the heir apparent of the Earl of Wemyss (who is also Lord Douglas of Neidpath) is known as Lord Neidpath. An exception is Lord Balfour of Burleigh. He is not known as Lord Burleigh, to save confusion with the English peerage of Lord Burghley, borne by the Marquess of Exeter and usually adopted as the courtesy title for his heir apparent.

As the terms of address for

a peer, peeress and their children *and*
a baronet and knight, and their wives

are complicated, the titles and styles are summarized below, with a few general notes. For full information, see the appropriate title or style.

Summary of Titles
PEER, BARONET, KNIGHT AND DAME

	Husband	Wife	Eldest Son	Other Sons	Daughters
Peer	The Duke of Blank	The Duchess of Blank	Courtesy peerage title	Lord John Brown	Lady Mary Brown
	The Marquess of Little-hampton	The March-ioness of Littlehampton	Courtesy peerage title	Lord John Smith	Lady Mary Smith
	The Earl of Worthing	The Countess of Worthing	Courtesy peerage title	The Hon. John Robinson	Lady Mary Robinson
	The Viscount Angmering	The Viscount-ess Angmering	The Hon. John Green	The Hon. John Green	The Hon. Mary Green
	The Lord Ferring	The Lady Ferring	The Hon. John Grey	The Hon. John Grey	The Hon. Mary Grey
Baronet	Sir John Findon Bt.	Lady Findon	Untitled	Untitled	Untitled
Knight	Sir John Black	Lady Black	Untitled	Untitled	Untitled
Dame	Untitled	Dame Mary	Untitled	Untitled	Untitled

CORRESPONDENCE

In social correspondence a peer or peeress is addressed with the prefix of 'The' before the title, as in the table above.[1]

In formal correspondence the following styles are adopted:

His Grace the Duke of . . .	Her Grace the Duchess of . . .
The Most Hon. the Marquess (of) . . .	The Most Hon. the Marchioness (of) . . .
The Rt. Hon. the Earl (of) . . .	The Rt. Hon. the Countess (of) . . .
The Rt. Hon. the Viscount . . .	The Rt. Hon. the Viscountess. . .
The Rt. Hon. the Lord . . .	The Rt. Hon. the Lady . . .
	(A Peeress in her own right may prefer the style of The Rt. Hon. the Baroness . . .)

Neither series of prefixes are accorded to those who by courtesy are known by a peerage title or style.

For Baronets, Knights, their wives and Dames, see these Sections.

VERBAL ADDRESS

A Duke or Duchess is always known by his or her exact title. Other peers, peeresses and those who by courtesy are known by a peerage title are referred to as Lord and Lady Blank. For Baronets, Knights, their wives and Dames, see these Sections.

COURTESY LORD

He assumes by courtesy the title of a peerage usually the second in rank held by the peer, but which must be of a lesser grade than that used by the peer, i.e. the eldest son of a Marquess may be styled Earl, Viscount, or Baron.

The eldest son of a courtesy lord of the rank of Marquess or Earl also assumes a courtesy title. This is usually the third in rank held by the peer, but of necessity of a grade junior to his father's.

They are treated socially as if they were peers, but in correspondence see below.

PEERESS IN HER OWN RIGHT

She is styled as for the wife of a peer, but a Baroness sometimes prefers to use that title instead of 'The Lady . . .'.

[1] It is optional whether the initial 'T' of 'The' is written with a capital or small letter when preceded by another word, with the exception of Members of the Royal Family who use the capital 'T', e.g. Her Royal Highness The Princess . . .

Her children have the same style as that accorded to the children of a peer of equivalent rank.

LIFE PEER OR PEERESS

He or she is addressed identically as an hereditary peer or peeress.

The children have the same style as those of an hereditary peer or peeress.

MARRIED DAUGHTERS OF A PEER

They take their husband's surname, e.g. Lady Mary Blank or The Hon. Mrs. Scarlet, unless they marry a peer or courtesy lord. See the appropriate section for a possible exception in the latter case.

WIDOW OF A PEER

She is known either as (a) The Dowager Countess of Worthing or appropriate rank (which is the official style), or (b) Mary, Countess of Worthing, which is more usually adopted. She does not have the first option if a Dowager Countess of Worthing is still living. On remarriage she loses any title derived from her late husband.

WIDOW OF A BARONET

She is known either as (a) Dowager Lady Findon, or (b) Mary, Lady Findon, with the same proviso as for the widow of a peer. On remarriage she loses any style derived from her late husband.

WIDOW OF A KNIGHT

She retains the same style as a knight's wife.

FORMER WIFE OF A PEER OR BARONET

She has the style of Mary, Countess of Worthing or Mary, Lady Brown, but on remarriage she loses any title or style derived from her former husband.

FORMER WIFE OF A KNIGHT

She retains the same style as a knight's wife, but on remarriage she loses such style derived from her former husband.

Part III

OTHER TITLES AND STYLES

Baronet, Baronetess, Baronet's wife, widow, and former wife

Widows of those who would have succeeded to a Baronetcy had their husbands survived

Knight, his wife, widow, and former wife

Dame

The Privy Council

Members of the Orders of Chivalry below the rank of Knight, and recipients of Decorations and Medals conferred by the Crown

Untitled gentleman, married and unmarried lady

Scottish titles and territorial designations

Irish Chieftainries and other Irish titles

Position of letters after the name

The Aga Khan, and the Maltese and Canadian Nobility

Foreign titles and styles

Usage in the United States

OTHER TITLES AND STYLES

Baronet

A baronetcy is an hereditary dignity the holder of which is accorded the prefix of 'Sir' and the suffix of Baronet to his name. The suffix is invariably abbreviated in correspondence. The usual abbreviation is 'Bt.' but the more old-fashioned 'Bart.' is sometimes preferred.

Scottish baronets sometimes use their territorial titles in conjunction with their surnames. In this case, Bt. should appear at the end, e.g. Sir John Macmillan of Lochmillan, Bt. See *Scottish Titles and Territorial Designations*, p. 87.

For summary of titles, see p. 59.

BEGINNING OF LETTER

Formal	(Dear) Sir[1]
Social	Dear Sir John
	If the acquaintanceship is slight, the surname may be used in addition, e.g. Dear Sir John Brown

ENDING OF LETTER

Formal	Yours faithfully (see also p. 2)
Social	Yours sincerely

ENVELOPE

Formal and Social	Sir John Brown, Bt.

See p. 49, note [1].

VERBAL ADDRESS

Formal and Social   Sir John
Employee Status   Sir John

DESCRIPTION IN CONVERSATION

Sir John

If distinction is necessary, or on introduction, he is described as Sir John Brown.

PRIVY COUNSELLOR

The Rt. Hon. Sir John Brown

It is unnecessary to include the letters P.C. since 'The Rt. Hon' is sufficient indication. See also *Privy Counsellor*, p. 78.

ECCLESIASTICAL, AMBASSADORIAL, OR SERVICE RANK

These should precede 'Sir':

The Hon. Sir John Brown, Bt
The Rev. Sir John Brown, Bt[1]
Major Sir John Brown, Bt.

All other letters after the name *follow* 'Bt.':

Lt.-Gen. Sir John Brown, Bt., K.C.B., C.B.E., D.S.O.
The Reverend Sir John Brown, Bt., D.C.L.

SIGNATURE

John Brown

STYLE FROM SOURCES OTHER THAN THE CROWN

It is not customary in *formal* usage to combine styles emanating from other sources with titles conferred by the Sovereign. Alderman Sir John Smith and Professor Sir William Brown are solecisms. In *social* usage this is not uncommon, though deprecated by purists.

BARONETESS

When a lady inherits a baronetcy she is known as a Baronetess, with the official style of 'Dame Mary Brown, Btss'.

Although a few baronetesses were created in the past, there is now only one lady on the Roll of the Baronets. Few baronetcies

---

[1] A Church of England clergyman who is a Baronet is styled 'Sir', whereas if a knighthood is conferred upon him he does not receive the accolade.

still in existence, all of them Scottish, can be inherited in the female line. Succession to a baronetcy follows the remainders specified in the letters patent of creation.

The form of address is the same as for a *Baronet's Wife,* with the exception of the envelope, which is addressed as follows:

Lady Dunbar of Hempriggs, Btss.

WIFE OF A BARONET

The wife of a baronet has the style of 'Lady' before her surname. The old-fashioned style of 'Dame', followed by her christian names and surname (e.g. Dame Edith Brown) is no longer in general use, but is retained for legal documents. It is useful for these purposes in that it allows for the identification of a particular Lady Brown by the use of her christian names. An alternative *legal* style is for the christian names to be placed before 'Lady'. See p. 8. For *correspondence,* where confusion with others of the same surname could arise, 'Lady' may be followed by the christian name in brackets, as mentioned below (under *Envelope*). This form is often used in publications.

If a baronet's wife has a courtesy style of Lady Mary, this is used in full, e.g. Lady Mary Brown.

If she has the courtesy style of 'The Honourable' this precedes 'Lady Brown', e.g. The Hon. Lady Brown.

The wife of a Scottish baronet who uses his territorial designation should be so addressed, e.g. Lady Macmillan of Lochmillan.

BEGINNING OF LETTER

Formal	(Dear) Madam[1]
Social	Dear Lady Brown[2]

ENDING OF LETTER

Formal	Yours faithfully (see also p. 2)
Social	Yours sincerely

ENVELOPE

Formal and Social	Lady Brown

If it is necessary, to distinguish a particular wife of a baronet from another with the same title and surname, such as at an hotel or conference, the christian name may be added in brackets,

[1] See p. 26, note [1].
[2] This is the feminine equivalent for both Dear Sir John Brown, and Dear Sir John.

e.g. Lady (Edith) Brown. This form should only be used in special circumstances.

<small>VERBAL ADDRESS</small>

Social	Lady Brown
Employee Status	My Lady *or* Your Ladyship[1]

<small>DESCRIPTION IN CONVERSATION</small>

Social	Lady Brown
Employee Status	Her Ladyship

WIDOW OF A BARONET

Officially the widow of a baronet immediately becomes the Dowager Lady Brown on the death of her husband, unless the widow of a senior baronet of the same creation is still alive, when she becomes Mary, Lady Brown.

Many dowager ladies prefer to use their christian name rather than the word 'Dowager', so the wishes of the lady concerned should be ascertained. If in doubt, I recommend the style of 'Mary, Lady Brown', which the majority prefer.

Should she remarry, she takes her style from her present husband.

By custom, when the present baronet is unmarried, the widow of the late baronet continues to call herself Lady Blank, the same style as when her husband was living. Should the present baronet marry, it is usual for the widow of the baronet to announce the style by which she wishes to be known, i.e. 'Dowager Lady Brown' or 'Mary, Lady Brown'.

The widow of a Scottish baronet who uses his territorial title should be so described, e.g. Dowager Lady Macmillan of Lochmillan, or Mary, Lady Macmillan of Lochmillan.

<small>BEGINNING OF LETTER</small>

Formal	(Dear) Madam[2]
Social	Dear Lady Brown

<small>ENDING OF LETTER</small>

Formal	Yours faithfully (see also p. 2)
Social	Yours sincerely

[1] See p. 36, note [3].
[2] See p. 26, note [1].

ENVELOPE

Formal and Social   Dowager Lady Brown *or*
                        Mary, Lady Brown
The word 'The' should not be included as a prefix as this
would imply that the lady was a Peeress.

VERBAL ADDRESS

Social   Lady Brown
Employee Status   My Lady *or* Your Ladyship[1]

DESCRIPTION IN CONVERSATION

Social, Lady Brown. If distinction is necessary, or on introduction,
she should be described as Mary, Lady Brown.
    Employee Status, Her Ladyship.

FORMER WIFE OF A BARONET

See *Widow of a Baronet* (p. 68).

She is addressed as the widow of a Baronet with the style Mary,
Lady Brown, provided that she does not remarry.

WIDOWS OF THOSE WHO WOULD HAVE SUCCEEDED TO A BARONETCY HAD THEIR HUSBANDS SURVIVED

The Queen may issue a Royal Warrant by which the lady concerned may enjoy the same title, rank, place, pre-eminence, and
procedure as if her late husband had survived and succeeded to the
title.
    This privilege is usually only granted when her late husband
died on active service.

CHILDREN OF A BARONET

They do not have any special style, but follow the rules for
addressing untitled ladies or gentlemen. Children who are or have
been adopted are not in line of succession to a baronetcy by
reason of such adoption.

[1] See p. 36, note [3].

Knight

The dignity of knighthood is the one which is most frequently conferred. It carries the prefix of 'Sir', but unlike a baronetcy it is only held for life.

The recipient is now allowed to use the prefix from the date of the announcement in the LONDON GAZETTE, and does not need to wait for the accolade to be conferred upon him.

There are two kinds of knighthood conferred by the Sovereign:

(1) Knights of the various Orders of Chivalry, identified by the appropriate letters after the name, see below, page 72; and (2) Knights Bachelor, which in ordinary correspondence, carry no letters after the name (see page 73).

For summary of titles, see p. 59.

BEGINNING OF LETTER

Formal	(Dear) Sir[1]
Social	Dear Sir John
	If the acquaintanceship is slight, the surname may be used, e.g. Dear Sir John Smith.

ENDING OF LETTER

Formal	Yours faithfully (see also p. 2)
Social	Yours sincerely

ENVELOPE

Formal and Social	Sir John Smith (with the appropriate letters after his name).

VERBAL ADDRESS

Formal and Social	Sir John
Employee Status	Sir John

DESCRIPTION IN CONVERSATION

Sir John. If distinction is necessary, or on introduction, he is described as Sir John Smith.

MEMBERSHIP OF THE PRIVY COUNCIL

The Rt. Hon. Sir John Smith.

[1] See p. 49, note [1].

It is unnecessary to include the letters P.C., since 'The Rt. Hon' is sufficient indication. See also *Privy Counsellor* (p. 78).

ECCLESIASTICAL, AMBASSADORIAL, OR SERVICE RANK

These precede 'Sir'.

The Hon. Sir John Brown, K.C.B.
Major Sir John Brown

A clergyman of the Church of England, if appointed a knight of one of the Orders of Chivalry, does not receive the accolade, and is thus not accorded the prefix '*Sir*' before his name but he places the appropriate letters of the Order of Chivalry concerned after his name, e.g.:

The Rt. Rev. the Lord Bishop of Sevenoaks, K.C.V.O.

Clergy of other Churches may receive the accolade and thus use 'Sir'.

SIGNATURE

John Smith

A PEER WHO RECEIVES A KNIGHTHOOD OF AN ORDER OF CHIVALRY

He adds the appropriate letters of the Order after his name, e.g.:

The Viscount Angmering, K.C.V.O.

STYLE FROM SOURCES OTHER THAN THE CROWN

It is not customary in *formal* usage to combine the style emanating from other sources with titles conferred by the Sovereign. Alderman Sir William Brown and Professor Sir Edward Hailstorm are solecisms. In social usage this is not uncommon, though deprecated by purists.

HONORARY KNIGHTHOOD

When a foreign national receives an honorary knighthood of an Order of Chivalry, he is not entitled to prefix *Sir* before his name, but he may place the appropriate letters after his name, e.g. General Omar Vanderbilt, K.C.B. Should he subsequently become a naturalised British subject, he will be entitled to receive the accolade. Having become a full knight of the appropriate Order, he will use '*Sir*' before his name.

1. KNIGHTS OF THE ORDERS OF CHIVALRY

The three senior Orders of Chivalry are very exclusive. Unlike the other Orders (see below), they consist of one class only. They carry the following letters after the name:

Knight of the Garter	K.G.[1]
Knight of the Thistle	K.T.
Knight of St. Patrick	K.P.[2]

The remaining Orders of Chivalry consist of several classes of which the first two classes of these Orders carry Knighthoods, viz.:

Class 1—Knight Grand Cross or Knight Grand Commander

Class 2—Knight Commander

The appropriate letters for the various Orders of Chivalry are as follows:

	Knight Grand Cross or Knight Grand Commander	Knight Commander
Order of the Bath	G.C.B.	K.C.B.
Order of the Star of India[3]	G.C.S.I.	K.C.S.I.
Order of St. Michael & St. George	G.C.M.G.	K.C.M.G.
Order of the Indian Empire[3]	G.C.I.E.	K.C.I.E.
Royal Victorian Order	G.C.V.O.	K.C.V.O.
Order of the British Empire	G.B.E.	K.B.E.

For lower classes of the Orders of Chivalry which do *not* carry Knighthoods, see *Members of the Orders of Chivalry below the rank of Knight* (p. 80).

There is no difference in the form of address of a Knight Grand Cross (or Knight Grand Commander) and a Knight Commander. In both cases the appropriate letters will be placed after the names.

Should a knight be promoted within the same Order, he ceases to use the appropriate titles of his lower rank, e.g. if General Sir John Brown, K.C.B. is raised to a G.C.B. he becomes General Sir John Brown G.C.B.

[1] Ladies of this Order do not have any letters after their names. L.G. is incorrect.
[2] No appointments have been made since 1921. There are only two surviving Knights, the Dukes of Gloucester and Windsor.
[3] No appointments have been made since 1947. but there are several surviving Knights of these Orders.

The same applies to a knight of an Order of Chivalry who previously belonged to the same Order, but of a class which did not carry a knighthood. Thus Colonel John Brown, C.B. on promotion to a K.C.B. becomes Colonel Sir John Brown, K.C.B. and henceforward drops the C.B.

When a knight receives more than one Order of the same class, the letters appear in order of precedence of the Orders concerned, and *not* according to the date he received them, e.g. a Knight Grand Cross of the Bath, the Royal Victorian Order and the British Empire, is addressed as follows:

Field Marshal Sir John Brown, G.C.B., G.C.V.O., G.B.E.

When a knight receives more than one Order of a different class, the higher grade of a junior Order is placed before the lower grade of a senior Order, e.g.:

Lt. Gen. Sir John Brown, G.B.E., K.C.M.G., C.B., C.V.O.

Where a knight has received several Orders of Chivalry, *all* the appropriate letters must be included after his name in correspondence. The old fashioned style of putting 'etc, etc.' after the first letters mentioned is no longer followed, and the omission is considered to be slighting both to the individual and to the Orders concerned.

2. KNIGHT BACHELOR

No letters are now usually placed after the name of a Knight Bachelor, except in legal and official documents, when 'Knight' may be added, but to add 'Kt.' which was formerly used is not incorrect.

'K.B.' should never be used in correspondence for a Knight Bachelor: this signified a Knight of the Bath before the Order was re-organized in 1815.

Knighthood does not affect the use of letters already borne, e.g. if a *Mr.* John Brown, C.B., C.V.O., O.B.E. is created a Knight Bachelor, he becomes *Sir* John Brown, C.B., C.V.O., O.B.E.

PRECEDENCE OF LETTERS

Victoria Cross[1]	V.C.
George Cross[1]	G.C.
Knight of the Garter	K.G.
Knight of the Thistle	K.T.

[1] Does not confer a Knighthood upon recipient.

Knight of St. Patrick[1]	K.P.
Knight Grand Cross of the Bath	G.C.B.
Order of Merit[2]	O.M.
Knight Grand Commander of the Star of India[1]	G.C.S.I.
Knight Grand Cross of the Order of St. Michael and St. George	G.C.M.G.
Knight Grand Commander of the Indian Empire[1]	G.C.I.E.
Knight Grand Cross of the Royal Victorian Order	G.C.V.O.
Knight Grand Cross of the British Empire	G.B.E.
Companion of Honour[2]	C.H.
Knight Commander of the Bath	K.C.B.
Knight Commander of the Star of India[1]	K.C.S.I.
Knight Commander of St. Michael and St. George	K.C.M.G.
Knight Commander of the Indian Empire[1]	K.C.I.E.
Knight Commander of Royal Victorian Order	K.C.V.O.
Knight Commander of the British Empire	K.B.E.

(Then follow letters below the rank of knight, commencing with C.B.)[3]; see *Members of the Orders of Chivalry below the rank of Knight* (p. 80).

WIFE OF A KNIGHT

The wife of a knight is known as 'Lady' followed by her surname, and she is addressed as is the wife of a baronet.

The old-fashioned style of 'Dame' followed by christian name and surname, e.g. Dame Edith Brown is no longer in general use, but is retained for legal documents. It is useful for these purposes in that it allows for the identification of the particular Lady Brown by the use of her christian names. An alternative *legal* style is for her christian names to be placed before 'Lady'. For *correspondence*, where confusion with others of the same surname could arise, 'Lady' may be followed by the christian name in brackets. This form is often used in publications. See *Envelope*. She should never be styled Lady Barbara Brown, unless the daughter of a Duke, Marquess, or Earl.

[1] No longer conferred.
[2] Does not confer a Knighthood upon recipient.
[3] Letters which signify membership of The Most Venerable Order of the Hospital of St. John of Jerusalem do not appear after the name. Bailiffs and Knights of Justice and of Grace do not receive the accolade.

If a knight's wife has the courtesy style of 'Lady Mary', this is used in full, e.g. Lady Mary Smith.

If a knight's wife has the courtesy style of 'The Honourable', this precedes 'Lady Smith', e.g. The Hon. Lady Smith.

The wife of a Church of England clergyman who receives a knighthood but is not eligible to receive the accolade continues to be addressed as Mrs. John Smith, but she has the precedence of a Knight's wife.

The wife of an honorary knight continues to be addressed as Mrs. John Braun.

BEGINNING OF LETTER

Formal	(Dear) Madam[1]
Social	Dear Lady Brown[2]

ENDING OF LETTER

Formal	Yours faithfully (see also p. 2)
Social	Yours sincerely

ENVELOPE

Formal and Social	Lady Brown

Note : Where there may be more than one lady of the same title and surname, such as at an hotel or conference, the christian name may be added in brackets, e.g. Lady (Edith) Brown. This form should, however, *only* be used in special circumstances.

VERBAL ADDRESS

Formal and Social	Lady Brown
Employee Status	My Lady or Your Ladyship[1]

DESCRIPTION IN CONVERSATION

Social	Lady Brown
Employee Status	Her Ladyship

WIDOW OF A KNIGHT

She is addressed as the wife of a knight, provided that she does not remarry, when she will take her style from her present husband.

[1] See p. 26, note [1].
[2] This is the feminine equivalent for both 'Dear Sir John' and 'Dear Sir John Brown'.

FORMER WIFE OF A KNIGHT

She is addressed as the wife of a knight, provided that she does not remarry, when she will take her style from her present husband.

CHILDREN OF A KNIGHT

They do not have any special style, but follow the rules for addressing untitled ladies and gentlemen.

Dame

A dame is the feminine equivalent of a knight of an Order of Chivalry. Similarly, the title is always used in conjunction with the christian name. For the legal use of 'Dame' see also p. 8.

Dames are appointed to the following Orders of Chivalry, and as for knights, there are two classes:

	Dame Grand Cross	Dame Commander
Order of St. Michael and St. George	G.C.M.G. (not yet bestowed)	D.C.M.G.
Royal Victorian Order	G.C.V.O.	D.C.V.O.
Order of the British Empire	G.B.E.	D.B.E.

The rule for promotion in the same Order of Chivalry and the precedence of the Orders applies as for a knight.[1]

A peeress (including holders of a peerage title by courtesy) who is appointed a dame adds the appropriate letters after her name, e.g. The Countess of Dorking, D.C.V.O.

The daughter of a Duke, Marquess, or Earl, with the style Lady Mary Brown, adds the appropriate letters after her name, e.g. Lady Mary Brown, D.B.E.

As a dame, the wife *or* widow of a baronet or knight is usually known as Dame Irene Smith, D.B.E., but a few ladies prefer to continue their former style of Lady Smith, D.B.E. (as did Baroness Spencer-Churchill when Lady Churchill). She should be addressed as Dame Irene Smith, D.B.E., unless her preference for the latter style is known.

---

[1] Letters which signify membership of The Most Venerable Order of the Hospital of St. John of Jerusalem are not included after the name. Dames Grand Cross and Dames of Justice and of Grace do not bear the title of 'Dame' before the name.

A lady styled 'The Hon.' is addressed 'The Hon. Dame Mary Jones, D.B.E.'. As a dame is the feminine equivalent of a knight, the style of 'Mrs.' is incorrect.

A husband does not derive any style or title from his wife.

When a dame of an Order of Chivalry is gazetted by her professional, rather than her legal, name she usually prefers to be so addressed, e.g. Dame Margot Fonteyn.

When a dame is the wife or widow of a knight, she generally prefers to separate the honour acquired in her own right from that derived from her husband; e.g., when Miss Daphne du Maurier (widow of Sir Frederick Browning) was raised to the rank of a Dame of the British Empire, she chose to be addressed either as Lady Browning, D.B.E., or Dame Daphne du Maurier, D.B.E.

For summary of titles, see p. 59.

BEGINNING OF LETTER

Formal	(Dear) Madam
Social	Dear Dame Mary
	When the acquaintanceship is slight, the surname may be used, e.g. Dear Dame Mary Smith

ENDING OF LETTER

Formal	Yours faithfully (see also p. 2)
Social	Yours sincerely

ENVELOPE

Formal and Social	Dame Mary Smith, D.B.E. (or applicable Order)

VERBAL ADDRESS

Social	Dame Mary
Employee Status	Dame Mary

DESCRIPTION IN CONVERSATION

Dame Mary. When distinction is necessary, or on introduction, she is described as Dame Mary Smith.

CHILDREN OF A DAME

They do not have any special style, but follow the rule for addressing untitled ladies and gentlemen.

The Privy Council

The Privy Council is the ancient executive governing body of the United Kingdom presided over by the Sovereign and exercises many functions, some of which have been entrusted to it by Acts of Parliament, which may be legislative, administrative or judicial. Its decisions are usually embodied in Orders in Council or Proclamations.

Membership is for life, with the style of 'Right Honourable'. Privy Counsellors are appointed by the Crown from persons distinguished in various walks of public life, at home and in the Commonwealth, including some members of the Royal Family, the Archbishops of Canterbury and York, the Bishop of London, The Lord Chancellor, many members of the Judiciary such as Lords of Appeal, all Cabinet Ministers, and some Overseas Prime Ministers. The Lord President of the Council is usually a senior member of the Cabinet.

A full Council is now only assembled for the Accession of a new Sovereign, and it is not usual for a member to attend any Council unless specially summoned. Those summoned are generally, though not invariably, members of the Government. A routine Council meeting is usually held at Buckingham Palace by the Sovereign (or, in Her absence abroad, by Counsellors of State), and must be attended by at least four Privy Counsellors and the Clerk of the Council.

The Cabinet owes its origin to the Privy Council, of which it was 'an inner Council' or committee.

Much of the work of the Privy Council is done in committee, of which the most important is the Judicial Committee, the final Court of Appeal outside the United Kingdom (where the House of Lords is the Supreme Court of Appeal), though certain Commonwealth countries have abolished appeals to the Privy Council (e.g. Canada, India and Pakistan) and established instead their own Supreme Courts of Appeal. The Queen does not preside at committee meetings of the Privy Council.

PRIVY COUNSELLOR

The spelling *Privy Councillor* is also used, but as the Privy Council Office prefer the above spelling it has been adopted throughout this book.

The letters P.C. follow all honours and decorations awarded

by the Crown. This is because membership of the Privy Council is an appointment or office held rather than an honour conferred.[1]

By precedence a Privy Counsellor immediately follows a Knight of the Garter or the Thistle (in Scotland), and the letters P.C. are often *incorrectly* given next position after K.G. or K.T. The position of letters after the name is not always identical with precedence, e.g. V.C. is given first place by Royal Warrant, though such precedence has not been accorded.

BEGINNING OF LETTER

Formal and Social	There is no special form used when writing to a member of the Privy Council e.g.
Formal	My Lord, (Dear) Sir,[2] (Dear) Madam[3]
Social	Dear Lord Blank, Dear Lady Blank, Dear Mr. Blank, Dear Mrs. Blank, Dear Miss Blank.

ENDING OF LETTER

Formal	Yours faithfully (see also p. 2)
Social	Yours sincerely.

ENVELOPE

Peer or Peeress

He (or she) is addressed according to his (or her) peerage rank, with the letters P.C. after the title and Orders conferred.

Formal	The Rt. Hon. the Earl of Dorking, K.C.V.O., P.C.
Social	The Earl of Dorking, P.C.
Social	The Baroness Jones, P.C.

Others

'The Rt. Hon.' is always placed before the name both in formal and social usage. There is no need to add the letters P.C. after the

---

[1] Valentine Heywood, in his *British Titles*, 1951, points out that there are many offices which give precedence. 'You may put a man's offices before, or after, his name and style, but you cannot put them in the middle of it. You cannot say "The Right Hon. Winston Spencer-Churchill, Prime Minister, C.H." You must say either "Prime Minister—The Right Hon. Winston Spencer-Churchill, C.H." or "The Right Honourable Winston Spencer-Churchill, C.H., Prime Minister" . . . although the office of Prime Minister gives precedence above C.H. Nor does it in any way alter this, if, on the analogy of the P.C., you abbreviate Prime Minister into P.M.' When Garter King of Arms proclaimed the styles of the Duke of Connaught at his funeral, after reciting fully his styles, he ended 'One of His Majesty's Most Honourable Privy Council, Field-Marshal in the Army.'
[2] See p. 49, note [1].
[3] See p. 26, note [1].

name, since 'The Rt. Hon.' is sufficient indication of membership of the Privy Council.

Other ranks such as ecclesiastical, ambassadorial, Service, etc., precede 'The Rt. Hon.'. (See below.)

Ladies who are Privy Counsellors drop the use of 'Miss' or 'Mrs.'.

Examples

The Rt. Hon. Sir John Smith, M.P.
Lt. Col. the Rt. Hon. John Jones
The Rt. Hon. Edward Heath, M.P.
The Rt. Hon. Barbara Castle, M.P.
The Rt. Rev. and Rt. Hon. the Lord Bishop of London
The Rt. Hon. Lord John Jones, M.P.
His Excellency the Rt. Hon. Christopher Soames.

VERBAL ADDRESS

Membership of the Privy Council does not affect verbal address in any way. A peer, peeress, baronet, knight, or an untitled lady or gentleman is addressed as any other person of the same rank who is not a Privy Counsellor, i.e. Lord Blank, Lady Blank, Admiral Blank, Mr. Blank, Mrs. Blank, or Miss Blank.

DESCRIPTION IN CONVERSATION

Membership of the Privy Council does not affect description in any way. The Rt. Hon. Sir John Smith is known as 'Sir John Smith', Lt. Col. the Rt. Hon. John Jones as 'Colonel Jones' and the Rt. Hon. Barbara Castle, M.P. as 'Mrs. Castle'.

WIFE (OR HUSBAND) OF PRIVY COUNSELLOR

They acquire no style or title.

Members of the Orders of Chivalry below the rank of Knight, and recipients of Decorations and Medals conferred by the Crown

They are addressed according to their rank, with the appropriate letters after their name in order of precedence. The use of all these letters is obligatory, e.g. John Brown, Esq., C.B.E., M.V.O., T.D.

Those promoted within the same Order of Chivalry do not continue to show the letters of the lower class of that Order, e.g. if Brigadier John Smith, O.B.E., is promoted to C.B.E. he is addressed as Brigadier John Smith, C.B.E., the O.B.E. being dropped.

Precedence of letters

The full list of honours and awards in order of precedence of letters is given below. A baronet has the letters Bt. or Bart. immediately after the name, and before any letters which signify honours. See *Baronet* (p. 65).

It should be noted that V.C. and G.C. have precedence over *all* letters signifying Orders (including knightly grades therein), Decorations and Medals.

The Order of Merit (O.M.) and Companion of Honour (C.H.) are important honours which bestow no title on the holder. The letters O.M. follow G.C.B., and C.H. follow G.B.E.

For membership of The Most Venerable Order of the Hospital of St. John of Jerusalem, see p. 74, note [3] and p. 76, note [1].

Precedence of letters signifying Orders, Decorations and Medals

The following is the complete list of letters of Orders, etc., conferred by the Crown below the rank of knight, in order of precedence.

The placing of the letters M.V.O. depends upon whether of fourth or fifth class, both of which have identical letters, see below.

Victoria Cross	V.C.	(precedes all letters including knights)
George Cross	G.C.	(after V.C., but precedes all other letters, including knights)
Order of Merit	O.M.	(follows G.C.B. see *Knightage*, p. 72)
Order of Victoria and Albert[1,2]	V.A.	(follows G.C.I.E. see *Knightage*, p. 72)
Order of the Crown of India[1,2]	C.I.	(before G.C.V.O. see *Knightage*, p. 72)
Companion of Honour	C.H.	(follows G.B.E. see *Knightage*, p. 72)
Companion of the Order of the Bath	C.B.	
Companion of the Order of the Star of India[1]	C.S.I.	

[1] No longer bestowed.
[2] Conferred exclusively upon ladies.

Companion of the Order of St. Michael and St. George	C.M.G.
Companion of the Order of the Indian Empire[1]	C.I.E.
Commander of Royal Victorian Order	C.V.O.
Commander of the Order of the British Empire	C.B.E.
Distinguished Service Order	D.S.O.
Member of Royal Victorian Order (if Class IV)	M.V.O.
Officer of Order of British Empire	O.B.E.
Imperial Service Order	I.S.O.
Member of Royal Victorian Order (if Class V)	M.V.O.
Member of Order of British Empire	M.B.E.
Indian Order of Merit (Military)[1]	I.O.M.
Royal Red Cross[2]	R.R.C.
Distinguished Service Cross	D.S.C.
Military Cross	M.C.
Distinguished Flying Cross	D.F.C.
Air Force Cross	A.F.C.
Associate, Royal Red Cross[2]	A.R.R.C.
Order of British India[1]	O.B.I.
Albert Medal[1]	A.M.
Distinguished Conduct Medal	D.C.M.
Conspicuous Gallantry Medal	C.G.M.
George Medal	G.M.
Edward Medal[1]	E.M.
Distinguished Conduct Medal of Royal West African Frontier Force and King's African Rifles[1]	D.C.M.

[1] See p. 81 for note.
[2] See p. 81 for note.

Indian Distinguished Service Medal[1]	I.D.S.M.	
Distinguished Service Medal	D.S.M.	
Military Medal	M.M.	
Distinguished Flying Medal	D.F.M.	
Air Force Medal	A.F.M.	
Medal for Saving Life at Sea	S.G.M.	
Indian Order of Merit (Civil)[1]	I.O.M.	
British Empire Medal	B.E.M.	(not part of the Order of the British Empire, and shown separately)
Canada Medal	C.M.	
King's Police Medal	K.P.M.[2]	
King's Police and Fire Service Medal	K.P.F.S.M.[2]	
Queen's Police Medal	Q.P.M.[3]	
Queen's Fire Service Medal	Q.F.S.M.[3]	
Meritorious Service Medal[1]	M.S.M.	(if awarded in the Navy before 20th July 1928)
Army Emergency Reserve Decoration	E.R.D.	
Volunteer Officer's Decoration[1]	V.D.	
Territorial Decoration	T.D.	
Efficiency Decoration	E.D.	
Decoration for Officers of the Royal Naval Reserve	R.D.	
Decoration for Officers of the Royal Naval Volunteers Reserve	V.R.D.	
Canadian Forces Decoration	C.D.	

ORDER OF CANADA

The formation of the Order of Canada was announced in 1967.

[1] No longer bestowed or bestowed posthumously.
[2] The designation of medals already awarded does not change from King's to Queen's during the present reign.
[3] The change from King's to Queen's was made on 19 May 1954.

The Order, of which The Queen is Sovereign, is divided into the following:

> Companion of the Order of Canada, with the letters C.C.
> The Medal of Courage, with the letters C.M. (which may be awarded posthumously)
> The Medal of Service, with the letters S.M.

All these letters follow the name after V.C. and G.C., before any other letters. Though membership of the Order is restricted to Canadian citizens, those of other countries may be appointed Companions or receive the Medal of Service on an honorary basis.

Untitled Gentleman

It is for the writer to decide whether one should be addressed as John Brown, Esq. or Mr. John Brown. For the history of these descriptions see Sir Anthony Wagner, *English Genealogy*, 1960, pp. 104–6. The former style is now customary in most walks of life in Great Britain and Ireland but in United States,[1] Canada, Australia, and New Zealand, the style of Mr. is generally used. John Brown is considered impolite, except for schoolboys. (See below.)

BEGINNING OF LETTER

Formal	(Dear) Sir[2]
Social	Dear Mr. Brown

ENDING OF LETTER

Formal	Yours faithfully (see also p. 2) *or*
Social	Yours sincerely

ENVELOPE

John Brown Esq.[3]
Mr. John Brown

VERBAL ADDRESS AND DESCRIPTION IN CONVERSATION

Mr. Brown.

---

[1] See also Usage in the United States, p. 118.
[2] See p. 49, note [1].
[3] Esqre, now regarded as an old-fashioned form, may be used if preferred.

On formal occasions the following distinction is made, unless a prefix, such as 'Captain', makes this unnecessary:

Head of the family	Mr. Brown
Others	Mr. John Brown
Employee Status	Sir

SCHOOLBOYS

The usual style of addressing the envelope is 'John Brown', but at Eton and some other public schools they are usually given 'Esq.' after the name. The style of 'Master John Brown', at one time given to boys up to the age of 12 or 13, has largely gone out of fashion. If adopted at all, it is now restricted to small boys up to the age of about 8 years, but is generally disliked by boys.

UNTITLED MARRIED LADY

It is incorrect for a widow to be addressed by her own christian names or initials, as this implies that her marriage was dissolved. This mistake is frequently made.

If the christian name of the lady's husband (living or dead) is unknown, it is considered better to address her as Mrs. Brown rather than Mrs. Mary Brown.

If the senior lady of the family has a title (e.g. Lady Mary Brown), this is sufficient identification for the next senior lady to be known as Mrs. Brown.

BEGINNING OF LETTER

Formal	(Dear) Madam[1]
Social	Dear Mrs. Brown

ENDING OF LETTER

Formal	Yours faithfully (see also p. 2)
Social	Yours sincerely

ENVELOPE

    (a) Wife or widow of the head of the family (provided no senior widow is living):

        Mrs. Brown

    (b) Wives or widows of other members of the family:

        Mrs. John Brown *or* Mrs. J. W. Brown
          (her husband's initials)

[1] See p. 26, note [1].

(c) Divorced ladies:
>   Mrs. Mary Brown *or*, as is usually preferred,
>   Mrs. M. J. Brown (her initials)

Mrs. Brown.
>   On formal occasions the following distinction is made:
>   (a) Wife or widow of the head of the family, and
>   divorced ladies:
>   Mrs. Brown
>   (b) Wives of younger sons:
>   Mrs. John Brown
>   Mrs. Edward Brown

Employee Status   Madam

The old description of a married lady as 'Mistress Brown' (i.e. Mrs.) is still prevalent in rural Scotland.

JUNIOR BRANCHES OF A FAMILY

Although the relationship of an individual to the head of the family would not be known to most acquaintances, the custom of restricting the use of the surname alone (e.g. Mrs. Waynflete) to the wife of the head of the family (or, if still living, the widow of the previous head), is still followed socially, especially in the country. In some families, where the various branches keep in touch with the senior line, wives of all these cousins style themselves by their husbands' christian names, e.g. Mrs. William Waynflete, and not as Mrs. Waynflete. As so many families are scattered and in consequence relationships not maintained, this custom is not kept up as much as in the past.

UNTITLED UNMARRIED LADY

Formal   (Dear) Madam[1]
Social   Dear Miss Brown

Formal   Yours faithfully (see also p. 2)
Social   Yours sincerely

[1] See p. 26, note [1].

ENVELOPE

Eldest unmarried daughter of the senior generation
Miss Brown

Otherwise   Miss Mary Brown

VERBAL ADDRESS AND DESCRIPTION IN CONVERSATION

Social   Miss Brown
On formal occasions, if she is not the senior unmarried lady:
 Miss Mary Brown[1].

Employee Status Madam

Scottish Titles and Territorial Designations

According to Scots law there are some special titles which are recognized by the Crown.

These fall into two divisions:

1. Those pertaining to the Peerage of Scotland with the title of Master. See *Scottish Title of Master* (p. 56).
2. Recognized chiefly styles and territorial designations of chieftains and lairds, which are strictly speaking part of their surname. These are under the jurisdiction of the Lord Lyon King of Arms. By statute these form part of the name, and should always be used.

These titles are as follows:
 Chiefs of Clans (Highlands)
 Chiefs of Names (Lowlands)
 A few independent Heads of considerable houses who are recognized as Chiefs (e.g. Fraser of Lovat, Macdonald of Clanranald, Macdonald of Sleat)
 Chieftains (branch chiefs)
 Lairds

Some of the above are feudal Barons, in addition, with precedence before esquires. They may be known by their baronial status (usually on the Continent, where baronets and the other designations mentioned above are not understood). For this

---

[1] If a younger branch adopts a family name to distinguish them from the senior line, the same rule applies. If members of this branch are known as the Berkeley Browns, the senior unmarried lady is Miss Berkeley Brown. Others are known as Miss Joan Berkeley Brown, etc. It is probable, however, that these details will not be known except to those in the same circle.

4

reason the fifth grade in Peerage of Scotland is a Lord of Parliament and *not* a Baron as in other Peerages. There is no English equivalent for the formal style of William Stirling, Baron of Keir.

The traditional prefix to which chiefs, chieftains, and lairds are entitled is 'The Much Honoured', which is not much used today.

A chief wears on ceremonial occasions three eagle's feathers, so he normally uses for his bonnet badge a circlet consisting of his crest and motto, surmounted by three silver feathers. A chieftain has two feathers.

Chiefships and chieftaincies descend to the nearest heir of the Blood and Name, unless there is a family settlement with a different line of succession. The ruling chief, may, if he thinks fit, nominate his successor, but in such a case Crown confirmation through the Lord Lyon's permitting such a successor to matriculate the chiefly Arms must be obtained.

Where a chiefship has long been dormant, and no heir can prove his right to the succession, Lyon in his ministerial capacity may grant and confirm the chiefly Arms to a suitable person of the Name who thus is officially recognized as chief (usually after a petition from the leading men of the clan), subject to challenge by an heir coming forward and proving his claim within twenty years.

If the name of a laird is recognized it does not necessarily imply that the estate is now in possession of the laird concerned, e.g. MacDonell of Glengarry. Subsequent owners with the same surname must use some other designation.

Scottish Chief, Chieftain or Laird

CHIEF, CHIEFTAIN OR LAIRD

Surnames were adopted by the Anglo-Normans in the twelfth and thirteenth centuries from either placenames or nicknames. In the Lowlands, Braes, and part of the Highlands, territorial surnames were adopted to match (e.g. Sir Matthew of Moncreiffe). The chief as head of the family and owning the name-place, described himself as 'Sir John of Moncreiffe of that Ilk' (which became standardized in charter Latin as 'dominus Johannes de Moncreiffe de eodem'). By the sixteenth century the 'of' became omitted before Moncreiffe (William Moncreiffe of that Ilk).

By the second half of the sixteenth century, Highland chiefs were styled by the Crown as 'of that Ilk', to make their chiefly status clear and they so styled themselves (e.g. MacGregor of that Ilk). Some varied between this form and a territorial designation (e.g. Maclean of Duart).

After the Union of 1707, Highland chiefs moved to a straightforward re-duplification of the name (e.g. Macdonald of Macdonald) because of the difficulty in explaining 'of that Ilk' in England. Most other families have since followed suit.

In recent years the Lord Lyon has recognized landless chiefs as 'of that Ilk', though their ancestors never bore that designation.

For centuries some chiefs have abbreviated their style, and adopted the initial 'The', e.g. Chisholm of Chisholm is known as 'The Chisholm', and Macnab of Macnab as 'The Macnab'. Others use 'The' as well as the clan or territorial designation, e.g. The Maclaren of MacLaren, The MacKinnon of MacKinnon, and The Macneil of Barra. The use of 'The' by certain chiefs, in place of the christian name, is officially recognized by Lyon.

Macdonald of Clanranald is formally styled The Captain of Clanranald, 'Captain' being a mediaeval word for 'Chief', literally 'Headman'. Similarly, the Mackintosh chief of Clan Chattan is formally styled The Captain of Clan Chattan.

The use of 'The' arose in two ways. Occasionally 'le' was a corruption of 'de', e.g. Robert of Bruce was incorrectly called Robert the Bruce. Usually it implied *The* Chief of the Clan or Name, much in the same way as today we speak of '*The* Mr. Ford'. Though this form was used both in the Highlands and Lowlands, its survival is now restricted to chiefs of Highland clans.

In Scotland the following chiefly designations are used:

1. *Direct re-duplification of the name*, e.g.
   Henry Borthwick of Borthwick
   The MacKinnon of MacKinnon
2. *Single designation*
   The Menzies
3. *'Of that Ilk'*
   Sir Iain Moncreiffe of that Ilk, Bt.
4. *Territorial designation*
   Colonel Donald Cameron of Lochiel
   The Macneil of Barra
   Biographies of Chiefs of Clans and Names appear in DEBRETT.

Chieftains (branch chiefs) and lairds have the appropriate territorial designation following their christian and surnames.

FORMS OF ADDRESS

In Scotland it is normal to write to chiefs, chieftains and lairds by their designation or estate and not by their surname. The English 'Esquire' is not added to the name on the envelope.

BEGINNING OF LETTER

Formal	(Dear) Sir
Social	Dear Chisholm[1]
	Dear Lochiel
	Dear Drum

A member of a Clan or Name writes to his Chief: Dear Chief.

ENVELOPE

The Chisholm
Colonel Donald Cameron of Lochiel, T.D.
The MacNeil of Barra
Henry Forbes Irvine of Drum
Peter Barclay of that Ilk

VERBAL ADDRESS

By clan or territorial designation, and not by the surname.
Lochiel
Mackintosh

On introduction, 'The' can be used, if applicable (e.g. The Macnab), or simply 'This is Lochiel'.

DESCRIPTION IN CONVERSATION

As for Verbal Address, except for those styled 'The' (e.g. The Chisholm) are so described.

CHIEF, CHIEFTAIN OR LAIRD (WOMAN)

There is no separate feminine equivalent for a lady who is a chief, chieftain, or laird, and a woman has exactly the same status as a man, except that one does not write to her by her estate only. See also *Wife of a Chief.*

[1] A non-Scotsman who writes to a Chief or Laird with a service rank, especially when younger of junior in rank. would write socially to The Mackintosh as 'Dear Admiral Mackintosh of Mackintosh'. This style is not incorrect as it includes the clan or territorial designation which is the essential part of the name.

Formal (Dear) Madam

Social Dear Madam Maclachlan of Machlachlan *or* Dear Mrs. Maclachlan of Machlachlan (whichever form is adopted, see *Wife of a Chief* below).

Dear Miss Rose of Kilravock

If she possesses a title, she is addressed as such. A letter to the Chief of Clan MacLeod, will be addressed 'Dear Dame Flora (MacLeod of MacLeod)'.

ENVELOPE

Madam Maclachlan of Maclachlan *or* Mrs. Stewart of Ardvorlich (whichever form is adopted, see *Wife of a Chief* below)

If she possesses a title, then as such, e.g.:

Dame Flora MacLeod of MacLeod, D.B.E.

Miss Rose of Kilravock

WIFE OF A CHIEF, ETC.

Until the end of the eighteenth century, a wife of a chief or laird was invariably described as 'Lady', followed by her husband's territorial designation, e.g. the wife of Cameron of Lochiel was called Lady Lochiel.

As the difference between 'Lady' plus the estate, and 'Lady' plus the surname (e.g. a knight's wife), was not understood by English officials, this title for a chief's wife died out early this century, becoming restricted to the peerage, baronetage and knightage. For the same reason, a chief's or laird's wife came to adopt her husband's full surname, and not just the territorial designation part.

Today, some wives of chiefs or chieftains use the designation of 'Mrs.'; others have adopted the Irish style of 'Madam', e.g. Madam Chisholm, which has met with the Lord Lyon's approval. To be certain of the designation preferred, one needs to check with an individual family.

WIDOW OF A CHIEF, ETC.

The style of the Dowager Madam (*or* Mrs.) Maclean of Ardgour is now seldom used, but when the widow of a previous chief, etc., is under the same roof as the wife of the current chief, this identification is useful.

ELDEST SON AND HEIR APPARENT OF A CHIEF

He is known by his father's territorial designation, with the addition of 'younger', abbreviated to 'yr.' (so that it will not be mistaken for a surname). This may either follow the surname, but it is more usually placed after the territorial designation, e.g.:

Ranald Macdonald of Castleton, yr., *or*
Ranald Macdonald, yr. of Castleton

If the christian name of the heir apparent is different from his father, 'yr.' may be omitted.

WIFE OF THE ELDEST SON

She is known by her husband's style, i.e. with 'yr.', but without his christian name, e.g. Mrs. MacGregor of MacGregor, yr., unless she is sufficiently distinguished from her mother-in-law, e.g. Lady Mary MacGregor of MacGregor.

OTHER SONS

They are not known by their father's territorial designation but as an esquire, e.g. John Macdonald, Esq., unless they are recognized as lairds in their own right, e.g. Sir Thomas Innes of Learney's younger son is Malcolm Innes of Edingight, being laird of that old family estate.

ELDEST DAUGHTER

As an unmarried daughter she uses the territorial designation of her house without her christian name, e.g. Miss MacLeod of Glendale, unless a senior lady is still living, such as an unmarried daughter of a previous chief, etc., when she will use her christian name as well as the territorial designation, as for younger daughters.

OTHER DAUGHTERS

All other unmarried daughters bear the designation of their house e.g. Miss Janet MacLeod of Glendale.

SIGNATURE

By statute, lairds were prevented from signing themselves like peers without a first name. It was laid down that they should sign with first name and surname including designation, e.g. Donald Cameron of Lochiel.

Irish Chieftainries

Chieftains of Irish Tribes and Septs are known by their titles.

About the beginning of the nineteenth century, some of the representatives of the last holders of these chieftainries resumed the appropriate designations which had lapsed with the destruction of the Gaelic order.

The use of 'The' as a prefix, though convenient, and generally used, lacks official recognition by the Chief Herald of Ireland.

The descent of the following by primogeniture in the male line from the last inaugurated or *de facto* chieftain has been examined by the Genealogical Office, Dublin Castle. Subject in some cases to the possible survival of senior lines at present unidentified, they are recorded at the Genealogical Office as Chiefs of the Name, and are recognized by courtesy. Certain chieftains or chiefs (the terms are synonymous in Ireland) whose pedigrees have not been finally proved, are included in the following list on account of their prescriptive standing:

The O'Neill of Clanaboy	O'Neill (descended from the Kings of Ulster)
The O'Brien of Thomond (*Lord Inchiquin*)	O'Brien (descended from the Kings of Munster)
The McMorrough Kavanagh	Dormant (descended from the Kings of Leinster)
The O'Conor Don	O'Conor (descended from the Kings of Connaught)
The MacDermot, Prince of Coolavin[1]	MacDermot
The MacDermot Roe	Dormant
The MacGillycuddy of the Reeks	MacGillycuddy
The O'Callaghan	O'Callaghan
The O'Donel of Tirconnell	O'Donel

[1] The word 'Prince' is not now generally used.

The O'Donoghue of the Glens	O'Donoghue
The O'Doneven[1]	O'Doneven
The O'Grady of Kilballyowen[2]	O'Grady
The O'Kelly of Gallagh and Tycooly[3]	O'Kelly
The O'Morchoe (Chief of his Sept)	O'Morchoe
O'Sionnaigh (called The Fox since 1552)	Fox
O'Toole of Fer Tire (*Comte O'Toole*)	O'Toole

BEGINNING OF LETTER

Formal	(Dear) Sir
Social	Dear O'Conor[4]

ENVELOPE

Service rank precedes the style, e.g.
    Lieut.-Colonel the O'Grady, M.C.

VERBAL ADDRESS

    O'Conor
On introduction, the full title is used, e.g.:
    The O'Conor Don

DESCRIPTION IN CONVERSATION

By the title, e.g.:
    The O'Conor Don

SIGNATURE

As a peer, e.g.:
    O'Grady

[1] Immediate past Chieftains spelt the name 'O'Donovan'.
[2] Often abbreviated to 'The O'Grady'.
[3] Often abbreviated to 'The O'Kelly'.
[4] A non-Irishman who writes to a Chieftain with a Service rank, especially when he is younger or junior in rank, would write 'Dear Colonel the O'Grady'.

WIFE OF AN IRISH CHIEFTAIN

She is referred to and addressed as Madam or Madame (pronounced Madam), according to the custom of the family, e.g.:

Madam O'Donoghue
Madame O'Doneven

The form of Madam(e) probably originated because several Roman Catholic chieftains of Jacobite sympathies left Ireland in the eighteenth century to live abroad. They usually spoke French through entering service abroad, being prevented as Catholics from holding commissions in the British Army. In France 'Madame' is the equivalent both to 'Lady' and 'Mrs.'.

CHILDREN OF AN IRISH CHIEFTAIN

They do not have any special form of address.

IRISH HEREDITARY KNIGHTS

There are three Irish hereditary Knights, feudal dignities which were conferred upon the FitzGerald family, viz. The Knight of Kerry (the Green Knight), The Knight of Glin (the Black Knight), and The White Knight. The last of these, whose surname became fixed as FitzGibbon, is dormant. The Knight of Kerry, who is a baronet, prefers to be addressed 'The Knight of Kerry', his older title.

BEGINNING OF LETTER

Formal	Dear Sir
Social	Dear Knight

ENVELOPE

The Knight of Glin
Major the Knight of Kerry, Bt.

VERBAL ADDRESS

Knight

DESCRIPTION IN CONVERSATION

The Knight of Glin
The Knight of Kerry

WIFE OF AN IRISH HEREDITARY KNIGHT

She is addressed as the wife of an Irish chieftain, viz.:
    'Madam' before her surname

The wife of the Knight of Kerry (who is also a Baronet) is addressed as Lady FitzGerald.

JOINT FORM OF ADDRESS

    The Knight of Glin and Madam FitzGerald
    The Knight of Kerry and Lady FitzGerald

Position of Letters After the Name

The abbreviations 'Bt.' or 'Bart.' (for a Baronet) and 'Esq.', if applicable, precede all other letters.

    The series of other letters are grouped either by regulations or by custom as follows:

1. Orders and Decorations conferred by the Crown.

2. Appointments in the following order, Privy Counsellor, Aide de Camp to Her Majesty, Honorary Physician to The Queen, Honorary Surgeon to The Queen, Honorary Dental Surgeon to The Queen, Honorary Nursing Sister to The Queen, and Honorary Chaplain to The Queen, viz. P.C., A.D.C., Q.H.P., Q.H.S., Q.H.D.S., Q.H.N.S. and Q.H.C.

3. University Degrees.

4. (a) Religious Orders, *or*
   (b) Medical Qualifications.

5. (a) Fellowships of Learned Societies,
   (b) Royal Academicians and Associates, *or*
   (c) Fellowships, Memberships, etc., of Professional Institutions, Associations, etc.

6. Appointments (other than 2 above), in the following order, Queen's Counsel, Justice of the Peace, Deputy Lieutenant and Member of Parliament, viz. Q.C., J.P., D.L., M.P.

7. Membership of one of the Armed Forces, such as R.N. or R.A.F.

———

The following notes are given for guidance.

It is important to keep the group order, even if the individual series of letters in Groups 3, 4, and 5 present difficulties. For further details see the appropriate section.

The nature of the correspondence determines which series of letters should normally be included under Groups 3, 4, and 5. For instance, when writing a professional letter to a doctor of medicine one would normally add more medical qualifications than in a social letter.

On a formal list all the appropriate letters are usually included after each name.

Those who have letters signifying Crown Honours and Awards are usually given only the principal letters in Groups 3, 4, and 5 (e.g. M.D., F.R.C.S., F.R.S.).

A peer who is a junior officer in the Armed Forces, is not usually addressed by his Service rank in social correspondence, unless he so wishes, or a letter is forwarded to him at a Service address or club.

1. ORDERS AND DECORATIONS

All the appropriate letters are obligatory in correspondence and lists. The order is laid down for Knights (p. 73), Dames (p. 76), and others (p. 81).

2. PRIVY COUNSELLORS AND APPOINTMENTS TO THE QUEEN

The letters P.C. for peers are obligatory. For other Privy Counsellors, 'Rt. Hon.' before the name is sufficient identification (see p. 78). As the other appointments to the Crown (Q.H.P., Q.H.S., etc.) are held for a limited period only, they are not always used by recipients.

3. UNIVERSITY DEGREES

Doctorates in the faculties of Divinity and Medicine (D.D., M.D.) and Masters degrees in the latter (e.g. M.S.) are given in all correspondence. Other Divinity degrees (e.g. B.D.) are sometimes included.

Other degrees in medicine (e.g. M.B., B.S.) are sometimes included, especially in professional correspondence, but if one progresses in the same degree only the higher is given.

Doctorates in other faculties are sometimes given, especially if the correspondence concerns the particular profession or subject (e.g. LL.D., D.Sc.). Alternatively, except for surgeons, the envelope may be addressed as 'Doctor' before his name, without giving his (or her) degrees.

Other degrees are seldom, and M.A. and B.A. never used in social correspondence, but they are generally included in a formal list.

For further information see *Medical Section* and *Academic Section*.

4 (a) RELIGIOUS ORDERS

Letters for members of religious communities, when used, should be included, e.g. S.J. Some Members of the Order of St. Benedict do not normally use the letters O.S.B. as the prefix of 'Dom' or 'Dame' is held to be a sufficient identification.

(b) MEDICAL QUALIFICATIONS

Fellowships are given in all correspondence (e.g. F.R.C.P., F.R.C.S.)

Other qualifications are sometimes given, especially those which are the highest held. They are usually included when writing professionally.

When all letters signifying qualifications are included, as for example in a nominal list, they should appear in the following order. (*Note:* Fellows and Members of each category precede the next category):

> Medicine
> Surgery (except M.R.C.S.)
> Obstetrics, Gynaecology and other specialities
> Qualifying diplomas (e.g. M.R.C.S., L.R.C.P.)
> Other diplomas (e.g. D.P.H., D.Obst. R.C.O.G.)

In practice, a maximum of three series of letters including M.D. (see Group 3 above) is usually sufficient in ordinary correspondence (e.g. M.D., M.S., F.R.C.S.). See also *Medical Section*.

5. (a) FELLOWSHIPS OF LEARNED SOCIETIES

Fellowships fall into two categories:

    (a) honorific, i.e. nomination by election,
    (b) nomination by subscription.

Normally only honorific fellowships are used in social correspondence (e.g. F.R.S., F.B.A.). Fellowships by subscription are generally restricted to correspondence concerning the same field of interest, e.g. a writer to a Fellow of the Zoological Society on the subject of zoology will include F.Z.S. after the name.

There is no recognized order for placing these letters. Strictly speaking, they should be arranged according to the date of foundation or incorporation of the societies concerned, but some hold that those with a Royal Charter should precede others.

In practice the following is usually adhered to:

(1) Where one society is indisputably of greater importance than another, the letters may be placed in that order; or alternatively the fellowship of the junior society may be omitted.

(2) If such precedence cannot be determined, the letters may be placed in order of conferment. Where this is not known, they may be placed in alphabetical order.

(3) Where a fellow is pre-eminent in a particular subject, his fellowship of a society connected with this interest may either be placed first, or his other fellowships omitted.

The following are some of the principal learned societies, with their dates of incorporation:

Fellow of The Royal Society	F.R.S.	1662
Fellow of The Society of Antiquaries	F.S.A.	1707
Fellow of The Royal Society of Edinburgh	F.R.S.E.	1783
Fellow of The Royal Society of Literature	F.R.S.L.	1823
Fellow of The British Academy	F.B.A.	1901

Presidents of some societies have special letters to signify their appointment, e.g. The President of the Royal Society has P.R.S. after his name, but these letters are only used within the particular society.

The Royal Society of Literature bestows an award limited to ten recipients, the Companion of Literature. The letters C.Lit. are placed before the Fellowship.

(b) ROYAL ACADEMY OF ARTS, THE ROYAL SCOTTISH ACADEMY, ETC.

It is not suggested that Royal Academicians yield in precedence to fellows of learned societies. In practice the two lists do not coincide.

The President and Past Presidents are indicated as follows:

President of the Royal Academy	P.R.A.
Past President of the Royal Academy	P.P.R.A.
President of the Royal Scottish Academy	P.R.S.A.
Past President of the Royal Scottish Academy	P.P.R.S.A.

Royal Academicians and Associaties are included as follows:

Royal Academician	R.A.
Royal Scottish Academician	R.S.A.
Associate of the Royal Academy	A.R.A.
Associate of the Royal Scottish Academy	A.R.S.A.

Similarly with other Academies, e.g. President Royal Hibernian Academy (P.R.H.A.) and Academicians (R.H.A.).

Honorary Academicians and Associates do not normally use the relevant letters.

(c) FELLOWSHIPS AND MEMBERSHIPS OF PROFESSIONAL INSTITUTIONS, ASSOCIATIONS, ETC.

These letters are usually restricted to correspondence concerning the particular profession.

It is not suggested that professional societies as such yield precedence to learned societies, but in point of fact the two groups do not coincide to any great extent. Most of the senior learned societies which elect fellows are senior in age and importance to the professional. Those whose fellowships are by subscription are generally only used in the particular field of interest. For example, if Mr. John Smith is a Chartered Engineer and a Fellow of the Royal Historical Society, he would normally be described professionally as John Smith, Esq., C.Eng., F.I.Mech.E. When corresponding on historical subjects he is normally described as John Smith, Esq., F.R.Hist.S. If both series of letters are placed after his name, it is usual to place first those which concern the particular function or subject.

As there is no recognized order for placing qualifications awarded by different bodies, a recipient usually places these letters on headed paper, business cards, etc. in order of importance to his particular profession.

Engineering Institutions, etc.

The fourteen qualifying Engineering Institutions, etc., are in the process of reorganisation by which Associate Members become Members, and Members become Fellows.

All Corporate Members, apart from those of the Royal Aeronautical Society, are Chartered Engineers, and hence C.Eng. is placed after their name, before the appropriate letters which signify a Fellow or Member (e.g. C.Eng., M.I.Mech.E.).

Note : Some Chartered Engineers are also Masters of Engineering (a University degree). These are shown as 'M.Eng., C.Eng.'.

Chartered Societies of the Land

Three chartered societies of the land, viz. :

> The Royal Institution of Chartered Surveyors
> The Chartered Land Agents' Society
> The Chartered Auctioneers' and Estate Agents' Institute

united in June 1970 to become the Royal Institution of Chartered Surveyors. Fellows and Professional Associates respectively have the letters F.R.I.C.S. and A.R.I.C.S.

The Incorporated Society of Auctioneers and Landed Property Agents united in April 1968 with The Valuers' Institution to form The Incorporated Society of Valuers and Auctioneers, with the letters F.S.V.A. and A.S.V.A.

6. APPOINTMENTS

The letters M.P. are always shown for a Member of Parliament.

The letters Q.C. are always shown for a Queen's Counsel including a County Court Judge, but *not* a High Court Judge.

The letters J.P. for a Justice of the Peace and D.L. for a Deputy Lieutenant may be included *in that order*. In practice they are often omitted for a peer, or for one with several honours and awards.

Note : There is no abbreviation for a Lord Lieutenant or a Vice-Lieutenant, see County section.

7. MEMBERSHIP OF ONE OF THE ARMED FORCES

> *Royal Navy.*—The letters 'R.N.' (or 'Royal Navy' which this Service prefers) are placed after the names of serving officers of and below the rank of Captain, and also after

retired Captains, Commanders, and Lieutenant-Commanders. Similarly R.N.R.

Army.—The appropriate letters which signify a Regiment or Corps may be placed after the name for officers on the active list of and below the rank of Lieutenant-Colonel, but are often omitted in social correspondence. These letters are not used for retired officers.

Corps have letter abbreviations (e.g. R.E., R.A.M.C., R.A.O.C., R.A.P.C.). Most regiments are written in full.

Royal Air Force.—The letters R.A.F. are placed after serving and retired officers, except for Marshals of The Royal Air Force. Officers above the rank of Group Captain do not often use these letters. Similarly with R.A.F.V.R.

Royal Marines.—The letters 'R.M.' (or 'Royal Marines' which some officers prefer) are placed after the names of serving and retired officers of and below the rank of Lieutenant-Colonel. Similarly R.M.V.R.

For further information, e.g. Women's Services, see Armed Forces section.

The Aga Khan

The Aga Khan received the personal title of His Highness from The Queen in 1957 on succeeding his grandfather His Highness the late Rt. Hon. the Aga Khan, G.C.S.I., G.C.I.E., G.C.V.O., and is therefore styled 'His Highness the Aga Khan.' The wife of the Aga Khan is styled 'Her Highness Begum Aga Khan.'

The widow of the late Aga Khan is styled 'Her Highness Begum Sultan Mohamed Aga Khan.'

Indian Princes

The principal Indian Princes and Chiefs, and their wives, may by courtesy be styled His *or* Her Highness, but the Princely Order in India was abolished by a presidential decree on Sept. 7th, 1970. These titles are recognized in Pakistan.

The Maltese Nobility

The Nobility of Malta consists of titles of the following degrees: Marquis, Count, and Baron. They take precedence among themselves according to the date of creation as a noble, irrespective of title. They are all addressed 'The Most Noble' followed by the title.[1] If the title of Marquis is of Italian origin, the Italian form comprising 'Marchese' is sometimes used in place of 'Marquis'.

The eldest sons and heirs apparent of nobles have the courtesy title of 'Marchesino', 'Contino', or 'Baroncino' before the title, depending on its degree. If the heir be a daughter, she has the courtesy title of 'Marchesina', 'Contina', or 'Baroncina'. They are addressed by these titles, which are untranslatable, followed by the family title (e.g. Marchesino St. George).

The younger sons and all daughters of nobles are styled by courtesy 'The Noble' before the christian name and title.

Other members of a noble's family are styled 'dei Marchesi', 'dei Conti', or 'dei Baroni,' followed by their christian name and surname or title. When a woman who has succeeded to a title marries an untitled commoner named Smith, she is addressed 'The Most Noble Countess Smith Montalto'. When a daughter, with the style of 'The Noble', marries Mr. Smith, she is styled 'The Noble Mrs. Smith'.

These titles are recognized and regulated by the Committee of Privileges of the Maltese Nobility, Archbishop Street, Valletta.[2]

The Canadian Nobility

There is one French title which is recognized by the British Crown, the Baron de Longueüil (of Longueüil in the Province of Quebec). This was created in 1700 by King Louis XIV for the services rendered in Canada by Charles Le Moyne, whose descendants still hold it.

Foreign Titles—Imperial, Royal and Ruling

FOREIGN AND COMMONWEALTH SOVEREIGNS STILL REGNANT

European.—Belgium (Kingdom), Denmark (Kingdom), Greece (Kingdom), Holland (Kingdom), The Holy See or Vatican (The Pope), Liechtenstein (Principality), Luxembourg

---

[1] Queen Victoria recognized the prefix of 'Most Noble,' which was communicated to the Governor of Malta by The Earl Granville on 23rd February, 1886.
[2] Before the Constitution of Independence, 1964, all titles were controlled by the Crown, but since then they have been regulated by the Committee of Privileges, Malta only, as the First Court, and the Civil High Court, Malta, in the case of an appeal.

(Grand Duchy), Monaco (Principality), Norway (Kingdom), Sweden (Kingdom).

It is important to use the correct official designation, e.g. The King of the Belgians (*not* of Belgium), The King of the Hellenes (*not* of Greece), and The Queen of the Netherland (*not* of Holland).

Others.—Ethiopia, Iran and Japan (Empires), Afghanistan, Bhutan, Jordan, Laos, Lesotho, Morocco, Nepal, Saudi Arabia, Sikkim, Swaziland, Thailand and Tonga (Kingdoms). The Supreme Head of Malaysia has the style of 'His Majesty.' He is elected for a term of five years by the rulers of the Malay states from among their number. There are also other rulers bearing various designations, such as the Sultans of Brunei and the Maldive Islands, the Head of State of Western Samoa, and the rulers of various Arab states in the Persian Gulf (i.e. Sultanate of Muscat and Oman, Amirates, Shaikhdoms, etc.)

FOREIGN SOVEREIGNS AND THEIR WIVES

Should a Sovereign no longer reign officially he is addressed as for a reigning sovereign, except that on the envelope his christian name is added, e.g. His Majesty King Leopold III of the Belgians. The form 'ex-King' (ex-Emperor, or appropriate title) is never used.

The exception is when a former sovereign receives a lesser title, e.g. after abdication His Majesty King Edward VIII became His Royal Highness The Duke of Windsor, and Her Majesty the Queen of The Netherlands became Her Royal Highness Princess Wilhelmina of The Netherlands.

BEGINNING OF LETTER

Emperor or Empress	Your Imperial Majesty *or* Sir/Madam
King or Queen	Your Majesty *or* Sir/Madam
Reigning Prince or Princess	Your Royal Highness/Your Highness/ Your Serene Highness *or* Sir/Madam

ENDING OF LETTER

Formal	I have the honour to remain (*or* to be), Sir/Madam, Your Majesty's (or appropriate title) obedient servant

Social	I have the honour to remain (*or* to be) Your Majesty's (or appropriate title) loyal (*or* devoted) friend

Envelope

His Royal Highness
The Grand Duke of Luxembourg

Her Serene Highness
The Princess of Monaco

VERBAL ADDRESS

Emperor or Empress	Your Imperial Majesty (for the first time), otherwise as for a King or Queen
King or Queen	Your Majesty (for the first time), subsequently Sir *or* Ma'am (to rhyme with Pam).
Reigning Prince or Princess	Your Royal Highness/Highness/Serene Highness (for the first time), subsequently Sir *or* Ma'am

DESCRIPTION IN CONVERSATION

Formal	His/Her Imperial Majesty *or* The Emperor/Empress. The country is mentioned for purposes of differentiation
	His/Her Majesty The King/Queen
	His Royal Highness/Highness/Serene Highness. The country may be mentioned for purposes of differentiation
Social	The Emperor/Empress
	The King/Queen
	The Prince/Princess[1]
	The country may be mentioned for purposes of differentiation

WIDOW OF A SOVEREIGN

She is addressed as Her Majesty The Dowager Queen of . . ., or the appropriate title with its proper prefix.

The widow of a previous Sovereign is known by her christian name, e.g. 'Her Majesty Queen Frederica of The Hellenes'.

[1] Prince and Princess are also non-Royal Titles, see 109.

If she is the mother of the reigning Sovereign, she is sometimes styled 'Her Majesty The Queen Mother of . . .'.

If the style is not known, the appropriate Embassy should be approached.

In other respects as for the wife of a Sovereign.

THE HUSBAND OF A REIGNING SOVEREIGN

Should the Sovereign of a Kingdom be a woman, her consort is usually accorded the style of 'His Royal Highness' and created a Prince.

THE ELDEST SON

He is known as His Royal Highness The Crown Prince of . . ., unless there is a special title for the heir apparent, such as The Prince of The Asturias.

The eldest son of the Grand Duke of Luxembourg is styled 'The Hereditary Grand Duke of Luxembourg' and the eldest sons of the Prince of Liechtenstein and the Prince of Monaco are also styled 'Hereditary Prince'.

BEGINNING OF LETTER

'Your Royal Highness', or 'Sir'.

ENDING OF LETTER

As for a Sovereign, with the substitution of 'Your Royal Highness's' for 'Your Majesty's'.

ENVELOPE

His Royal Highness
The Crown Prince (or appropriate title).

VERBAL ADDRESS

'Your Royal Highness' for the first time, and subsequently 'Sir' (as for the British Royal Family).

DESCRIPTION IN CONVERSATION

Formal   His Royal Highness

Social The Crown Prince,
or The Duke of . . ., as appropriate.
The country may be mentioned for purposes of differentiation or on introduction outside his own country.

WIFE OF THE ELDEST SON, OR A CROWN PRINCESS IN HER OWN RIGHT

She is known as 'Her Royal Highness the Crown Princess of . . .' or by her husband's title, e.g. 'Her Royal Highness the Duchess of . . .'.

Forms of address are as for her husband, with the substitution of 'Madam' for 'Sir' in the written form, and 'Ma'am (pronounced to rhyme with Pam) in the spoken form.

YOUNGER SONS, AND PRINCES OF YOUNGER BRANCHES

They are known as, e.g. 'His Royal Highness Prince Richard of . . .' unless a Dukedom has been created for him, when he is known as 'His Royal Highness the Duke of . . .'. Other forms of address are as for the eldest son, with the substitution of his christian name or title. The social form is 'Prince Richard', or by his title if appropriate. His wife is known as 'Her Royal Highness Princess Richard' or by his title. The social form is 'Princess Richard' or, The Duchess of . . . Other forms of address are as for the wife of the eldest son, with the substitution of her husband's christian name or title.

DAUGHTERS, AND PRINCESSES OF YOUNGER BRANCHES

They are known as, e.g. 'Her Royal Highness Princess Louise of . . .'. Other forms of address are as for the wife of the eldest son, with the substitution of her christian name. The social form is 'Princess Louise'. Married princesses take their style from their husband unless they marry commoners, when they usually retain their own style in conjunction with their married name, e.g.:

Her Royal Highness
Princess Elizabeth, Mrs. John Smith

otherwise a princess may give up her Royal Style and become Mrs. John Smith.

MEMBERS OF FORMER REIGNING FAMILIES

Members of families who reigned in the past (including those within the German Empire with Royal prefixes[1]), continue to inherit the same ranks and titles, e.g. Prince, Archduke, Duke and Margrave, unless a family council has authorised any changes. There is one exception: the head of a family who himself has never reigned does not succeed to the title of King or Grand Duke.

The title of Archduke is confined to members of the Habsburg family. That of Grand Duke has become extinct in Germany, and almost so in the Romanov family. Before 1917 nearly all members of the Russian Imperial Family were either Grand Dukes or Grand Duchesses. This title is now confined to the Head of the family (The Grand Duke Vladimir), his wife and children.[2] Many of those who would have succeeded as Grand Dukes in Germany have revived the old title of Margrave, such as Baden (with the style 'H.R.H.'). Members of the Russian Imperial Family are known as 'His Highness Prince or Princess Constantine of Russia', or 'His (Her) Highness Prince or Princess Constantine Romanov'.

Forms of address are as for members of a Royal Family but some prefer a simpler form.

The head of the former ruling House of France is the Comte de Paris, addressed as 'Monseigneur'. His title is never translated as 'Count of Paris'.

NON-ROYAL TITLES

Although foreign titles are often the same as those used in Britain, their structure and laws of succession are markedly different, notably in the use of adopting, purchase, recognition, etc. In Europe, a family once enobled includes every member of it and their descendants in perpetuity, whether titled (which they usually are) or untitled. Unlike the British peerage, no one, however junior in line, is a commoner, though they do not as a rule resort to courtesy titles as we know them. There is no such institution as our peerage.

The devolution of titles is different and often much wider than our peerage. Those of the Holy Roman Empire descend to all male descendants in the male line and all their issue, and those of

[1] Including such prefixes as 'His (or Her) Serene Highness' (H.S.H.), 'His (or Her) Highness' (H.H.), etc.
[2] Austrian Archdukes and Archduchesses have the style 'His (Her) Imperial and Royal Highness' (H.I. & R.H.), and The Grand Duke Vladimir of Russia, is 'His Imperial Highness' (H.I.H.).

certain of the old Italian states can be given, or left by will, by the holder. In the main, all sons and daughters are known by the family title before their christian name and surname, but in some countries (e.g. Spain and France), certain titles may pass to their children, including a daughter if there is no son.

The titles of Earl, Lord, Lady, and Sir, are exclusively British, and cannot be used by foreign nobles.

It is always advisable to refer to a well-known authority, such as an Embassy, or the publications of the *Genealogisches Handbuch des Adels* (published by C. A. Starke & Co., Limburg a.d. Lahn, Germany), notably the *Genealogische Handbuch der Fürstlicher Haüser*, which has virtually replaced the defunct *Almanach de Gotha*.

Status of Foreign Titles Borne by British Subjects

Only those held in accordance with a Royal Warrant are officially recognized. Royal Warrants are no longer granted for this purpose.

Status of Foreign Titles

The position is complicated in that many countries have formally abolished the use of titles (e.g. Austria and Japan). Some States, such as those in Eastern Europe, ignore their existence, whereas others, like the Federal Republic of Germany, continue to recognize them. The only European countries where titles are still conferred are Belgium, the Netherlands, Spain, the Holy See, and (rarely) Sweden, Liechtenstein, Luxembourg, and Monaco. Titles formerly recognized by former rulers or heads of states are generally accorded.

The following titles are usually written in English, except on the envelope:

> Prince and Princess—(N.B., this is not exclusively a Royal title)
>
> Duke and Duchess
> Count and Countess
> Baron and Baroness

Other foreign titles are written in the language of the country concerned, including that of Viscount which is confined to France, Belgium, Spain and Portugal. See table below for the principal titles.

France/Belgium	*Italy*	*Spain*	*Portugal*
(The feminine form is placed in brackets)			
Prince de	Principe di	Principe de	Principe de
(Princesse de)	(Principissa di)	(Princesa de)	(Princeza de)[1]
Duc de	Duca di	Duque de	Duque de
(Duchesse de)	(Duchessa di)	(Duquesa de)	(Duqueza de)
Marquis de	Marchese di	Marqués de	Marquez de
(Marquise de)	(Marchesa di)	(Marquesa de)	(Marquêza de)
Comte de	Conte de	Conde de	Conde de
(Comtesse de)	(Contessa di)	(Condesa de)	(Condessa de)
Vicomte de	—	Vizconde de	Visconde de
(Vicomtesse de)		(Vizcondesa de)	(Viscondessa de)
Baron de	Barone di	Barón de	Barão de
(Baronne de)	(Baronessa di)	(Baronesa de)	(Baronesa de)

Germany and Austria

Prince	Fürst[2]	Duke	Herzog
Princess	Fürstin	Duchess	Herzogin
Count	Graf	Baron	Freiherr[3]
Countess	Gräfin	Baroness	Freifrau[3]

All these titles may be written in English, except on the envelope, but Graf and Gräfin are often written in German. Graf is sometimes abbreviated to Gf. and Freiherr to Frh.

The nobility of the Holy Roman Empire (dissolved in 1806) consists of Reichsfürst (Prince), Reichsgraf (Count) and Reichsfreiherr (Baron).

Other titles include that of knight, viz. Chevalier, Ritter, Cavaliere, etc., which is sometimes hereditary, such as in Belgium, Austria and Italy.

TITLES AND STYLES IN FOREIGN COUNTRIES

See also Foreign equivalents of 'Mr.' (see p. 117).

France

'Monsieur', 'Madame', and 'Mademoiselle', followed by the christian name and surname, are used in place of the title, both

---

[1] This is only borne by members of the former Royal House of Braganza.
[2] The head of the family is Fürst (Fürstin), but Prinz (Prinzessin) is used for other members of the family. All royal princes are Prinz, and princesses are Prinzessin. All are translated into English as Prince (Princess).
[3] Some families are known as Baron (Baroness), see p. 116. In English usage no distinction is made, and they are all termed Baron (Baroness).

in writing and speech, except verbally by employees,[1] but a Duke or Duchess is addressed as 'Monsieur le Duc' or 'Madame la Duchesse'.

Titles may be used socially on the envelope, or on an invitation card.

'Monsieur' is appended before all appointments and names, e.g. Monsieur le President de la Republique, Monsieur le Docteur.

Ambassadors are addressed as 'Excellence'.

When writing or speaking to an officer of the armed forces, he is referred to as 'Mon Colonel', 'Mon Général', but, Monsieur le Maréchal.

The wife of those with high office is often colloquially referred to by her husband's rank, e.g. Madame la Générale. The widow of a Marshal of France is referred to for all purposes as 'Madame la Maréchale'.

Monsieur is *not* abbreviated to M., nor Madame to Mme., and Mademoiselle to Mlle. in correspondence. Mons. is never used.

'Monsieur', 'Madame', and 'Mademoiselle' are universally used in speech to everyone, whatever their status.

Belgium

The envelope is normally addressed 'Comte de . . .' or 'Comtesse de . . .'. It is not usual to add 'Monsieur', 'Madame', or 'Mademoiselle' before the title, with the following exception.

In Belgium members of the Royal Family and their Households, whether or not they are titled, are officially addressed on the envelope:

Monsieur
    Monsieur le Comte de Bruges, *or*

Madame
    Madame la Comtesse de Bruges

This form was once adopted on the envelope for all those with titles, but is now considered old fashioned.

Monsieur is appended before appointments and names, as in France.

Monsieur, Madame, and Mademoiselle are *not* abbreviated in correspondence.

The Netherlands

There are four hereditary titles, Graaf, Baron, Ridder and

[1] Who use the form 'Madame la Marquise', etc.

Jonkheer. Graaf and Gravin are usually translated as Count and Countess, and Baronesse as Baroness. Ridder is confined to one or two families only. The word 'Jonkheer' is placed before the initials or christian name. His wife has Mevrow, and unmarried daughters 'Jonkvrouwe', before the name.

Dutch titles are not used in speech. All are referred to as Mijnheer (Mr.), Mevrouw (Mrs.), and Freule (Miss) van Dam. For acceptable translations of Mr. see p. 117.

Italy

Titles were abolished by the 1947 Constitution and no longer have official status or legal protection, the only trace of them remaining being a territorial designation which may continue to be recognized as an adjunct to the surname. Titles are, however, used socially, and are complicated in that they were conferred in a variety of states, and cannot be treated as an entity. Rules governing the use of a title by other members of the family accordingly varies. If the title has a Frankish origin in remote feudal times, it is based upon the German custom of equal sharing between males. Titles of the Holy Roman Empire are borne both by males and females. Generally Italian titles are restricted to the head of the family, and all recent letters patent embody this system.

Some great families have several territorial titles (from fiefs held). Some are known by their title and surname (e.g. Il Principe Colonna); others are styled formally by their title and fief (e.g. Il Principe di Montesole), or less formally by their title, fief and surname (e.g. Il Principe di Montesole Castagnaro), which is useful for purposes of identification.

Members of certain families of the nobility bear the styles of Don and Donna, which form four main groups, viz. in Lombardy, Rome, Naples and Sardinia. In *Lombardy* (where titles were reviewed by the Empress Maria Theresa, also Duchess of Milan) they are borne by children and other collaterals of certain families, which may belong to any of the ranks of the nobility. In *Rome* they are borne by the children and collaterals of Princes and Dukes. In some families, Donna is used by all females, and in others the style is somewhat restricted. In *Naples* the styles are used by the children and collaterals of Princes and Dukes, both by males and females. In *Sardinia* a grade of the nobility is styled Nobile, Cavaliere, Don, but they are addressed in speech as Don and Donna.

Children of a noble without the styles of Don and Donna, and without a territorial title are styled, e.g. 'Nobile Antonio dei Conti Selvatichelli', and with a territorial title 'Nobile Antonio Selvatichelli dei Conti di Acquatorta' (dei = of the family).

There are also municipal titles conferred by cities up to the time of the French Revolution, which saw the end of the residual forms of medieval urban self-government. Up to that time they were replenished as families became extinct. These titles are Patrician (Patrizio) and Noble (Nobile), and are now highly prized for their rarity. The Nobili, apart from being the style of members of the 'feudal' nobility, may thus denote membership of the body of nobles of a city. In large cities there were two tiers, governing families with the title of Patrizio in addition to the Nobili. Both are used by males and females, but only in writing, e.g. a noble of a city is addressed on the envelope 'Giovanni Argentari, Nobile di Vigevano' and not 'Giovanni Argentari di Vigevano', which has the appearance of a feudal territorial title. A patrician likewise is addressed 'Andrea Pagliardi, Patrizio di Perugia'. The spoken form is Signor (Giovanni) Argentari or Signor (Andrea) Pagliardi.

Personal styles may be listed as under, (1) Cavaliere ereditario (hereditary knights, which are usual in Sardinia, Lombardy and Venice), (2) Nobile, Cavaliere, Don (Sardinia), (3) Nobile, as a title, and (4) Nobile, as a member of a noble family. Wives of those in group 1 are addressed, both in writing and speech, as Signora . . .

Papacy

The Holy See confers titles of Prince, Marchese, and Count, but not Baron, on Roman Catholics, in countries all over the world, e.g. Count John McCormack.

Spain

All Dukes, some Marqueses and Condes, and a few Vizcondes are Grandees of Spain. All Grandees and their consorts are Excellencies. The form of address of Excellency is also given to holders of Grand Crosses of various Orders, Ambassadors, Generals, Bishops, and eldest sons of Grandees of Spain, and their wives.

An envelope to a person with the style of Excellency is addressed Excelentissimo Señor, usually abbreviated to Excmo. Sr., followed by his title, e.g. 'Excmo. Sr. Duque de . . .'. If he has no title, this is followed by Don, e.g. Excmo. Sr. General Don, followed by his christian name and surname. Married ladies are addressed similarly as Excelentisima Señora, usually abbreviated to Exma. Sra.

Nobles who are not Grandees are addressed on the envelope 'El Visconde de . . .' or the appropriate title.

Grades of various Orders below Excellency rank are addressed Illustrious, viz. Ilustrisimo (feminine Ilustrisima), of which the abbreviations are Ilmo. and Ilma.

Don is a customary form of respect, rather equivalent to our Esquire. It is used in polite speech when referring to a person by his christian name, e.g. Don Juan. An envelope is addressed Señor Don Juan before his surname. Doña, the feminine form, is used in the same way, both in speech and on the envelope.

Señor (Sr.), Señora (Sra.) and Señorita (Srta.) are the usual forms of address for those without titles. 'Señora' is always followed by the addition of 'de' before the surname on the envelope. A married lady may also be addressed by her maiden surname, with her husband's appended, e.g. Sra. Doña Maria Luisa (then her maiden name) de (followed by her husband's surname). An unmarried lady is called and addressed 'Señorita Doña Maria Luisa' (followed by her surname). A man's surname is often followed by his mother's maiden name, e.g. Señor Don Francisco Moreno y Garcia, both in correspondence and on visiting cards.

Portugal

Those with titles are addressed formally as:

Excelentíssimo Senhor

Conde de . . . (or appropriate title)

but envelopes are now often addressed:

Dom Manuel de Bragança

'Dom' is restricted to a few families, but the feminine equivalent 'Doña' is customarily used for all ladies, whether married or single. The abbreviation D. is frequently used for both Dom and Doña.

Excelentíssimo (or the feminine form Excelentíssima) is written in full for a distinguished person, such as a Minister, Ambassador, etc. For others, including wives of ministers, etc., the abbreviations Exmo. and Exma. are used.

It is customary for those with appointments to be addressed 'Senhor Professor . . .' ('Prof.' is abbreviated for ordinary schoolmasters), 'Senhor Doutor (Doctor) . . .', etc., with their degrees and university appended after the name. Those with degrees of Licenciado (Master) or Bacharel (Bachelor) are styled 'Dr.' 'Doutor' is only written in full for one with a Doctor's degree.

Portuguese men may add their mother's name *before* the surname. A married lady may retain her maiden surname before her married surname.

Latin America

Though the language of all countries is Spanish, except for Brazil, which is Portuguese-speaking, forms of address vary according to the country. In some countries accents have been abolished. Mr., Mrs. and Miss are translated in Spanish-speaking countries as Senor, Senora and Senorita, and in Brazil, Senhor, Senhora and Senhorita. Here, unmarried ladies who are senior in age are addressed as Senhora.

The prefixes of Excelentísimo and Excelentísima (ladies) are given in some countries, often abbreviated to Exmo. and Exma. or Excmo. and Excma. In Brazil, Ilustríssimo and Ilustríssima are used, often abbreviated to Ilmo. and Ilma.

The use of Don (Dom in Brazil) and Dona varies according to the country. In *Brazil*, Dom is not used as a form of address, apart from special instances, such as to priests. Dona is placed after Senhora, when writing formally. It is also used in speech to slight acquaintances, e.g. Dona Maria . . . In *Mexico*, Don and Doña are less used than in Colombia but often formally in the provinces. In *Peru*, don (note small 'd') is used on envelopes, e.g. Señor don Pablo Sanchez, but doña is only used in special instances. In *Chile*, Don and Doña are not generally used.

It is a general rule to include Doctor, Professor, etc. between Senor and Don, or between Senor and the name.

Germany

The Republican Constitution of 1920 did not abolish titles of nobility but stipulated that they were to be an integral part of the name. This was confirmed by the Federal Republic 1949. Thus the christian name is used before the title on the envelope.

Graf is often not translated to Count. It is sometimes followed by the family name (e.g. Wolff-Metternich), but more often by von, or very occasionally 'von' and 'zu' (e.g. 'von und zu Bodman'). It is suggested that a handbook on the nobility be consulted for the exact wording.

Baron, in place of the older German title of Freiherr, is used extensively in South Germany, and also in the Baltic states where some families migrated from the east. Both are normally translated in English to Baron.

The prefix 'zu' is only used in writing. A Baron with both designations, would be announced either as 'Baron von . . .', or 'Herr von . . .', but would not introduce himself with either prefix.

For those with an appointment such as Professor, Doctor, etc. it is customary to refer to them as Herr Professor or Frau Doktor.

BEGINNING OF SOCIAL LETTER

Dear Graf (von) Blank (feminine form, Gräfin)
Dear Baron (von) Blank (Baronesse is translated Baroness)

These titles are also borne by sons and unmarried daughters before their christian names. They are not retained by daughters who have married outside the nobility.

ENVELOPE

German	*English*
Moritz, Graf/Freiherr/Baron (von) . . .	Graf (von) . . . (or appropriate title)
Anna, Grafin/Freifrau/Baron-esse (von) . . .	Gräfin (von) . . . (or appropriate title)

Sons and daughters are addressed, both in German and English, by their titles before their christian names, e.g. Graf Luitpold von Blank and Gräfin Anna von Blank.

Austria

Titles are not recognized under the Constitution but are used socially.

Russian, Polish, and Hungarian Families

They share the ranks of Prince, Count and Baron, which all precede the family name, e.g. Prince Orlov, Count Potocki, and Baron Orczy.

In Russia, unless a name has a foreign origin, when it is indeclinable, the feminine form ends in 'a', e.g. Trubetskoy, Trubetskaya. Names from the Ukraine which end with 'o' are also indeclinable. It is usual to add the father's name before the patronymic, viz. Count Ivan Ivanovich Tolstoy, Countess Anna

Alexandrovna Tolstaya. Many families who have settled outside Russia do not use the feminine ending.

In Poland, the usual ending is 'ki', with the feminine form 'ka', e.g. Count Potocki, Countess Potocka. Certain names, such as Dubis, have the feminine form 'owa' (pronounced 'ova'), i.e. Dubisowa. Others are indeclinable, e.g. Debiec for both sexes.

FOREIGN EQUIVALENTS OF 'MR.'

It is permissible to address citizens of other countries as under, these being the forms used by the Foreign and Commonwealth Office.

English

Mr. (Mrs., Miss)   Commonwealth countries
Asian countries, including Turkey
Algeria
Morocco
United Arab Republic (Egypt)
Other African countries, except those which were formerly part of the French Empire, those which are French-speaking or are administered by Portugal.

French

Monsieur (Madame, Mademoiselle)   All European countries[1] (including Switzerland) *except* for Germany, Austria, Italy, Spain, Portugal
Ethiopia
Indonesia
Countries which were formerly part of the French Empire (e.g. Tunis, Laos, Lebanon, Gabon, but *not* Algeria or Morocco)

German

Herr (Frau, Fraulein)   Germany
Austria

Italian

Signor (Signora, Signorina)   Italy

[1] This is adopted officially for the Soviet Union, though sometimes 'Mr.' is used.

Spanish

Señor (Señora, Señorita)	Spain
	Other Spanish-speaking countries (e.g. Central and South American republics (except Brazil), Cuba, Dominican Republic, Philippines)

Portuguese

Senhor (Senhora, Senhorita)[1]	Portugal
	Brazil

Other styles

Sayed is used in Sudan, and U in Burma (except for military ranks).

Usage in the United States

THE HONORABLE

The Honorable is used by the following when they are addressed by name. It appears on the first line of the envelope, followed by the name on the second line. Alternative usage is the omission of 'The', 'Honorable' being followed by the name on the same line.

AMERICAN AMBASSADORS[2]

American Ministers (including those with personal rank)
American Representatives on International Organizations
Deputy and Assistant Heads of Independent Government Agencies
Assistant Secretaries of Executive Departments and Officers of comparable rank
Assistants and Special Assistants to the President[3]
Boards, Members of equal rank
Cabinet Officers
Clerk of United States House of Representatives
Commissioners
The Commissioner of the District of Columbia[4]

[1] Unmarried ladies in Portugal are known as Senhora, but Senhorita is used in Brazil.
[2] The use of 'His Excellency' when addressing American Officials is not in accordance with American custom.
[3] Titles of Presidential Assistants vary with each Administration, 'The Honorable' is given usually to the ranking Presidential advisers and assistants.
[4] Popularly known as 'Mayor'.

Counsellor of the Department of State
Foreign Ministers
Governors of States and Territories
Heads of major organizations within the Federal Agencies, i.e. The Federal Bureau of Investigation, Immigration and Naturalization Service, etc.
Heads of International Organizations (unless entitled to His Excellency, by reason of a position previously held), alternates, Deputies and Assistant Heads
High officers of State Governments
Judges (Justices of the Supreme Court excepted)
Legal Adviser and officers of comparable rank.
Mayors of Cities
Ministers Resident
President of the United States (if addressed by name)
Public Printer
Secretary of United States Senate
Press Secretary to The President
Senators
Sergeant at Arms of United States Senate and House of Representatives
State Cabinet and Legislative officials
Under Secretaries and Officers of comparable rank of Executive Departments
United States Representatives, Alternates and Deputies of International Organizations and organs of such organizations
Vice-President (if addressed by name)

MR.

This is the generally accepted prefix in the United States. It is used before President, Vice-President, and Ambassador at the commencement of social letters (e.g. Dear Mr. President) and in speech.

ESQUIRE

In New York, Washington, Boston, Philadelphia, and Baltimore, and generally in the eastern part of the United States, 'Esq.' after the name denotes an attorney-at-law, and as such appears on a letter heading or list, but this usage is less common in other parts of the United States. In Department of State usage, the term is

5

reserved for Foreign Service officers serving abroad, and is not usually given to attorneys.

PROFESSOR

Those with a Doctor's degree are generally known as 'Dr . . .', otherwise as 'Mr . . .'. The term 'Professor' is regarded as old fashioned.

DOCTOR OF MEDICINE

Although he is referred to as 'doctor' verbally and at the beginning of a letter, he is addressed on the envelope, 'John Smith, M.D.'.

THE USE OF NUMERALS, SENIOR, AND JUNIOR AFTER A NAME

This practice for important families is widespread in the United States. When a father, who was not previously known as Junior (Jr.) or by a numeral, has a son who is given the same christian name, the son is called Jr. The father may be referred to as Sr. after his name (e.g. Mr. John Howard Sr. and Mr. John Howard Jr.), but some consider that in the best American usage, 'Sr.', is not used by a man, who would continue to be known as Mr. John Howard. His widow might then add 'Sr.' to distinguish her from her daughter-in-law.

When the first John Howard dies, his son drops his Jr. (after a limited time to prevent confusion), unless he decides to retain it out of courtesy to his father's widow. If John Howard Jr. has a son named John who was born during the first John Howard's lifetime, he is known as John Howard III.

Hereafter the usage is optional. If John III has a son born during the lifetime of the first two Johns, the child would be known as John IV. Upon the death of John Sr., leaving behind both a Jr. and a III, the Jr. might become known as Sr., but the III would not normally use Jr. It is common for the III to retain his numeral until her parents' and grandparents' deaths, after which time he would drop his numeral. John IV then has the option of deciding whether to continue with his numeral or to be known as John Jr.

Some families maintain their numerals for several generations with impressive results. There is a John Bishop VI, and until recently there was a Henry Peter Borie VIII, who retained that style until his father the VII decided to become Sr. instead, when the VIII reverted to the style of Henry Peter Borie Jr.

As explained above, the usage of II is not adopted by the Sr.'s son (Jr.), but refers to some other relative of the same christian and surname, often a grandson or nephew, not necessarily in direct succession. Henry Ford's grandson is Henry Ford II, the intervening generation not having the same christian name. Since the numerals and Sr./Jr. for distinguishing purposes and do not form part of the name, they tend to be dropped after a period of time when no confusion would result. However, usage varies according to the family concerned.

Letters are addressed to:

Mr. John D. Brown III (Mrs. John D. Brown III)

Mr. John D. Brown, Jr. (Mrs. John D. Brown, Jr.)

Part IV

STYLES BY OFFICE

The Churches Section

The Diplomatic and Commonwealth Section

The Armed Forces Section

Political and Civil Service Section

Legal Section

Medical Section

Nursing Section

Civic Section

County Section

Police Section

Merchant Navy and Airline Officers Section

Academic Section

STYLES BY OFFICE

CHURCHES SECTION

Retired officers of the Armed Forces who enter Holy Orders in any Church within the United Kingdom are not addressed by their Service rank, either in the body of the letter or on the envelope, but this practice is customary in Australia and Canada.

Church of England and Associated Churches in the Anglican Communion

As a result of the Lambeth Conference 1968, under the guidance of the Archbishop of Canterbury, a simplified form of Address for the clergy of the Church of England was announced as given in this section.

Ordained clergymen of the Church of England, and other Churches within the Anglican Communion, do not receive the accolade of knighthood, though the letters signifying an order of knighthood are placed after the name, e.g. The Right Reverend the Lord Bishop of Brompton, K.C.V.O.[1]

Doctorate Degrees should be added on the envelope where appropriate.

If a clergyman succeeds to a title or has a courtesy title or style, the ecclesiastical style precedes the temporal, e.g.:

1. The Venerable Sir John Jones, Bt.
2. The Reverend the Hon. John Brown.
3. The Very Reverend the Earl of Southend.

Wives of the clergy do not have any special form of address.

[1] Often abbreviated to 'The Rt. Rev.'. Some clergymen prefer 'The Reverend' to be written in full. Others prefer the abbreviation 'The Revd.' but the 'The Rev.' is usually adopted.

ARCHBISHOPS OF CANTERBURY AND YORK

They are Privy Counsellors, and accordingly are addressed 'The Most Reverend and Right Honourable . . .'.

BEGINNING OF LETTER
> Dear Archbishop[1]

ENDING OF LETTER
> Yours sincerely

ENVELOPE
> The Most Reverend and Right Hon. the Lord Archbishop of Canterbury/York

VERBAL ADDRESS

Formal	Your Grace
Social	Archbishop

DESCRIPTION IN CONVERSATION
> The Archbishop (of York)

ARCHBISHOPS OF OTHER PROVINCES,

ARCHBISHOPS OF OTHER PROVINCES, INCLUDING THE CHURCH OF IRELAND

There are two Archbishops of the Church of Ireland: Armagh and Dublin.

Certain Archbishops of Overseas Churches are styled '*in*' and not '*of*', e.g. The Archbishop *in* Jerusalem.

BEGINNING OF LETTER
> Dear Archbishop[1]

ENDING OF LETTER
> Yours sincerely

ENVELOPE
> The Most Reverend the Lord Archbishop of Blank

[1] Prior to October 1968, the formal style in use was 'My Lord Archbishop', which may still be adopted if preferred.

Formal   Your Grace
Social   Archbishop

DESCRIPTION IN CONVERSATION
The Archbishop (of Blank)

RETIRED ARCHBISHOP OF CANTERBURY

On retirement he is usually created a Peer. (So far, no Archbishop of York has retired.)

BEGINNING OF LETTER
Dear Archbishop *or* Lord Fisher of Lambeth

ENDING OF LETTER
Yours sincerely

ENVELOPE
The Most Reverend and Right Hon. Archbishop Lord Fisher of Lambeth, G.C.V.O., P.C., D.D.

VERBAL ADDRESS
Formal   Your Grace
Social   Archbishop *or*
                                        Lord Fisher

DESCRIPTION IN CONVERSATION
Lord Fisher of Lambeth

RETIRED ARCHBISHOPS

Other retired Archbishops revert to the status of a Bishop.

BISHOP OF LONDON

He is always a Privy Counsellor, and accordingly is addressed as "Right Reverend and Right Honourable . . .".

BEGINNING OF LETTER
  Dear Bishop[1]

ENDING OF LETTER
  Yours sincerely

ENVELOPE
  The Right Reverend and Right Hon. the Lord Bishop of London

VERBAL ADDRESS
  Bishop[1]

DESCRIPTION IN CONVERSATION
  The Bishop (of London)

BISHOPS, DIOCESAN AND SUFFRAGAN, CHURCH OF ENGLAND AND CHURCH IN WALES

The Bishops of London, Durham, and Winchester have seats in the House of Lords. Until 1841 the other Diocesan Bishops of the Church of England also had seats, but since that date, only 21 sit in the Upper House. When a vacancy arises it is filled by the senior Diocesan Bishop without a seat, and the vacated See is then placed at the foot of the list of those awaiting seats. Translation of a Bishop from one See to another does not affect his right to sit in the House of Lords. The Bishop of Sodor and Man has a Seat in the Manx House of Keys but not in the House of Lords.

In each Diocese of the Church of England, Suffragan Bishops are appointed on the recommendation of the Bishop to assist him. These are styled by the name of some ancient town within the See. While enjoying full episcopal rights, they do not qualify for membership of the House of Lords.

There has been some controversy as to whether a Suffragan Bishop is entitled to the style of 'Lord' Bishop (i.e. whether this title is ecclesiastical or temporal), but although the prefix is usually given by custom or courtesy, he is not so styled in an official document.

[1] Prior to October 1968, the formal style was 'My Lord', which may still be adopted if preferred.

The Church was disestablished in Wales in 1920.

BEGINNING OF LETTER
Dear Bishop[1]

ENDING OF LETTER
Yours sincerely

ENVELOPE
The Right Reverend the Lord Bishop of Blank

VERBAL ADDRESS
Bishop[1]

DESCRIPTION IN CONVERSATION
The Bishop (of Blank)

ASSISTANT AND RETIRED BISHOPS

BEGINNING OF LETTER
Dear Bishop[1]

ENDING OF LETTER
Yours sincerely

ENVELOPE
The Right Rev. John Smith
If a Privy Counsellor (e.g. a retired Bishop of London), The Right Rev. and Right Hon. John Smith.

VERBAL ADDRESS
Bishop[2]

DESCRIPTION IN CONVERSATION
The Bishop, *or* by name, e.g. Bishop Smith

[1] Prior to October 1968 the formal style for a Diocesan Bishop was 'My Lord', and for other Bishops 'My Lord' or 'Right Reverend Sir'. The latter alternative was used by those who did not agree that a non-Diocesan Bishop should be described as a 'Lord Bishop'. These forms may still be adopted if preferred.
[2] Prior to October 1968, the formal style was 'My Lord' or 'Right Reverend Sir', which may still be adopted if preferred. See *Bishops. Diocesan and Suffragan, above.*

BISHOPS, EPISCOPAL CHURCH IN SCOTLAND

Since the Episcopal Church is not the State Church of Scotland, a Bishop has no *official* precedence and recognition. He is therefore addressed as 'The Right Rev. John Smith, Bishop of X', and not as 'The Right Rev. the Bishop of X'.

Socially he is styled as for a Diocesan Bishop of the Church of England (p. 128), except for the Primus of Scotland who acts as the Presiding bishop. He is elected by the other bishops and has no Metropolitan power. He is styled Most Reverend the Primus.

The following is the form of address for the Primus:

BEGINNING OF LETTER
> Dear Primus

ENDING OF LETTER
> Yours sincerely

ENVELOPE
> The Most Reverend the Primus

VERBAL ADDRESS
> Primus

DESCRIPTION IN CONVERSATION
> The Primus

BISHOPS, CHURCH OF IRELAND

The Church of Ireland was united with The Church of England by the Act of Union 1800, but was disestablished in 1869.

Bishops are styled as in the Church of England (p. 128), with the following exception:
> The Bishop of Meath (Premier Bishop of the Church of Ireland) is styled 'The Most Reverend' instead of 'The Right Reverend'.

BISHOPS OF OVERSEAS CHURCHES

They are styled as for Bishops in the Church of England (p. 128) with the following exceptions:

The Metropolitan of the Church of India, Pakistan, Burma and Ceylon, has the following style:
> The Most Reverend the Bishop of Calcutta (or his appropriate See)

The Presiding Bishop of the Episcopal Church in the United States has the following style:
> The Most Reverend the Presiding Bishop

Certain Bishops of Churches Overseas have the style 'in' or 'on' instead of 'of', e.g.:
> The Bishop on the Niger Delta
> The Bishop in Egypt
> The Bishop in Iran
> The Bishop in Argentina with Falkland Islands

DEAN

A Dean is the incumbent of a Cathedral or Collegiate Church. The style is also used in certain colleges (see Academic Section).

BEGINNING OF LETTER
> Dear Dean[1]

ENDING OF LETTER
> Yours sincerely

ENVELOPE
> The Very Reverend the Dean of Ely[2]

VERBAL ADDRESS
> Dean[3]

DESCRIPTION IN CONVERSATION
> The Dean (of Ely)

RETIRED DEAN

After retirement, he is addressed as for other clergy, i.e. 'The Reverend' instead of 'The Very Reverend' as above, unless he

---

[1] Prior to October 1968, the formal style was 'Very Reverend Sir', and the social style was 'Dear Mr. Dean', which may still be adopted if preferred.
[2] For abbreviation of Reverend see p. 125, note [1].
[3] Prior to October 1968, the verbal address was 'Mr. Dean', which may still be adopted if preferred.

remains an Archdeacon, Canon, or Prebendary, or is appointed to emeritus rank, when he is addressed according to the appropriate rank. The word 'emeritus' is only used in official documents.

PROVOST

The incumbent of a Cathedral in a diocese created in the twentieth century is invariably appointed a Provost rather than a Dean. In other respects his duties are the same. The style is also used in certain non-ecclesiastical appointments, such as the Heads of certain colleges (see Academic Section).

BEGINNING OF LETTER

Dear Provost[1]

ENDING OF LETTER

Yours sincerely

ENVELOPE

The Very Reverend the Provost of Guildford

VERBAL ADDRESS

Provost[2]

DESCRIPTION IN CONVERSATION

The Provost (of Guildford)

RETIRED PROVOST

After retirement he is addressed as other clergy, i.e. 'The Reverend', instead of 'The Very Reverend' (p. 125), unless he remains an Archdeacon, Canon, or Prebendary, or is appointed to emeritus rank, when he is addressed as such. The word 'emeritus' is only used in official documents.

ARCHDEACON

An Archdeacon is a senior clergyman whose duty it is to advise and help his brother clergy, and to administer part of a diocese,

[1] Prior to October 1968, the formal style was 'Very Reverend Sir', and the social style, 'Dear Mr. Provost', which may still be adopted if preferred.
[2] Prior to October 1968, the verbal style was 'Mr. Provost'. which may still be adopted if preferred.

hence his territorial designation. As well as his visitation duties he is in charge of the fabric of parish churches and their contents.

BEGINNING OF LETTER
   Dear Archdeacon[1]

ENDING OF LETTER
   Yours sincerely

ENVELOPE
   The Venerable[2] the Archdeacon of Exeter.

VERBAL ADDRESS
   Archdeacon[3]

DESCRIPTION IN CONVERSATION
   The Archdeacon (of Exeter)

RETIRED ARCHDEACON

After retirement he is addressed as other clergy, i.e. 'The Reverend' in place of 'The Venerable' as above, unless he remains, a Canon or Prebendary, or is appointed to emeritus rank, when he is addressed accordingly. The word 'emeritus' is only used in official documents. He is often incorrectly referred to as 'Archdeacon Smith' but the word 'archdeacon' signifies an office not a rank. Strictly speaking there cannot be an Archdeacon Emeritus though the title is often used.

CANON

A Canon is either residentiary, with duties in his Cathedral, or honorary. The latter usually holds a benefice within the Diocese.

   A Minor Canon is a cleric attached to a cathedral or collegiate church to assist in the daily services. He is addressed as for other clergy (p. 135).

[1] Prior to October 1968, the formal style was 'Venerable Sir' and the social style was 'Dear Mr. Archdeacon', which may still be adopted if preferred.
[2] Often abbreviated to 'The Ven.'.
[3] Prior to October 1968, the verbal address was 'Mr. Archdeacon', which may still be adopted if preferred.

BEGINNING OF LETTER

>Dear Canon *or*
>Dear Canon Smith

ENDING OF LETTER

>Yours sincerely

ENVELOPE

>The Reverend Canon John Smith

VERBAL ADDRESS

>Canon *or*
>Canon Smith

DESCRIPTION IN CONVERSATION

>The Canon *or*
>Canon Smith

RETIRED CANON

After his retirement he is addressed as other clergy (p. 135) unless he is appointed a Canon Emeritus when he is addressed as previously. The word 'emeritus' in only used in official documents.

Honorary Canons usually retain their title unless they specifically resign it on leaving the diocese or retiring from the Church.

PREBENDARY

Prebendaries have a Prebendal Stall in certain Cathedrals or Collegiate Churches. The appointment is similar to a non-residentiary Canon.

BEGINNING OF LETTER

>Dear Prebendary *or*
>Dear Prebendary Smith

ENDING OF LETTER

>Yours sincerely

ENVELOPE

>The Reverend Prebendary John Smith

VERBAL ADDRESS

Prebendary *or*
Prebendary Smith

DESCRIPTION IN CONVERSATION

Prebendary *or*
Prebendary Smith

RETIRED PREBENDARY

After retirement he is addressed as other clergy (below) unless he is appointed to emeritus rank. In this case he continues to be addressed as Prebendary. The word 'emeritus' is only used in official documents.

RURAL DEAN

No special form of address but he is usually an honorary canon— see *Canon* (p. 133) or *Other Clergy* (below), as applicable.

OTHER CLERGY

BEGINNING OF LETTER

Dear Mr. Smith *or*
Dear Father Smith, according to personal preference.
When writing to beneficed clergy, the form 'Dear Rector' or 'Dear Vicar' may be used.[1]

ENDING OF LETTER

Yours sincerely,

ENVELOPE

The Reverend John Smith[2]
The form 'The Reverend Smith' or 'Reverend Smith' is incorrect and should never be used.

VERBAL ADDRESS

'Mr. Smith' *or* 'Father Smith', according to his personal preference.

[1] The difference between a Rector and a Vicar is now purely nominal. A Rector was in receipt of greater and lesser tithes, and a Vicar of the lesser tithes only. Tithes were virtually abolished in 1936. Vicars are appointed to all new livings.
[2] For abbreviation of Reverend, see p. 125, note [1].

'Mr. Smith' *or* 'Father Smith', according to his personal preference, or 'The Rector' or 'The Vicar', if applicable.

RELIGIOUS COMMUNITIES, CHURCH OF ENGLAND (MEN)

Ordained members of Religious Orders are addressed as Father, and lay members as Brother.

The letters signifying the religious Order are given on p. 139.

The Head of a Community includes the following offices:

The Right Reverend the Abbot
The Reverend the Prior
The Reverend Superior-General
The Reverend Pro-Superior
The Reverend Superior

BEGINNING OF LETTER

Superior

By his office, e.g.:

Dear Father Abbot
Dear Father Prior
Dear Father Superior (including Superior-General and Pro-Superior)

Other Ordained Members

Dear Reverend Father (this covers all ordained members); alternatively, the name may be used, e.g.:

Dear Father Smith
Dear Father David (for Orders where surnames are not used)
Dear Dom Andrew (Benedictine)

Lay Members

Dear Brother Andrew
Dear Brother (if the name is not known)
Dear Dom Andrew (Benedictine)

ENDING OF LETTER

Yours sincerely

ENVELOPE

By his office, followed by the letters to denote his Order, e.g.:

The Right Reverend the Lord Abbot, O.S.B.
The Reverend the Prior, C.G.A.

Note.—A few communities do not have letters.

Other Ordained Members

> The Reverend Andrew Thompson, O.G.S., *or*
> The Reverend Fr. Andrew Thompson, O.G.S.
> The Reverend Fr. Andrew S.S.F. (if the surname is not used).
> The Reverend Dom John Smith, O.S.B. (Benedictine)

Lay Members

> Brother John (with his surname, if used by his Order)
> Dom John Smith, O.S.B. (Benedictine)

VERBAL ADDRESS

Superior

> Father Abbot
> Father Prior
> Father Superior (including Superior-General and Pro-Superior)

Other Ordained Members

> Father David (with his surname, if used by his Order)
> Dom John Smith, Dom John, *or* Father Smith (Benedictine)

Lay Members

> Brother John *or*
> Brother
> Dom John (Benedictine)

The surname or religious name may be used if distinction is necessary or on introduction.

DESCRIPTION IN CONVERSATION

Superior

> The Abbot
> The Prior (or appropriate office)

Other Ordained Members

> Father Smith
> Father David
> Dom Andrew Smith (Benedictine)

Lay Members

> Brother Andrew (and his surname if used by his Order)
> Dom John Smith

RELIGIOUS COMMUNITIES, CHURCH OF ENGLAND (WOMEN)

For the appropriate letters for Religious Orders, see p. 139.

Superiors by her office, e.g.:
>   Dear Lady Abbess
>   Dear Mother Superior
>   Dear Prioress
>   Dear Reverend Mother
>   Dear Sister Superior
>   Dear Reverend Sister

Other Sisters
>   Dear Sister Agnes
>   Dear Dame Mary (Benedictine, having taken final vow)
>   Dear Sister Mary (Benedictine)

ENVELOPE
Superiors
By her office, followed by the letters of her Order (a few Communities do not have letters), such as:
>   The Right Reverend the Lady Abbess, O.S.B.
>   The Reverend the Prioress
>   The Reverend Mother Superior
>   The Reverend Mother
>   The Reverend Mother General
>   The Reverend Sister Superior
>   The Reverend Mother Audrey Mary

Other Sisters
>   Sister Agnes, followed by the letters of her Order
>   The Reverend Dame Mary Smith O.S.B. (Benedictine if final vows are taken)
>   Sister Mary Smith O.S.B. (Benedictine)

VERBAL ADDRESS
Superiors by her office, e.g.:
>   Reverend Mother (in some communities 'Mother')

Other Sisters
>   Sister Agnes (in some communities 'Sister')

DESCRIPTION IN CONVERSATION
Superiors by her office, e.g.:
>   The Lady Abbess

Other Sisters
>   Sister Agnes
>   Dame Mary Smith (Benedictine, if final vows are taken)
>   Sister Mary Smith (Benedictine)

RELIGIOUS ORDERS, CHURCH OF ENGLAND

Men

C.R.	Community of the Resurrection (Mirfield, Yorks.)
C.S.W.G.	Community of the Servants of the Will of God (Crawley Down, Sussex)
O.G.S.	Oratory of the Good Shepherd (Greenford, Middlesex)
O.S.B.	Benedictine Community of Nashdom Abbey (Burnham, Bucks)
O.S.P.	Order of St. Paul (Alton)
S.S.F.	Society of St. Francis
S.S.J.E.	Cowley Fathers (Society of Mission Priests of St. John the Evangelist, Oxford)
S.S.M.	Society of the Sacred Mission (Kelham, Newark)

Men and Women

C.G.A.	Community of the Glorious Ascension (Burton-on-Trent)

Women

C.A.H.	Community of All Hallows (Bungay, Suffolk)
C.B.V.M.	Community of the Blessed Virgin Mary (Rottingdean, Sussex)
C.E.	Community of the Epiphany (Truro)
C.H.C.	Community of Holy Cross (Haywards Heath, Sussex)
C.H.F.	Community of the Holy Family (St. Leonards-on-Sea)
C.H.N.	Community of the Holy Name of Jesus (Malvern)
C.H.R.	Community of the Holy Rood (Middlesbrough)
C.J.G.S.	Community of the Companions of Jesus the Good Shepherd (Newton Abbot)
C.J.N.	Community of Jesus of Nazareth (Kingham, Oxford)
C.P.	Community of the Presentation (Hythe)
C.R.	Community of the Resurrection of Our Lord (London and Grahamstown, S. Africa)
C.R.J.B.S.	Community of Reparation to Jesus in the Blessed Sacrament (London)
C.S.C.	Community of Servants of the Cross (Lindfield, Sussex)
C.S.C.	Community of the Sisters of the Church (Ham Common, Surrey)
C.S.Cl.	Community of St. Clare (Freeland, Oxon.)

C.S.D.	Community of St. Denys (Warminster, Wilts.)
C.S.F.	Community of St. Francis (S. Petherton, Somerset)
C.S.J.B.	Community of St. John the Baptist (Clewer, Windsor)
C.S.K.	Community of St. Katharine of Egypt (Henley-on-Thames)
C.S.L.	Community of St. Laurence (Belper)
C.S.M.V.	Community of St. Mary the Virgin (Wantage)
C.S.P.	Community of St. Peter (Woking)
C.S.P.	Community of the Sacred Passion (Chelmsford and Tanzania)
C.S.P.H.	Community of St. Peter (Horbury, Yorks.)
C.S.W.	Community of St. Wilfrid (Warminster, Wilts.)

CHAPLAINS TO H.M. FORCES

A chaplain serving with H.M. Forces is addressed by his ecclesiastical rank, and never in speech by his relative Service rank, which is only for administrative purposes. It is not necessary or usual to write the Service rank, but when used it must appear in brackets after the ecclesiastical title and before the chaplain's christian name or initials.

The Chaplain of the Fleet, the Chaplain General to the Forces, Army, and the Chaplain-in-Chief, Royal Air Force, are Archdeacons, and therefore 'The Venerable' is placed before the name. Letters begin with his appointment or name, e.g. 'Dear Chaplain General' or 'Dear Archdeacon Smith'. Envelopes are addressed accordingly, e.g. 'The Chaplain of the Fleet', 'The Chaplain General', 'Chaplain-in-Chief' or 'The Venerable John Smith', followed by his appointment. Verbally he is addressed by his appointment, or as Archdeacon as may be appropriate.

The Deputy Chaplain General to the Forces, Army, the Principal Chaplain, Church of Scotland and Free Churches, Royal Navy, or Royal Air Force and the Principal Roman Catholic Chaplain, Royal Navy, Army or Royal Air Force are addressed in correspondence by name, or by appointment. Principal Roman Catholic Chaplains are Monsignori, and are addressed accordingly, see Roman Catholic Church.

Other chaplains are addressed by name or by appointment in correspondence as may be appropriate, e.g. 'Dear Canon Jones', 'Dear Mr. Jones', 'Dear Assistant Chaplain General', etc. When the name is used, the appointment held should be placed after the name, e.g.:

The Reverend John Jones, O.B.E., M.A., C.F.
      Assistant Chaplain General,
          H.Q., Blankshire Command.

The letters R.N. and R.A.F. are placed after the names of chaplains to these Services, following any letters for decorations, etc. Army chaplains have the letters 'C.F.' after the name (following any letters for decorations, etc.). Verbally a chaplain may be addressed by name or by appointment or by ecclesiastical title or, informally as 'Padre'.

When the chaplain's name is not known, correspondence should be addressed to e.g.:

      The Church of England Chaplain,
          R.A.F. Station,
          Blanktown.
      The Roman Catholic Chaplain,
          H.M.S. Blankshire, etc.

Correspondence to the Jewish Chaplain is addressed, e.g.:

      The Reverend David Smith, C.F.,
          Senior Jewish Chaplain,
          Blanktown Garrison, etc.

Verbally he is addressed as Rabbi, as Minister or 'Padre' as may be appropriate.

ARCHBISHOPS' AND BISHOPS' SIGNATURES

CHURCH OF ENGLAND

Archbishops and Bishops sign, after a cross, by their christian names followed by their Province or See, sometimes in Latin, or a Latin abbreviation (see below), e.g.:

      + Michael Cantuar
      + Mervyn Worcester

The following sign, after the christian name, as below. Other Sees are accorded the usual spelling.

Archbishops

Canterbury	Cantuar
York	Ebor

Bishops

Bath and Wells	Bath et Well
Carlisle	Carliol
Chester	Cestr
Chichester	Cicestr

Durham	Dunelm
Ely	Elien
Gloucester	Gloucestr
London	Londin
Norwich	Norvic
Oxford	Oxon
Peterborough	Petriburg
Rochester	Roffen
Salisbury	Sarum
Truro	Truron
Winchester	Winton

Retired Bishops

They sign their name after a cross, followed by Bishop.

CHURCH IN WALES

The Archbishop and Metropolitan signs, after a cross, his christian name followed by 'Cambrensis'. A Bishop of any Welsh diocese may be elected as Archbishop of Wales.

EPISCOPAL CHURCH IN SCOTLAND

Bishops, including the Primus, sign after a cross, their christian name, followed by their dioceses, except that the Bishop of Moray, Ross and Caithness signs 'Moray' and the Bishop of St. Andrews, Dunkeld and Dunblane signs 'St. Andrews'—without the other dioceses.

The Bishop of Edinburgh signs by his christian name followed by 'Edenburgen'.

CHURCH OF IRELAND

Archbishops sign, after a cross their christian name, followed by their Province; Bishops sign, after a cross, by their christian name, followed by the first diocese in their title.

CHANCELLORS, DIOCESAN

(See *Legal Section*.)

The Church of Scotland

This is the Established Church in Scotland, and is Presbyterian by constitution. The Church is presided over by a Moderator, who is chosen annually by the Assembly. The Sovereign is represented by the Lord High Commissioner to the General Assembly who is appointed annually by the Crown. The same styles are used whether a man or woman is appointed to this office.

THE LORD HIGH COMMISSIONER TO THE GENERAL ASSEMBLY

BEGINNING OF LETTER
    Your Grace
This form of address is adhered to even when the Lord High Commissioner is a member of the Royal Family.

ENDING OF LETTER
    I have the honour to remain,
    Your Grace's most devoted and obedient servant.

ENVELOPE
    His (or Her) Grace the Lord High Commissioner
If a member of the Royal Family, His (or Her) Royal Highness the Lord High Commissioner.

VERBAL ADDRESS
    Your Grace

DESCRIPTION IN CONVERSATION
    The Lord High Commissioner

MODERATOR OF THE GENERAL ASSEMBLY

BEGINNING OF LETTER
Formal   Dear Sir *or*
                            Dear Moderator
Social   Dear Mr. (Dr.) Smith *or*
                            Dear Moderator

ENDING OF LETTER
Formal   Yours faithfully (see also p. 2)
Social   Yours sincerely

ENVELOPE
    The Rt. Rev. the Moderator of the General Assembly of the
        Church of Scotland, *or*
    The Rt. Rev. John Smith

VERBAL ADDRESS
Moderator

DESCRIPTION IN CONVERSATION
The Moderator

FORMER MODERATORS

After his year of office a former Moderator is styled, The Very Reverend John Smith. Otherwise as for *Other Clergy* (Church of Scotland) below.

THE DEAN OF THE THISTLE AND THE DEAN OF THE CHAPEL ROYAL

They are styled 'The Very Reverend' (See *Dean, Church of England*, p. 131). Sometimes both appointments are held by one person.

OTHER CLERGY

BEGINNING OF LETTER

Formal   Dear Sir *or*
                                        Dear Minister

Social   Dear Mr. Smith *or*
                                        Dear Minister

ENDING OF LETTER

Formal   Yours faithfully (see also p. 2)
                                        Yours sincerely

ENVELOPE
    The Reverend John Smith
    The Minister of Blanktown (if a Minister of a Parish)
If a lady be ordained she would be styled 'The Reverend Mary Smith' (Mrs. or Miss is not used).

VERBAL ADDRESS
    Mr. Smith *or*
    Minister

DESCRIPTION IN CONVERSATION
Mr. Smith *or*
The Minister

CHAPLAIN TO THE FORCES

See p. 140

The Methodist Church, and Free Churches of Other Denominations

(See also *Presbyterian Churches of England* (p. 146), *of Wales* (p. 147), and *in Ireland* (p. 147), *The Salvation Army* (p. 147) and the *Moravian Church in Great Britain and Ireland* (p. 149).)

CLERGY

BEGINNING OF LETTER

Formal	Dear Sir or Madam
Social	Dear Dr., Mr., Mrs. *or* Miss Smith

ENDING OF LETTER

Formal	Yours faithfully (see also p. 2)
Social	Yours sincerely

ENVELOPE

The Reverend John Smith (The Reverend Dr. John Smith, *or* with the appropriate letters signifying a Doctor's degree). There are no women Ministers in the Methodist Church at the present time. Those of other Free Churches are addressed as, The Reverend Mary Smith ('Mrs.' or 'Miss' is not used.)

VERBAL ADDRESS

Mr. (or Dr.) Smith

On the platform the President of the Methodist Church, the Methodist Church in Ireland, etc., and the President of the Baptist Union (who may be a layman) are referred to as Mr. President.

The President and the Chairman of the Congregational Church in England and Wales,[1] are referred to as Mr. (or Madam)

[1] Until this Church changed its constitution in 1966, it was known as The Congregational Union of England and Wales.

President and Mr. (or Madam) Chairman. The Chairman of the Congregational Union in Scotland is referred to as Mr. (or Madam) Chairman.

DESCRIPTION IN CONVERSATION
> Mr., Dr., Mrs., or Miss Smith *or*
> The Minister, The Pastor, The President, etc.

CHAPLAIN TO THE FORCES

See p. 140.

DEACONESS OF THE METHODIST CHURCH

She is referred to as Sister Jane Smith, and is known in her community as Sister Jane, but in a written description she may be referred to as Deaconess Jane Smith which distinguishes her from a nursing sister.

The Presbyterian Church of England

THE MODERATOR

BEGINNING OF LETTER

Formal	Dear Moderator
Social	Dear Moderator

ENDING OF LETTER

Formal	Yours faithfully (see also p. 2)
Social	Yours sincerely

ENVELOPE
> The Rt. Rev. John Smith

VERBAL ADDRESS
> The Moderator

DESCRIPTION IN CONVERSATION
> The Moderator

FORMER MODERATORS

After his year of office, a Moderator reverts to 'The Rev.'.

MINISTERS

As for the Church of Scotland (p. 142), except that the form 'Dear Minister' is not used.

If a lady, she is styled The Rev. Mary Smith (Mrs. or Miss is not used).

The Presbyterian Church of Wales

Moderators of the General Assembly of the Presbyterian Church of Wales continue to be styled 'The Reverend'.

It is not customary to address the Moderator of this Church by name.

BEGINNING OF LETTER

> Dear Moderator

Ministers are styled as for the Presbyterian Church of England.

The Presbyterian Church in Ireland

Moderators of the General Assembly of the Presbyterian Church in Ireland are addressed as for the Presbyterian Church of England, viz. The Right Reverend.

Former Moderators are styled 'The Very Reverend'.

BEGINNING OF LETTER

> Dear Doctor Smith *or*
> Dear Moderator

Ministers are styled as for the Presbyterian Church of England.

The Salvation Army

After a two years' residential course as a cadet, a student is commissioned as an officer, as the movement terms its Ministers. Ranks are as follows:

> Commissioner
> Lieutenant-Commissioner
> Colonel

Lieutenant-Colonel
Brigadier
Major
Captain
Lieutenant

N.B. The rank of Brigadier is junior to that of Lieutenant-Colonel.

One Commissioner is appointed to be Chief of the Staff of the Salvation Army.

The senior officer of the Movement within other countries is the territorial commander, or officer commanding in smaller territories, who holds the rank of a Commissioner, Lieutenant-Commissioner, or Colonel.

The senior officer of the whole Movement is the General of the Salvation Army who is elected by the High Council.

Married Officers

Commissioned officers marry within the commissioned ranks of the Salvation Army. If they marry outside these ranks they opt out of officership of the Salvation Army, though they may continue as lay members.

BEGINNING OF LETTER

According to their rank, as follows:

Dear General
Dear Chief (i.e. Chief of the Staff)
Dear Commissioner (includes Lieutenant-Commissioner)
Dear Colonel (includes Lieutenant-Colonel)
Dear Brigadier
Dear Major
Dear Captain
Dear Lieutenant

An officer's wife may be referred to by her name (e.g. Mrs. Smith) or by her husband's rank (e.g. Mrs. Major Smith).

ENVELOPE

According to the exact rank held (e.g. Major John Jones or Captain Mary Brown), except for married ladies.

Married ladies take their husband's rank on marriage, e.g. the wife of Major Frank Briggs is addressed on the envelope 'Mrs. Major Frank Briggs'.

The Moravian Church in Great Britain and Ireland

BISHOP

BEGINNING OF LETTER
Dear Bishop (within this Church the term 'Brother' is used)

ENDING OF LETTER
Formal   Yours faithfully (see also p. 2)
Social   Yours sincerely

ENVELOPE
The Rt. Rev. John Smith

VERBAL ADDRESS
Bishop Smith

DESCRIPTION IN CONVERSATION
Bishop Smith

PRESBYTERS AND DEACONS
(See *Clergy of the Methodist Church* (p. 145).)

The Roman Catholic Church
The territorial designation and the term 'My Lord' are not officially recognized within the United Kingdom, and accordingly are not used in official communications and documents. Hence in these communications Archbishops, Bishops, Abbots and Priors are addressed by name and not by their Province, Diocese, etc. Letter endings have tended to be more informal than in the past. For the Order of Benedict and The Society of Jesus see these sections.

THE POPE
BEGINNING OF LETTER
Your Holiness *or*
Most Holy Father

ENDING OF LETTER
For Roman Catholics   I have the honour to be,
Your Holiness's most devoted
and obedient child (or 'most
humble child')

For non-Roman Catholics	I have the honour to be (or 'to remain'), Your Holiness's obedient servant

ENVELOPE
   His Holiness
      The Pope

VERBAL ADDRESS
   Your Holiness

DESCRIPTION IN CONVERSATION
   His Holiness *or*
   The Pope

CARDINAL

If appointed to a See, he may be addressed by his appointment, e.g. 'His Eminence The Cardinal Archbishop of Westminster', otherwise as 'His Eminence Cardinal Smith'. The territorial designation is not *officially* used (see p. 149), when such letters are addressed to the person and not territorially to his Province or Diocese.

BEGINNING OF LETTER

Formal	Your Eminence (usual) *or* My Lord Cardinal
Officially Recognized	Your Eminence
Social	Dear Cardinal Smith

ENDING OF LETTER

Very Formal	
Roman Catholic	I have the honour to be (or 'to remain'), My Lord Cardinal Your Eminence's devoted and obedient child
Roman Catholics in Holy Orders write 'servant' instead of 'child'	
Formal	I remain, Your Eminence ('My Lord Cardinal' is sometimes used in place of 'Your Eminence'), Yours faithfully

Officially Recognized	I have the honour to be (*or* 'to remain'), Your Eminence's obedient servant
Social	Yours sincerely

ENVELOPE
Formal and Social

(if an Archbishop)	His Eminence the Cardinal Archbishop of Westminster
(if not an Archbishop)	His Eminence Cardinal Smith
Officially Recognized	His Eminence Cardinal Smith

VERBAL ADDRESS

Formal	Your Eminence
Social	Cardinal (Smith)

DESCRIPTION IN CONVERSATION

Formal	His Eminence
Social	The Cardinal *or* Cardinal Smith

ARCHBISHOP

On retirement from his office, a Roman Catholic Archbishop is appointed to a titular See, and is then normally addressed by name.[1]

BEGINNING OF LETTER

Formal	My Lord Archbishop
Officially Recognized	Most Reverend Sir
Social	Dear Archbishop

ENDING OF LETTER

Very Formal (Roman Catholic)	I have the honour to be (or 'to remain'), Your Grace's devoted and obedient child

Roman Catholics in Holy Orders write 'servant' instead of 'child'

---

[1] See p. 152, note [1]. A titular See is not normally used in ordinary correspondence, but if desired, it may be given on the next line of the envelope, e.g.:
  The Right Reverend John Smith,
    Bishop of Laodicea.

Formal	I remain, Your Grace, Yours faithfully *or* Yours faithfully (see also p. 2)
Officially Recognized	I have the honour to be, Most Reverend Sir, Your obedient servant
Social	Yours sincerely

ENVELOPE

Formal and Social	His Grace the Archbishop of Sydney
Officially Recognized	The Most Reverend Archbishop Smith[1]
Titular Archbishop	The Most Reverend Archbishop Smith

VERBAL ADDRESS

Formal	Your Grace
Social	Archbishop

DESCRIPTION IN CONVERSATION

Formal	His Grace
Social	The Archbishop (of Blank)

BISHOP

In lists prepared by non-Roman Catholic organizations, a Roman Catholic Bishop should be mentioned by his name (e.g. The Right Reverend Bishop Brown). If the territorial designation is given, and there is an Anglican Bishop whose See has the same name, it should be stated 'Roman Catholic Bishop of Lancaster'.

Letter endings have tended to be more informal than in the past.

On retirement from his See or office, a Bishop is appointed to a titular See, and addressed by name. Though it is not the usual practice, the titular See may be appended on the envelope after the name if desired.[1]

[1] By tradition a retiring Bishop is given the honorary title of a disused Diocese. In the past former Christian Sees in Asia Minor and Africa were used, with the Latin phrase 'in partibus infidelium'. Today English-speaking retired Bishops are assigned to titular English-speaking dioceses which have fallen into abeyance, and the Latin phrase discontinued. In 1969, for example, the retired Bishop of Rochester N.Y., was appointed titular Archbishop of Newport (Monmouthshire), a See which was replaced by Cardiff in 1916.

BEGINNING OF LETTER
Formal   My Lord (usual) *or*
                                  My Lord Bishop

Officially Recognized   Right Reverend Sir

Social   Dear Bishop *or*
                                  Dear Bishop Smith

ENDING OF LETTER
Very Formal
    Roman Catholic   I have the honour to be,
                                  Your Lordship's obedient child

    Roman Catholics in Holy Orders write 'servant' instead of
    'child'.

Formal   I remain,
                                  My Lord,
                                  Yours faithfully
                                  ('My Lord Bishop' may be used
                                     in place of 'My Lord') *or*
                                  Yours faithfully (see also p. 2)

Officially Recognized   I have the honour to be (or 'to
                                     remain'),
                                  Right Reverend Sir,
                                  Your obedient servant

Social   Yours sincerely

ENVELOPE
Formal and Social   His Lordship the Bishop of
                                     Blank *or*
                                  The Right Reverend John Smith,
                                     Bishop of Bramber
                                  The Right Reverend John Smith
                                     Auxiliary Bishop of . . .
Officially Recognized   The Right Reverend Bishop
                                     Smith

In Ireland the word 'Dr.' is included on the envelope before
the name, e.g. 'The Right Reverend Dr. John Smith, Bishop of
Kildare'.

VERBAL ADDRESS	
Formal	My Lord (usual) *or*
	My Lord Bishop
Social	Bishop

DESCRIPTION IN CONVERSATION	
Formal	His Lordship
Social	The Bishop

ABBOT
(See also *Order of St. Benedict,* p. 160.)

BEGINNING OF LETTER	
Formal	My Lord Abbot *or*
	Right Reverend and dear Father Abbot
Officially Recognized	Right Reverend Sir
Social	Dear Father Abbot

ENDING OF LETTER	
Very formal	I beg to remain, my Lord Abbot, Your devoted and obedient servant,
Formal	Yours faithfully (see also p. 2)
Social	Yours sincerely

ENVELOPE	
Formal and Social	The Right Reverend the Abbot of Blank (followed by the initials of his Order)
Officially Recognized	The Right Reverend John Smith (followed by the initials of his Order)

VERBAL ADDRESS	
Formal	Father Abbot
Social	Abbot

DESCRIPTION IN CONVERSATION
The Abbot (of Blank)

MONSIGNOR
This title is held by virtue of a particular office, usually a Domestic Prelate, Protonotary Apostolic or Privy Chamberlain. By a

recent pronouncement, Monsignori are addressed as The Reverend instead of the Right Reverend or The Very Reverend.

BEGINNING OF LETTER

Formal	Reverend Sir
Social	Dear Monsignor Smith (usual) *or*
	Dear Monsignore

ENDING OF LETTER

Formal	Yours faithfully (see also p. 2)
Social	Yours sincerely

ENVELOPE

    The Reverend Monsignor John Smith[1] *or*
    The Reverend Monsignore
If he is a Canon:
    The Very Reverend Monsignor (Canon) John Smith

VERBAL ADDRESS

    Monsignor Smith (usually adopted) *or*
    Monsignore
If he is a Canon, he is usually known as 'Monsignor Smith'.

DESCRIPTION IN CONVERSATION

    Monsignor Smith

PROVINCIAL

The Provincial is the Superior of a Province in a Religious Order, such as the Dominicans, the Franciscans, or the Jesuits.

BEGINNING OF LETTER

Formal	Very Reverend Father Provincial
	or
	Very Reverend Father
Social	Dear Father Provincial *or*
	Dear Father Smith

CONCLUSION OF LETTER

Formal	Yours faithfully (see also p. 2)
Social	Yours sincerely

[1] Often abbreviated to Mgr.

ENVELOPE
> The Very Reverend Father Provincial (followed by the letters of his Order) *or*
>
> The Very Reverend Father Smith (followed by the letters of his Order)

VERBAL ADDRESS
> Father Provincial

DESCRIPTION IN CONVERSATION
> Father Provincial

PRIOR

(See also *Order of St. Benedict*, p. 161.)

BEGINNING OF LETTER

Very formal	Very Reverend and Dear Father Prior
Formal and social	Dear Father Prior

ENDING OF LETTER

Formal	Yours faithfully (see also p. 2)
Social	Yours sincerely

ENVELOPE
> The Very Reverend the Prior of Blank *or*
> The Very Reverend John Smith
> (followed by the initials of his Order)

VERBAL ADDRESS
> Father Prior

DESCRIPTION IN CONVERSATION
> The Prior (of Blank)

PROVOST

The form of address is as for a Canon, with the substitution of Provost for Canon. See *Canon* below.

CANON

If he is a Monsignor, see *Monsignor* (p. 154).

BEGINNING OF LETTER
Formal   Very Reverend Sir
Social   Dear Canon Smith *or*
                             Dear Canon

ENDING OF LETTER
Formal   Yours faithfully (see also p. 2)
Social   Yours sincerely

ENVELOPE
   The Very Reverend Canon John Smith

VERBAL ADDRESS
   Canon Smith

DESCRIPTION IN CONVERSATION
   Canon Smith

PRIEST

A Regular (member of a Religious Order) or Secular Priest is
addressed as 'Father'. (See also *Order of St. Benedict*, p. 160, Friar,
p. 163, and Society of Jesus, p. 164.)

BEGINNING OF LETTER
Formal   Dear Reverend Father
Social   Dear Father Smith

ENDING OF LETTER
Formal   Yours faithfully (see also p. 2)
Social   Yours sincerely

ENVELOPE
   The Reverend John Smith (usual) *or*
   The Reverend Fr. Smith
   If a Regular, the initials of his Order should be inserted after
his name.

VERBAL ADDRESS
   Father
   The surname may be used if distinction is necessary or on
introduction.

DESCRIPTION IN CONVERSATION
Father Smith *or*
Father John (for Regulars where only the christian or religious name is used).

LAY BROTHERS
They are verbally addressed as 'Brother' and referred to as 'Brother John'. (See also *Order of St. Benedict*, p. 162, and Friar, p. 163.)

CHAPLAIN TO THE FORCES
See p. 140.

Religious Communities (Women)

The appropriate letters of the Orders are placed after the name.

Although previously a religious name was usually adopted on taking vows, and the christian name and surname not used, it is becoming the practice in some Orders to retain both christian name and surname.

An Abbess is addressed 'The Lady Abbess' and in some Orders 'The Right Reverend and Lady Abbess'.

(See also *Order of St. Benedict*, p. 162.)

REVEREND MOTHER OR REVEREND SISTER SUPERIOR

BEGINNING OF LETTER
According to her office:
Dear Reverend Mother *or*
Dear Sister Superior

ENVELOPE
According to her office:
The Reverend Mother Prioress
The Reverend Mother
The Sister Superior

VERBAL ADDRESS
According to her office:
Reverend Mother
Sister Superior

<small>DESCRIPTION IN CONVERSATION</small>
According to her office:
  The Mother Prioress
  The Reverend Mother
  The Sister Superior

SISTER OF ORDERS
<small>BEGINNING OF LETTER</small>
  Dear Sister Mary

<small>ENVELOPE</small>
  The Reverend Sister Mary, D.C.
  The Reverend Sister Mary O'Brien, with letters of her Order

<small>VERBAL ADDRESS</small>
  Sister Mary

<small>DESCRIPTION IN CONVERSATION</small>
  Sister Mary (O'Brien)

RELIGIOUS ORDERS (ROMAN CATHOLIC) IN ENGLAND AND WALES
(This list is not complete.)

A.A.	Assumptionist
O.Carm.	Calced Carmelite
O.Cart.	Carthusian
O.C.R.	Cistercian (Reformed)
O.D.C.	Discalced Carmelite
O.F.M.	Franciscan (Friar Minor)
O.F.M. Cap.	Franciscan (Capuchin Friar Minor)
O.F.M. Conv.	Franciscan (Friar Minor Conventual)
O.P.	Dominican
O.S.A.	Augustinian
O.S.B.	Benedictine
O.S.B.M.	Ordo Sancti Basili Magni
O.S. Cam.	Camillan
O.S.F.	Order of St. Francis
O.S.J.D.	Order of St. John of God
O.S.M.	Servite
P.S.S.C.	Pious Society of St. Charles
S.J.	Jesuit (Society of Jesus)
S.M.	Marist

Order of St. Benedict

As the result of recent developments within the Order of St. Benedict, monks, whether clerical or lay, are to be addressed as 'Dom'. The style of 'Reverend' is to be extended to lay brothers by courtesy. At the present time all Benedictine Monasteries have not yet adopted this system. Custom varies considerably from congregation to congregation and even from monastery to monastery.

The following notes are intended as a guide for use in Great Britain. American Benedictines of the two American Congregations do not use 'Dom' but are styled 'The Reverend John Smith, O.S.B.'.

Lay Brothers are referred to as Claustral Brothers.

The form of addressing 'Juniors' (or 'Clerics' as they are called in some monasteries), i.e. monks studying for the priesthood. Custom varies according to the monastery. In one the new monk is 'Dom John' from his novitiate until his ordination, when he becomes 'Father John'. In another, the student monk is 'Reverend Father John' until his ordination, when he becomes 'Dom John'.

Today, monks who are priests could be addressed verbally, and in informal letters as 'Father'; those who are not priests as 'Brother'. In formal letters and usage, 'Dom' may be applied to all. Many Benedictines are content not to have O.S.B. appended to the name, 'Dom' being sufficient distinction.

BENEDICTINE ABBOT

Benedictine Abbots in Great Britain are not 'Lord' Abbots. The head of a Benedictine Congregation is generally referred to as the Abbot President.

BEGINNING OF LETTER
Dear Father President

ENVELOPE
The Right Reverend the Abbot President,
X Abbey

VERBAL ADDRESS
Father Abbot

DESCRIPTION IN CONVERSATION
The Abbot President

TITULAR ABBOTS

It is customary, though not invariably so, for a retired Abbot to take the title of an extinct Abbey. Titular Abbacies may also be conferred on individual monks. Such Abbots, if they have a local title, may be addressed as 'The Right Reverend the Abbot of X', but by practice and custom in the English Congregation they are usually addressed 'The Right Reverend Dom John Smith'. Letters may be begun 'Dear Father Abbot', 'Dear Father John', or even 'Dear Abbot John'.

It has hitherto been customary to refer to Abbots by their surnames, e.g. Abbot Smith, but the more recent practice is to refer to them by the religious name 'Abbot John'. This practice is invariably adopted among American Benedictines.

ABBOT VISITOR OR ABBOT GENERAL

Where these offices exist, they are so addressed.
VERBAL ADDRESS
    Father Abbot.

PRIOR

Conventional Priors (independent monasteries) and Priors of dependent Priories, who are also superiors of monasteries but subject to the founding Abbey, are addressed identically.

CLAUSTRAL PRIORS

They are second-in-command to the Abbot of a monastery, and are addressed as other Priors. The envelope is addressed The Very Reverend The Prior X Abbey.

TITULAR PRIORS

In the English Benedictine Congregation, titular Priors bear the titles of old cathedral monasteries. They are formally addressed as 'The Very Reverend', followed by, Prior of X, but by practice and custom in the English Congregation 'The Very Reverend Dom John Smith' is most usual. Letters begin 'Dear Father Prior'.

PRIESTS

BEGINNING OF LETTER
Formal   Dear Dom Julian
Social   Dear Father Julian

ENDING OF LETTER
Yours sincerely

ENVELOPE
The Reverend Dom Julian Smith, O.S.B.
The use of 'The Reverend' and 'O.S.B.' is optional

VERBAL ADDRESS
Formal   Dom John
Social   Father
                                  If distinction is necessary or on
                                      introduction 'Father Smith'.
He may be called by those who know him 'Dom', but this is
not usual.

'Dom' with the surname is peculiar to French Benedictines, and
even there is going out of use.

DESCRIPTION IN CONVERSATION
Dom John Smith
Parochially he is often referred to as Father Smith.

CLAUSTRAL (OR LAY) BROTHERS
BEGINNING OF LETTER
Formal   Dear Reverend Brother
Social   Dear Brother John

Benedictine Nuns

The following is the practice in the English Congregation. The
letters O.S.B. may be appended after the name.

ABBESS

She is referred to as Lady Abbess.

BEGINNING OF LETTER
Dear Lady Abbess

ENVELOPE
The Lady Abbess
Blank Abbey
The courtesy style of 'The Right Reverend' is not normally
used.

VERBAL ADDRESS
Lady Abbess *or* Mother Abbess

DESCRIPTION IN CONVERSATION
The Lady Abbess

PRIORESS
COMMENCEMENT OF LETTER
Dear Mother Prioress

ENVELOPE
The Mother Prioress
Blank Abbey

VERBAL ADDRESS AND DESCRIPTION IN CONVERSATION
Mother Prioress

NUN IN SOLEMN VOWS
BEGINNING OF LETTER
Dear Dame Jane

ENVELOPE
Dame Jane Smith,
Blank Abbey

VERBAL ADDRESS
Dame Jane

DESCRIPTION IN CONVERSATION
Dame Jane

NOVICES, JUNIORS, CLAUSTRAL SISTERS AND EXTERN SISTERS
They are addressed as Sisters.
  The envelope is addressed:
  Sister Jane Smith
  X Abbey

Friar

Members of certain Religious Orders, especially the Mendicant Orders of Franciscans (Grey Friars), Dominicans (Black Friars),

Augustinians (Austin Friars) and Carmelites (White Friars) ar
known as friars and not monks, primarily due to their flexibility
of movement within the Order. Each order is organized with a
Father Provincial for each Province, and a Father Prior (or Father
Guardian in the case of the Franciscan Order) for each House.
Though friar means brother, the term covers all priests and lay
brothers. Forms of address are as for those of other Religious
Orders.

The Society of Jesus

Jesuits do not normally accept ecclesiastical dignities. To do so
would be contrary to the views expressed by their founder, St.
Ignatius Loyola. The General, Provincials, Vice-Provincials and
Major Superiors (normally those in charge of a mission area) are
entitled to the prefix 'The Very Reverend'. All others are
addressed as 'The Reverend'.

An exception to the above is when a Jesuit receives an appointment within the Roman Catholic Church, e.g. as an Archbishop
or Bishop, which occasionally happens. He then takes the appropriate ecclesiastical style for such Office.

Members of the Order append S.J. after their names. The Order
is restricted to men.

The Jewish Community
The Orthodox Synagogues

They include the United Synagogue.

THE CHIEF RABBI
His appointment is Chief Rabbi of the United Hebrew Congregation of the British Commonwealth of Nations.

BEGINNING OF LETTER
Formal   Dear Sir, *or*
                                  Dear Chief Rabbi
Social   Dear Chief Rabbi

ENDING OF LETTER
Formal   Yours faithfully (see also p. 2)
Social   Yours sincerely

ENVELOPE
The Chief Rabbi Dr. Immanuel Jakobovits

The prefix 'The Very Reverend' is formally correct, but is not used by the present Chief Rabbi.

VERBAL ADDRESS
Chief Rabbi

DESCRIPTION IN CONVERSATION
The Chief Rabbi

THE CHIEF RABBI EMERITUS

As for the Chief Rabbi, but with the addition of 'Emeritus'.
The Prefix 'The Very Reverend' is formally correct, but is not normally used.

ENVELOPE
Chief Rabbi Emeritus Sir Israel Brodie, K.B.E.

RABBI

BEGINNING OF LETTER
Formal   Dear Sir
Social   Dear Rabbi Wiseman
                     Dear Dr. Wiseman (if a doctor)

ENDING OF LETTER
Formal   Yours faithfully (see also p. 2)
Social   Yours sincerely

ENVELOPE
Rabbi J. Wiseman
Rabbi Dr. J. Wiseman (if a doctor).
The 'Reverend' before Rabbi is not now used.

VERBAL ADDRESS
Rabbi Wiseman
Dr. Wiseman (if a doctor)

DESCRIPTION IN CONVERSATION
Rabbi Wiseman
Dr. Wiseman (if a doctor)

MINISTER

Readers and Cantors also use the title The Reverend.

BEGINNING OF LETTER

Formal	Dear Sir *or*
	Reverend Sir
Social	Dear Mr. Wiseman
	Dear Dr. Wiseman (if a doctor)

ENDING OF LETTER

Formal	Yours faithfully (see also p. 2)
Social	Yours sincerely

ENVELOPE

The Reverend David Wiseman
The Reverend Dr. David Wiseman (if a doctor)

VERBAL ADDRESS

Mr. Wiseman
Dr. Wiseman (if a doctor)

DESCRIPTION IN CONVERSATION

Mr. Wiseman
Dr. Wiseman (if a doctor)

CHAPLAIN TO THE FORCES

(See p. 140.)

The Sephardi Synagogue

The Sephardi (Spanish and Portuguese) Community in Great Britain has several Synagogues. The oldest synagogue in the country is the Spanish and Portuguese Congregation in London established in Creechurch Lane in the City of London in 1657. All the Sephardi Synagogues in Great Britain, and the Sephardi Community in Salisbury, Rhodesia, are under the spiritual jurisdiction of the Haham, the traditional title of the Chief Rabbi in Great Britain.

There are a number of Sephardi Rabbis who are not Ecclesiastical officials of Congregations.

The form of address for the Haham is as follows:

BEGINNING OF LETTER
Formal and Social   Dear Haham

ENDING OF LETTER
Formal   Yours faithfully (see also p. 2)
Social   Yours sincerely

ENVELOPE
    The Very Reverend the Haham, Dr. S. Gaon

For Rabbis and Ministers, see pp. 165 and 166.

Reform and Liberal Synagogues

The Reform Synagogues of Great Britain and the Union of Liberal and Progressive Synagogues are separate organizations. However, they have a United Council of Reform and Liberal Rabbis whose Chairman for the time being is their Ecclesiastical Representative.

The Ecclesiastical Representative and other Rabbis are addressed identically as Rabbis (p. 165).

Ministers are addressed identically as those on p. 166.

DIPLOMATIC AND COMMONWEALTH SECTION

A FOREIGN AMBASSADOR ACCREDITED TO THE UNITED KINGDOM AND A COMMONWEALTH HIGH COMMISSIONER

An Ambassador accredited to the Court of St. James's is accorded the style of His (or Her) Excellency within the United Kingdom.

The wife of an Ambassador is not entitled to the style of 'Her Excellency' and is referred to and addressed by her name.

Precedence within the Diplomatic Corps is accorded to an Ambassador from the date of his handing into the Foreign and Commonwealth Office the *copie d'usage* of his Letters of Credence.

A Commonwealth High Commissioner in the United Kingdom is accorded the same style and precedence as an Ambassador, but his precedence dates from the moment he sets foot on United Kingdom soil.

The Ambassador from the United States of America is colloquially known as the American Ambassador, but in a written communication he is referred to as the 'Ambassador of the United States'. An American Ambassador uses the style of 'The Honorable' before his name. Similarly, the Ambassador from Ireland is coloquially known as the Irish Ambassador, but in a written communication he is referred to as the 'Ambassador of the Irish Republic'.

BEGINNING OF LETTER

Formal	Your Excellency
Social	(My) dear Ambassador
	(My) dear High Commissioner

ENDING OF LETTER

Formal	I have the honour to be, with the highest consideration,
	Your Excellency's obedient servant
Social	Believe me,
	My dear Ambassador/High Commissioner,
	Yours (very) sincerely

ENVELOPE

His Excellency always precedes all other styles, titles or ranks, *except those of Royal or Serene Highness.* Señor, etc., precedes Don or Doctor. A Service rank immediately follows His Excellency, e.g.:

> His Excellency General . . .
> His Excellency Doctor . . .
> His Excellency Monsieur, Mr., Herr, Signor, Senor, Senhor
> . . ., etc.

(See *Foreign Equivalents of 'Mr.'*, p. 117.)

If an Ambassador is His Royal Highness, His Highness or His Serene Highness, 'His Excellency' is unnecessary.

'Esquire' cannot be used after 'His Excellency'.

Formal	His Excellency
	The Finnish Ambassador
Social	His Excellency
	Monsieur Pierre Duclos, K.C.V.O. (or appropriate letters)

VERBAL ADDRESS
Formal   Your Excellency should be mentioned at
                          least once in conversation, thereafter
                          'Sir' *or* by name.
Social   Ambassador, *or* by name
                          High Commissioner, *or* by name

DESCRIPTION IN CONVERSATION
Formal   His Excellency
Social   The French Ambassador, *or*
                          The Ambassador
                          or by name (as applicable)

                          The Canadian High Commissioner
                          The High Commissioner
                          or by name (as applicable)

JOINT FORM OF ADDRESS
    His Excellency the Andorran Ambassador and Madame de
        Blanc (or appropriate title)
    Similarly a High Commissioner and his wife.

BRITISH AMBASSADOR ACCREDITED TO A FOREIGN COUNTRY

A British Ambassador accredited to the Court of a foreign country
is known as 'His Excellency' within the country to which he is
accredited. When outside that country he is not accorded the
style or precedence of an Ambassador.

The wife of an Ambassador is not entitled to the style of 'Her
Excellency', and is addressed and referred to by her name.

BEGINNING OF LETTER
Formal   Sir
Social   (My) dear Ambassador

ENDING OF LETTER
Formal   I have the honour to be,
                          Sir,
                          Your Excellency's obedient Servant,

Social   Believe me,
                          My dear Ambassador,
                          Yours (very) sincerely,

ENVELOPE

Peer	His Excellency the Viscount Flintshire, K.C.M.G.
Privy Counsellor	His Excellency the Rt. Hon. John Jones C.M.G.
Knight	His Excellency Sir William Smith
Esquire	His Excellency Mr. John Smith, C.M.G.
	His Excellency Major-General John Brown, C.M.G.
	'Esq.' is not used with His Excellency

VERBAL ADDRESS

Formal	Your Excellency should be mentioned at least once in conversation, thereafter, Sir, *or* by name
Social	Ambassador, *or* by name

DESCRIPTION IN CONVERSATION

Formal	His Excellency
Social	The British Ambassador, *or*
	The Ambassador
	or by name (as applicable)

BRITISH HIGH COMMISSIONER IN A COMMONWEALTH COUNTRY

A High Commissioner is accorded the same style and precedence as an Ambassador, and is styled 'His Excellency'.

MINISTER

In the Diplomatic Service there are two kinds of Minister. A Minister Plenipotentiary, and a Minister who assists an Ambassador including Minister (Economic) and Minister (Commercial).

A Minister Plenipotentiary accredited to the United Kingdom or Her Majesty's Minister Plenipotentiary, accredited to a foreign country, is not styled 'His Excellency', which is reserved for Ambassadors and High Commissioners.

The official residence of a Minister Plenipotentiary is a Legation and not an Embassy. Today very few Ministers Plenipotentiary are appointed, since nearly all have been upgraded to the rank of Ambassador.

MINISTER PLENIPOTENTIARY

BEGINNING OF LETTER
Formal   Sir
Social   (My) dear Minister, *or* by name

ENDING OF LETTER
Formal   I have the honour to be,
    Foreign   with high consideration,
                Your obedient Servant,

    British   I have the honour to be,
                Sir,
                Your obedient Servant,
Social   Yours sincerely

ENVELOPE
    John Smith, Esq., C.M.G.
    H.M. Minister,
    British Legation,

VERBAL ADDRESS
    Minister *or* by name

DESCRIPTION IN CONVERSATION
    The Minister,
    The British Minister
    or by name (as applicable)
There is no special form of address for a Minister at an Embassy.

CHARGÉ D'AFFAIRES AND ACTING HIGH COMMISSIONERS

As a British Chargé d'Affaires of an Embassy or Legation does not represent the Crown, or a foreign Chargé d'Affaires his Head of State, he is not accorded the style 'His Excellency', even when, as 'Chargé d'Affaires en titre' he is permanently in charge of his country's diplomatic mission.

A Chargé d'Affaires within the British Commonwealth is not accorded the style of 'Her Majesty's' or 'H.M.' before his appointment.

A Chargé d'Affaires temporarily in charge of his country's Diplomatic Mission is officially known as 'Chargé d'Affaires ad interim' (which may be abbreviated to 'a.i.').

BEGINNING OF LETTER

Formal	Sir
Social	(My) dear Chargé d'Affaires
	or by name

An Acting High Commissioner is addressed by name and not by his appointment.

CONCLUSION OF LETTER

Formal	
Foreign	I have the honour to be, with high consideration, Your obedient Servant,
British	I have the honour to be, Sir, Your obedient Servant,
Social	Yours sincerely

ENVELOPE

John Brown, Esq.,
Chargé d'Affaires,
British Embassy, . . .

Monsieur Jean Le Brun,
Chargé d'Affaires,
. . . Embassy

Monsieur Georges Van
  Cleef,
Chargé d'Affaires
. . . Embassy

John Brown, Esq.,
Acting High Commissioner,
British High Commission, . . .

K. Singh, Esq.,
Acting High Commissioner,
. . . High Commission

VERBAL ADDRESS

Chargé d'Affaires
or by name

DESCRIPTION IN CONVERSATION
> The Guatamalan Chargé d'Affaires, *or*
> The Chargé d'Affaires
> The British Chargé d'Affaires
> *or* by name (as applicable)

> The Acting High Commissioner
> *or* by name

CONSUL-GENERAL, CONSUL, OR VICE-CONSUL

A Consul-General, Consul, or Vice-Consul who holds Her Majesty's Commission is entitled to the letters 'H.M.' before the appointment. The formal style of 'H.B.M.' (Her Britannic Majesty) is not now used.

Other Consuls, Vice-Consuls, and Consular Agents, appointed other than by the Crown, are known as the British Consul, Vice-Consul, etc., and do not have the prefix 'H.M.'.

The officer in charge of a Consular appointment, during the absence of the incumbent, takes for the time being the rank of the incumbent, but is addressed as 'The Acting British Consul-General, Consul', etc.

Consuls of the other Commonwealth Countries are addressed as 'The Australian Consul', etc.

The American Consul-General, Consul, etc., is addressed as 'Consul-General, Consul, etc., for the United States of America' but colloquially he is known as The American (or the United States) Consul-General, Consul,' etc.

ENVELOPE
> John H. Brown, Esq., C.M.G.,
> H.M. Consul-General,
> British Consulate-General

> William Smith, Esq.,
> H.M. Consul,
> British Consulate

> William Jones, Esq.,
> British Consul,
> British Consulate

Otherwise as an Esquire or appropriate style.

OTHER DIPLOMATIC OFFICERS AND SERVICE ATTACHES

These do not have any special form of address. They are addressed according to rank.

AGENT-GENERAL

Each Province in Canada and each State of Australia is represented in London by an Agent-General.

An Agent-General is not accorded any special form of address, but his appointment should be placed after his name.

> John Jones, Esq.,
> Agent-General for . . .

When more than one Agent-General for the Provinces in Canada are listed they should be placed according to the alphabetical order of the Provinces.

Agents-General for the States of Australia should be placed in the following order:

> New South Wales
> Victoria
> Queensland
> South Australia
> Western Australia
> Tasmania

Placement for Canadian Agents-General is sometimes done by seniority of tenure of Office in London.

TRADE COMMISSIONER

He is not accorded any special form of address.

GOVERNOR-GENERAL, GOVERNOR OR LIEUTENANT-GOVERNOR

A Governor-General or Governor is styled 'His Excellency', which precedes all other titles and ranks, while administering a Government and within the territory administered.

The Lieutenant-Governors of Jersey, Guernsey, and the Isle of Man are accorded the same style. A Lieutenant-Governor of a Canadian Province is accorded the style of 'The Honourable' for life.

The Governor-General of Canada has the rank of 'Right Honourable' for life.

Since 1924 the wife of a Governor-General but *not* of a Governor, has been accorded the style of 'Her Excellency' within the country administered by her husband.

BEGINNING OF LETTER

Formal	Sir
	My Lord (if a peer)
Social	Dear Lord Smith (if a peer)

Dear Sir John (Smith) (if a Knight)
Dear Mr. Smith (if an Esquire)
or My dear Lieutenant-Governor (Canada)

CONCLUSION OF LETTER
Formal
I have the honour to be,
Sir (My Lord, if a peer),
Your Excellency's obedient servant,
Social
Yours sincerely

ENVELOPE
Peer
His Excellency
The Lord Blank, K.C.B.,
Governor-General of Australia

Knight
His Excellency
Sir John Brown, K.C.B.,
Governor of New South Wales

Esquire
His Excellency
Mr. William Robinson, C.M.G.,
Governor of St. Helena

The Hon. John Smith,
Lieutenant Governor of (Canada).

VERBAL ADDRESS
Formal   Your Excellency
Social   By name

DESCRIPTION IN CONVERSATION
Formal
His Excellency *or*
The Governor (General)

Social
The Governor (General) *or*
by name
The Lieutenant-Governor
or by name

PRECEDENCE OF CONSULAR OFFICERS AND OFFICERS OF THE ARMED SERVICES

Consuls General rank with
but after   Rear-Admirals
                           Major-Generals
                           Air Vice-Marshals

Consuls rank with but after	Captains R.N. Colonels Group Captains
Vice-Consuls rank with but after	Lieutenant-Commanders Majors Squadron Leaders
Consular Agents rank with but after	Lieutenants R.N. Captains (Army) Flight Lieutenants

The officer in charge of a consular post, during the absence of the titular holder, takes the rank of that officer.

ARMED FORCES SECTION

TITLED OFFICERS

If an officer has a title, or a courtesy title or style, he is addressed in the beginning of the letter and in speech as for others with the same style, i.e.

CORRESPONDENCE	*Formal*	*Social*
Peer or a peer by courtesy	My Lord	Dear Lord Blank
Courtesy style of 'lord' before his christian name	My Lord	Dear Lord John (the surname may be added if the acquaintanceship is slight)
Baronet or Knight	(Dear) Sir	Dear Sir Guy (the surname may be added if the acquaintanceship is slight)

See the appropriate title for further information.

Some officers who have inherited or received a title or style prefer to be addressed by their Service rank. If Admiral Sir Guy Jones expresses his preference to be addressed 'Dear Admiral Jones' instead of 'Dear Sir Guy', this should be followed.

ENVELOPE

According to his title or style. The Service rank appears before his title, except 'His Excellency'. The appropriate letters which signify Orders, Decorations, etc., immediately follow the name, except that if he is a Baronet, the abbreviation Bt. or Bart. immediately follows his name followed by letters which signify orders, etc.:

His Excellency Admiral the Lord Chiswick, K.C.B.
Colonel Lord Edward Brown, D.S.O., M.C.
Wing Commander the Hon. Edward Smith, D.F.C., R.A.F.
Lieutenant-Commander Sir John Brown, Bt., D.S.O., Royal Navy (or R.N.)

VERBAL ADDRESS
According to his title or style, unless the officer prefers to be addressed by his Service rank. 'The Honourable' is never used in speech, e.g. Major the Honourable John Smith is known as Major Smith.

USE OF AN OFFICER'S RANK WITHOUT THE SURNAME

Within the Services, in informal correspondence, certain officers are sometimes addressed only by their rank (e.g. 'Dear Admiral' in place of 'Dear Admiral Smith'), generally when the writer is a casual acquaintance of the addressee. But though accepted within the Services, some officers dislike this practice from those outside.

Use of such rank without a surname is limited to the following:
Royal Navy.—Officers of Flag Rank (Rear-Admiral and above).
Army.—Major and above.
Royal Air Force.—Squadron Leader and above.

RETIRED OFFICERS WHO HAVE ENTERED HOLY ORDERS

(See p. 125.)

RELATIVE RANKS IN THE ARMED FORCES

Royal Navy	*Army*	*Royal Air Force*
Admiral of the Fleet	Field Marshal	Marshal of the Royal Air Force
Admiral	General	Air Chief Marshal
Vice-Admiral	Lieutenant-General	Air Marshal
Rear-Admiral	Major-General	Air Vice-Marshal

Commodore	Brigadier	Air Commodore
Captain	Colonel	Group Captain
Commander	Lieutenant-Colonel	Wing Commander
Lieutenant- Commander	Major	Squadron Leader
Lieutenant	Captain	Flight Lieutenant
Sub-Lieutenant	Lieutenant	Flying Officer
	Second Lieutenant	Pilot Officer

Officers rank according to their seniority or date of appointment.

Royal Navy

'ROYAL NAVY' or 'R.N.' PLACED AFTER THE NAME

All officers of the Royal Navy below the rank of Rear-Admiral are entitled to the words 'Royal Navy' or 'R.N.' after their name and decorations, etc., whether on the active or retired lists. The Royal Navy prefer this to be written in full, but the abbreviation 'R.N.' is customarily used.

RETIRED OFFICERS

The word 'retired' (abbreviated to 'Ret.' or 'Rtd') should not be used in ordinary correspondence or in lists, but only when it is necessary to indicate that an officer is on the retired list. The exception to this rule is that when a retired officer is employed in a civilian capacity at a Service establishment he may be addressed with (Ret.) or (Rtd.) to facilitate postal arrangements.

ADMIRAL OF THE FLEET

This is a rank held for life. (See also *Titled Officers*, p. 176.)

BEGINNING OF LETTER

According to his title (he would almost certainly be a peer, baronet, or knight).[1]

Formal

If a Peer	My Lord
Otherwise	(Dear) Sir

Social

If a Peer, Baronet, or Knight	Dear Lord Blank Dear Sir John (the surname may be added if the acquaintanceship is slight)
Otherwise	Dear Admiral Smith

ENDING OF LETTER

Formal	Yours faithfully (see also p. 2)
Social	Yours sincerely

ENVELOPE

According to rank, with the appropriate letters after his name, e.g.:
   Admiral of the Fleet the Earl of Flintshire, G.C.B., K.B.E.
   Admiral of the Fleet Sir John Brown, G.B.E., K.C.B.

VERBAL ADDRESS

According to his title[1]:
   Lord Brown
   Sir John
He may prefer to be known by his naval rank, which is socially abbreviated to 'Admiral'.
A younger man, or a more junior officer in any of the Armed Forces addresses him as 'Sir'.

DESCRIPTION IN CONVERSATION

   Lord Flintshire
   Sir John Brown
If reference is made to his rank, Admiral of the Fleet is used in full.

ADMIRAL, VICE-ADMIRAL, REAR-ADMIRAL

All three ranks are known socially as Admiral. The exact rank is given within the Royal Navy, on the envelope or in a formal description.
   (See also *Titled Officers*, p. 176.)

BEGINNING OF LETTER

Formal	(Dear) Sir
Social	
If a Knight	Dear Sir William[1] (the surname may be added if the acquaintanceship is slight)
Otherwise	Dear Admiral Robinson

CONCLUSION OF LETTER

Formal	Yours faithfully (see also p. 2)
Social	Yours sincerely

[1] If he prefers his Naval rank to be used, letters begin 'Dear Admiral Blank', and the verbal address is 'Admiral Blank' or 'Admiral'. (See also *Use of Officer's Rank Without the Surname*, p. 177.)

ENVELOPE

This is addressed to the exact rank, with the appropriate letters following the name, e.g.

>Admiral Sir William Smith, G.C.B.
>Vice-Admiral Sir John Brown, K.B.E., M.V.O.
>Rear-Admiral John Robinson, V.C., C.B., O.B.E.

VERBAL ADDRESS

If a Knight	Sir William[1]
Otherwise	Admiral Robinson

A younger man, or a more Junior Officer in any of the Armed Forces addresses him as 'Sir'.

DESCRIPTION IN CONVERSATION

If a Knight	Sir William Smith
Otherwise	Admiral Robinson

Should social reference be made to only one Admiral, Vice-Admiral, or Rear-Admiral he may be called informally 'the Admiral'.

COMMODORE OR CAPTAIN

A Commodore reverts to the rank of Captain on conclusion of his appointment.

BEGINNING OF LETTER

Formal	(Dear) Sir
Social	Dear Commodore Smith
	Dear Captain Smith

These ranks should not be abbreviated.

ENDING OF LETTER

Formal	Yours faithfully (see also p. 2)
Social	Yours sincerely

ENVELOPE

>Commodore John Smith, C.B.E., Royal Navy (or R.N.)
>Captain John Brown, C.B., Royal Navy (or R.N.)

These ranks should not be abbreviated.

VERBAL ADDRESS

>Commodore Smith
>Captain Smith

---

[1] If he prefers his Naval rank to be used to that appropriate for his knighthood, letters begin 'Dear Admiral Blank', and the verbal address is 'Admiral Blank' or 'Admiral'. (See *Titled Officers*, p. 176, and *Use of an Officer's Rank Without the Surname*, p. 177.)

A younger man, or a more junior officer in any of the Armed Forces, addresses him as 'Sir'.

DESCRIPTION IN CONVERSATION
Commodore Smith
Captain Smith

COMMANDER OR LIEUTENANT-COMMANDER

In the Royal Navy he is styled Commander or Lieutenant-Commander, as applicable, but socially both are styled Commander. The exact rank is given on the envelope or in a list.

BEGINNING OF LETTER
Formal   (Dear) Sir
Social   Dear Commander Smith (this rank should not be abbreviated)

ENDING OF LETTER
Formal   Yours faithfully (see also p. 2)
Social   Yours sincerely

ENVELOPE
Commander John Smith, O.B.E., Royal Navy (or R.N.)
Lieutenant-Commander John Jones, Royal Navy (or R.N.)
These ranks should not be abbreviated.

VERBAL ADDRESS
Commander Smith
A younger man, or a more junior officer in any of the Armed Forces addresses him as 'Sir'.

DESCRIPTION IN CONVERSATION
Commander Smith

LIEUTENANT

As for a Commander, with the substitution of Lieutenant.

SUB-LIEUTENANT

BEGINNING OF LETTER
Formal   (Dear) Sir
Social   Dear Mr. Smith

ENDING OF LETTER
Formal   Yours faithfully (see also p. 2)
Social   Yours sincerely

ENVELOPE
Sub-Lieutenant John Smith, Royal Navy (or R.N.)
This rank should not be abbreviated.

VERBAL ADDRESS
Mr. Smith

DESCRIPTION IN CONVERSATION
Mr. Smith

WOMEN MEDICAL AND DENTAL OFFICERS

These are officers of the Royal Navy, and are addressed according to their rank.

MIDSHIPMAN OR CADET

A Midshipman or Cadet is addressed as for a Sub-Lieutenant, with the exception of the envelope which is addressed according to his rank, i.e.:
Midshipman John Smith, Royal Navy (or R.N.)
Cadet John Smith, Royal Navy (or R.N.)

CHAPLAINS TO THE ROYAL NAVY

(See *Chaplains to H.M. Forces*, p. 140.)

NON-COMMISSIONED RATES

The principal rates, excluding technical and specialist rates, are as follows:
Fleet Chief Petty Officer
Chief Petty Officer (C.P.O.)
Petty Officer (P.O.)
Leading Seaman (Ldg. Smn.)
Able-Bodied Seaman (A/B)

BEGINNING OF LETTER
Dear Mr. Smith (Fleet Chief Petty Officer), otherwise according to rate, e.g. Dear Chief Petty Officer Smith.

ENVELOPE
According to rate, with Royal Navy or R.N. after the name.
Ranks should not be abbreviated to prevent confusion with initials of christian names.

VERBAL ADDRESS
According to rate.

Royal Marines

Forms of address are as for the Army.
Those of the rank of Lieutenant-Colonel and below place R.M. (some prefer 'Royal Marines' in full) after their name.
Retired Royal Marine Officers may place R.M. after their names.

NON-COMMISSIONED RANKS

The principal ranks are as follows:
  Regimental Sergeant-Major (equivalent to W.O. I)
  Quartermaster-Sergeant (equivalent to W.O. II)
  Staff Bandmaster (equivalent to W.O. II)
  Colour Sergeant
  Sergeant
  Corporal
  Lance Corporal
  Marine

BEGINNING OF LETTER

Regimental Sergeant-Major	Dear Mr. Smith
Quartermaster-Sergeant	Dear Q.M.S. Smith
Staff Bandmaster	Dear Staff Bandmaster Smith
Colour Sergeant	Dear Colour Sergeant Smith

Otherwise, as for the Army.

ENVELOPE
According to rank.

VERBAL ADDRESS
As for beginning of letter (omitting 'Dear').

The Army
FIELD MARSHAL
This rank is held for life.
(See also *Titled Officers*, p. 176.)

BEGINNING OF LETTER
According to his title (he would almost certainly be a peer, baronet, or knight).[1]
Formal

If a Peer	My Lord
Otherwise	(Dear) Sir

Social

If a Peer	Dear Lord Blank
Otherwise	Dear Sir John (the surname may be added if the acquaintanceship is slight)

ENDING OF LETTER

Formal	Yours faithfully (see also p. 2)
Social	Yours sincerely

ENVELOPE
According to rank with the appropriate letters after his name, e.g.:
Field Marshal (the Rt. Hon.) the Lord Blank, G.C.B.
Field Marshal Sir John Brown, K.C.B.

VERBAL ADDRESS
According to his title[1]:
Lord Black
Sir John
A younger man, or a more junior officer in any of the Armed Forces addresses him as 'Sir'.

DESCRIPTION IN CONVERSATION
Lord Horsham
Sir John Brown *or* The Field Marshal
If reference is made to his rank, Field Marshal is used in full.

GENERAL, LIEUTENANT-GENERAL,
MAJOR-GENERAL OR BRIGADIER-GENERAL
All four ranks are referred to as General, except on the envelope, or formally, such as in a list, when the exact rank is given.

[1] When he prefers his Military rank to be used, letters are commenced 'Dear Field-Marshal Blank' and the verbal address is 'Field-Marshal Blank' or 'Field-Marshal'. (See also *Use of an Officer's Rank Without the Surname*, p. 177.)

The rank of Brigadier-General was abolished in the United Kingdom in 1921. It is included because a few retired Brigadier-Generals are still living. The rank of Brigadier-General (in place of Brigadier) has recently been restored to the Canadian Armed Forces. (See *Commonwealth Armed Forces*, p. 202.)

(See *Titled Officers*, p. 176.)

BEGINNING OF LETTER

Formal	(Dear) Sir
Social	
If a knight	Dear Sir John[1] (the surname may be added if the acquaintanceship is slight)
Otherwise	Dear General Smith

ENDING OF LETTER

Formal	Yours faithfully (see also p. 2)
Social	Yours sincerely

ENVELOPE

According to the exact rank, with the appropriate letters after the name, e.g.:

    General Sir Edward Jones, G.C.B.
    Lieutenant-General Sir John Smith, K.C.B.
    Major-General John Jones, C.B., C.B.E.
    Brigadier-General William Robinson, C.I.E., D.S.O.
The ranks should not be abbreviated.

VERBAL ADDRESS

If a Knight	Sir John[1]
Otherwise	General Jones *or* General

A younger man, or a much junior officer in any of the Armed Forces addresses him as 'Sir'.

(See *Titled Officers*, p. 176.)

DESCRIPTION IN CONVERSATION

If a Knight	Sir John Smith[2]
Otherwise	General Jones

Should social reference be made to only one General Officer, he may be called 'the General'.

---

[1] If he prefers his military rank to be used letters begin 'Dear General Blank', and the verbal address is 'General Blank', or 'General'. (See also *Use of an Officer's Rank Without the Surname*, p. 177.)
[2] See also *Use of an Officer's Rank Without the Surname*, p. 177.

BRIGADIER

This rank was adopted in 1928.

BEGINNING OF LETTER
Formal   (Dear) Sir
Social   Dear Brigadier Smith[1]
This rank should not be abbreviated.

ENDING OF LETTER
Formal   Yours faithfully (see also p. 2)
Social   Yours sincerely

ENVELOPE
Brigadier John Brown, D.S.O., M.C.
This rank should not be abbreviated.

VERBAL ADDRESS
Brigadier Brown *or* Brigadier
A younger man, or a more junior officer in any of the Armed
Forces, addresses him as 'Sir'.

DESCRIPTION IN CONVERSATION
Brigadier Brown
Should social reference be made to only one Brigadier he may
be called 'the Brigadier'.

COLONEL OR LIEUTENANT-COLONEL

Both ranks are referred to as Colonel, except on the envelope, or
in a formal description, such as a list when the exact rank is
given.

BEGINNING OF LETTER
Formal   (Dear) Sir
Social   Dear Colonel Robinson[1]
This rank should not be abbreviated.

ENDING OF LETTER
Formal   Yours faithfully (see also p. 2)
Social   Yours sincerely

---

[1] See also *Use of an Officer's Rank Without the Surname*, p. 177.

ENVELOPE

The Regiment or Corps (or abbreviations) may be added to an officer on the active list.

Lieutenant-Colonel Edward Black, M.C.,
Grenadier Guards

These ranks should not be abbreviated.

VERBAL ADDRESS

Colonel Brown *or* Colonel

A younger man, or a more junior officer in any of the Armed Forces, addresses him as 'Sir'.

DESCRIPTION IN CONVERSATION

Colonel Brown

MAJOR OR CAPTAIN

The form of address is as for a Colonel, with the substitution of Major or Captain.

A letter should not begin 'Dear Captain' (see p. 177).

LIEUTENANT OR SECOND LIEUTENANT

BEGINNING OF LETTER

Formal	(Dear) Sir.
Social	Dear Mr. Jones

ENDING OF LETTER

Formal	Yours faithfully (see also p. 2)
Social	Yours sincerely

ENVELOPE

The Regiment or Corps may be added on the next line, as for a Lieutenant-Colonel.

John Brown, Esq.,
Grenadier Guards[1]

VERBAL ADDRESS

Mr. Brown

The verbal use of the terms 'Cornet' for a 2nd Lieutenant of

---

[1] It is now the practice in some regiments to include the rank of the officer on the envelope to a military address, e.g. '2nd Lieutenant John Brown, . . . Regt.'.

The Blues and Royals, and 'Ensign' for a 2nd Lieutenant of Foot Guards is restricted to within the Household Division.

DESCRIPTION IN CONVERSATION
    Mr. Brown

WOMEN MEDICAL AND DENTAL OFFICERS
They are officers of the R.A.M.C., otherwise forms of address are as for The Women's Royal Army Corps (see p. 197.)

OFFICER CADET
The form of address is as for a Lieutenant, but the envelope is addressed as follows:

Professional	Officer Cadet (or Senior Cadet) John Jones
Social	John Jones, Esq.

CHAPLAIN
(See *Chaplains to H.M. Forces*, p. 140.)

NON-COMMISSIONED RANKS

In all cases it is not the practice within the Service to mark abbreviations with full stops i.e. CSM.

Some ranks vary according to the Regiment or Corps.

The Household Division, which comprises The Household Cavalry and The Guards' Division, differs considerably from the rest of the Army, see below.

The principal ranks in the British Army (apart from the Household Division) are:

> Warrant Officer Class 1 (e.g. Regimental Sergeant Major (R.S.M.), Staff Sergeant Major (S.S.M.), Conductor (R.A.O.C.), etc.)
> Warrant Officer Class II (e.g. Regimental Quartermaster Sergeant (R.Q.M.S.), Company Sergeant Major (C.S.M.), Staff Quartermaster Sergeant (S.Q.M.S.), Quartermaster Sergeant (Q.M.S.), etc.)
> Staff Sergeant (SSgt.) and Colour Sergeant (CSgt.)
> Sergeant (Sgt.)
> Corporal (Cpl.)
> Lance Corporal (LCpl.) or Lance Bombardier (L.Bdr.)

Private (Pte) or equivalent rank (e.g. Gunner (Gnr.), Sapper (Spr.), Fusilier (Fus.), Rifleman (Rfn.), Signalman (Sig.), Driver (Dvr.), Craftsman (Sig.), Ranger (Rgr.)).

BEGINNING OF LETTER
Ranks are not abbreviated.

Warrant Officer Class I	Dear Mr. Smith
Warrant Officer Class II	Dear Sergeant Major Smith
Staff Sergeant	Dear Staff Sergeant Smith
Sergeant	Dear Sergeant Smith
Corporal and Lance Corporal	Dear Corporal Smith
Private and equivalent ranks	Dear Private (Gunner, etc.) Smith

ENVELOPE
According to rank, which may be abbreviated. Initials rather than a christian name are used, e.g.:

R.S.M. J. Jones, M.C., M.M.
C.S.M. W. Jones
Sgt. J. Brown

VERBAL ADDRESS
According to Corps and Regimental custom.

A Warrant Officer Class I is called 'Mr. Smith'. If he has the appointment of Regimental Sergeant Major, alternatively he may be called either 'Regimental Sergeant Major' or 'R.S.M. Jones'.

A Warrant Officer Class II who has the appointment of Company Sergeant Major, may be called either 'Sergeant Major' or 'C.S.M. Brown'. Other Warrant Officers Class II by their appointment, e.g. 'R.Q.M.S. Brown'.

N.C.O.s are called according to their rank. A Lance Corporal is called 'Corporal'. These ranks may be used with or without the surname.

For Privates or equivalent rank, the surname must always be added.

THE ARMY, HOUSEHOLD DIVISION

This comprises the Household Cavalry and The Guards' Division.

(a) *Household Cavalry* (The Life Guards, and The Blues and Royals).

The principal ranks are as follows:
 Warrant Officer Class I, Regimental Corporal Major (R.C.M.)
 Warrant Officer Class II, Squadron Corporal Major (S.C.M.)
 Staff Corporal (S.Cpl.)
 Corporal of Horse (C.o.H.)
 Corporal (Cpl.)
 Lance Corporal (LCpl.)
 Trooper (Tpr.)

BEGINNING OF LETTER
Ranks or appointments are not abbreviated.

Warrant Officer Class I, (Regimental Corporal Major)	Dear Mr. Smith
Warrant Officer Class II, (Squadron Corporal Major)	Dear Corporal Major Smith
Corporal of Horse	Dear Corporal Smith

 Otherwise as for the Army in general.

ENVELOPE
According to rank, which may be abbreviated, e.g. C.S.M.

VERBAL ADDRESS

As for beginning of letter (omitting 'Dear').

(b) *The Guards' Division (formerly The Brigade of Guards)*

The principal ranks are as follows:
 Warrant Officer Class I (R.S.M.)
 Warrant Officer Class II (C.S.M., etc.)
 Colour Sergeant (C.Sgt.) and Company Quartermaster
  Sergeant (C.Q.M.S.)
 Sergeant (Sgt.)
 Lance Sergeant (L.Sgt.)
 Lance Corporal (L.Cpl.)
 Guardsman (Gdsm.)

BEGINNING OF LETTER
Ranks or appointments are not abbreviated.

Regimental Sergeant Major	Dear Sergeant Major Brown

Other Warrant Officers	By their appointment, and name
Colour Sergeant and Company Quartermaster Sergeant	By their rank and name
Sergeant and Lance Sergeant	Dear Sergeant Smith
Lance Corporal	Dear Corporal Smith

ENVELOPE
According to rank, which may be abbreviated, e.g. Sgt.

VERBAL ADDRESS
As for beginning of letter (omitting 'Dear'). Alternatively some ranks may be abbreviated (e.q. C.Q.M.S. Brown).

N.C.O.s may be addressed with or without their surname. Guardsmen are always addressed with their surname.

The Royal Air Force

MARSHAL OF THE ROYAL AIR FORCE
This rank is held for life. (See also *Titled Officers*, p. 176.)

BEGINNING OF LETTER
According to his title (he would almost certainly be a peer, baronet or knight).[1]
Formal

If a Peer	My Lord
Otherwise	(Dear) Sir

Social

If a Peer	Dear Lord Blank
Otherwise	Dear Sir John (the surname may be added if the acquaintanceship is slight.) Dear Marshal Smith

ENDING OF LETTER

Formal	Yours faithfully (see also p. 2)
Social	Yours sincerely

ENVELOPE

Marshal of the Royal Air Force (the Rt. Hon.) Viscount Dorking, G.C.B.
Marshal of the Royal Air Force Sir John Jones, G.C.B.

[1] When he prefers his Air Force rank to be used, letters are commenced 'Dear Marshal Blank' and the verbal address is 'Marshal Blank' or 'Marshal'. (See also *Use of an Officer's Rank Without the Surname*, p. 177.)

VERBAL ADDRESS
According to his title[1]:
> Lord Dorking
> Sir John

A younger man, or a more junior officer in any of the Armed Forces addresses him as 'Sir'.

DESCRIPTION IN CONVERSATION
> Lord Dorking
> Sir John Jones

AIR CHIEF MARSHAL, AIR MARSHAL, OR AIR VICE-MARSHAL

All these ranks are referred to as Air Marshal except on the envelope or in a formal description, such as in a list, when the exact rank is given.

(See also *Titled Officers*, p. 176.)

The letters R.A.F. may follow the name, and any letters signifying orders, etc.

BEGINNING OF LETTER

Formal	(Dear) Sir
Social	
If a knight	Dear Sir John[1] (the surname may be added if the acquaintanceship is slight)
Otherwise	Dear Air Marshal Smith

ENDING OF LETTER

Formal	Yours faithfully (see also p. 2)
Social	Yours sincerely

ENVELOPE
According to the exact rank, with the appropriate letters after the name, e.g.:
> Air Chief Marshal Sir John Brown, G.B.E., R.A.F.
> Air Vice-Marshal Edward Grey, C.B., C.B.E., R.A.F.

These ranks should not be abbreviated.

VERBAL ADDRESS

If a Knight	Sir John[1]

[1] When he prefers, his Air rank to that appropriate for his knighthood, letters are commenced 'Dear Marshal Brown', and the verbal address is 'Marshal Brown' or 'Marshal'. (See also *Use of an Officer's Rank Without the Surname*, p. 177.)

Otherwise   Air Marshal Grey

A younger man, or a more junior officer in any of the Armed Forces addresses him as 'Sir'.

DESCRIPTION IN CONVERSATION
If a knight   Sir John Brown
Otherwise   Air Marshal Grey

Should social reference be made to only one Air Chief Marshal, Air Marshal, or Air Vice-Marshal he may be called 'the Air Marshal'.

AIR COMMODORE, GROUP CAPTAIN, WING COMMANDER, SQUADRON LEADER OR FLIGHT LIEUTENANT

These ranks are always used in full. The letters R.A.F. follow the name, and any letters which signify Orders, etc.

BEGINNING OF LETTER
Formal   (Dear) Sir
Social[1]   Dear Air Commodore Davis
               Dear Group Captain Smith
               Dear Wing Commander Jones
               Dear Squadron Leader Robinson
               Dear Flight Lieutenant Brown

ENDING OF LETTER
Formal   Yours faithfully (see also p. 2)
Social   Yours sincerely

ENVELOPE
     Air Commodore David Davis, C.B., R.A.F.
     Group Captain John Smith, C.B.E., R.A.F.
     Wing Commander John Jones, D.F.C., R.A.F.
     Squadron Leader Richard Robinson, M.B.E., R.A.F.
     Flight Lieutenant John Brown, R.A.F.

VERBAL ADDRESS
     Air Commodore Davis
     Group Captain Smith
     Wing Commander Jones

[1] See *Use of an Officer's Rank Without the Surname*, p. 177.

Squadron Leader Robinson
Flight Lieutenant Brown
A younger man, or more junior officer in any of the Armed Forces, addresses him as 'Sir'.

DESCRIPTION IN CONVERSATION
As for verbal address.

FLYING OFFICER OR PILOT OFFICER

The letters R.A.F. follow the name, and any letters which signify orders, etc.

BEGINNING OF LETTER
Formal   (Dear) Sir
Social   Dear Mr. Smith

ENDING OF LETTER
Formal   Yours faithfully (see also p. 2)
Social   Yours sincerely

ENVELOPE
John Smith, Esq., A.F.C., R.A.F. *or*
Flying Officer John Smith A.F.C., R.A.F.

VERBAL ADDRESS
Mr. Smith

DESCRIPTION IN CONVERSATION
Mr. Smith

WOMEN MEDICAL AND DENTAL OFFICERS

Women officers in the Medical and Dental branches are members of the R.A.F., and accordingly have the letters R.A.F. after their names. To avoid confusion in addressing correspondence to a woman medical or dental officer, a christian name may be used (e.g. Flight Lieutenant Marion G. Broad, M.B., Ch.B., R.A.F.) instead of the initials customary in the case of a W.R.A.F. officer. Otherwise, the conventions are the same as those applicable to the W.R.A.F.

OFFICER CADET

As for a Flying Officer or Pilot Officer, except on the envelope.

ENVELOPE
Professional
According to his rank, i.e.:
      Senior Under-Officer John Jones
      Under-Officer William Smith
      Senior Flight Cadet George Brown
      Flight Cadet Edward Robinson
   R.A.F. is not placed after the name.
Social
      John Jones, Esq.

CHAPLAIN TO THE ROYAL AIR FORCE

(See *Chaplains to H.M. Forces*, p. 140.)

NON-COMMISSIONED RANKS

The principal ranks are as follows:
      Warrant Officer
      Flight Sergeant (Flt. Sgt.)
      Chief Technician (Chief Tech.)
      Sergeant (Sgt.)
      Corporal (Cpl.)
      Junior Technician (Jnr. Tech.)
      Senior Aircraftman (S.A.C.)
      Leading Aircraftman (L.A.C.)
      Aircraftman (A.C.)

BEGINNING OF LETTER

Warrant Officer (formally)	Dear Warrant Officer Smith
(otherwise)	Dear Mr. Smith
Other ranks	According to rank

ENVELOPE
According to rank, with 'R.A.F.' after the name.

VERBAL ADDRESS
As for beginning of letter (omitting 'Dear').

Women's Services, Relative Ranks

W.R.N.S.	*W.R.A.C.*	*W.R.A.F.*
Commandant[1]	Brigadier[2]	Air Commodore[3]
Superintendent	Colonel	Group Captain
Chief Officer	Lieutenant-Colonel	Wing Commander
First Officer	Major	Squadron Leader
Second Officer	Captain	Flight Lieutenant
Third Officer	Lieutenant	Flying Officer
Probationary Third Officer	2nd Lieutenant	Pilot Officer

Women's Royal Naval Service

An officer of the W.R.N.S. is addressed by her appropriate rank and name, similar to those of the other Women's Services. The letters W.R.N.S. should always be added, since some rates are identical with the Merchant Navy. Socially, though she may always be called by her Service rank if she wishes, when she is not on duty it is usual for her to be called in writing and in speech, Miss (Mary) Brown or Mrs. (John) Smith. If a letter is addressed to her at an official address or upon a Service matter, she is addressed by her rank and name.

Within the W.R.N.S., those junior to her in rank write 'Dear Ma'am'. They also address her verbally as Ma'am.

NON-COMMISSIONED RATES

There are five rates:
> Fleet Chief Wren
> Chief Wren
> Petty Officer Wren (P.O. Wren)
> Leading Wren
> Wren

BEGINNING OF LETTER AND VERBAL ADDRESS
Dear Miss *or* Mrs. Smith (for Fleet Chief Wren), otherwise according to rank.

ENVELOPE
According to rank. Miss or Mrs. is ignored. The letters W.R.N.S. are not added after the name.

[1] The Director W.R.N.S. holds this rank.
[2] The Director W.R.A.C. holds this rank.
[3] The Director W.R.A.F. holds this rank.

Miss *or* Mrs. Smith (for Fleet Chief Wren), otherwise according to rate.

Women's Royal Army Corps

W.R.A.C. officers have Army ranks, with W.R.A.C after the name. They are always addressed by their Service rank.

BEGINNING OF LETTER
Formal	Dear Madam
Social	Dear Major Smith

These ranks should not be abbreviated.

Titled officers are addressed as such, e.g. Dear Dame Mary, or if the acquaintanceship is slight, Dear Dame Mary Brown. Unless the writer knows the recipient, her Service rank is used in preference, e.g. Colonel Dame Martha Wright is usually addressed 'Dear Colonel Wright' or 'Dear Colonel'.

ENDING OF LETTER
Formal	Yours faithfully (see also p. 2)
Social	Yours sincerely

ENVELOPE
Initials, rather than christian names, are customarily used:
Major J. K. Brown, W.R.A.C.
Ranks should not be abbreviated.

VERBAL ADDRESS
According to rank, except for Lieutenants and 2nd Lieutenants, who follow the Army practice of not being addressed by these ranks. They are referred to as Miss (or Mrs.) Jones.

DESCRIPTION IN CONVERSATION
According to rank.

NON-COMMISSIONED RANKS

They have Army ranks.

BEGINNING OF LETTER
Warrant Officers   Dear Miss (or Mrs.) Smith
Others according to rank, e.g. Dear Corporal Jones

ENVELOPE

Address according to rank, with W.R.A.C. after the name.
Initials are normally used in preference to christian name.

VERBAL ADDRESS

    Warrant Officers   Miss (or Mrs.) Smith
    Others according to rank.

Women's Royal Air Force

W.R.A.F. Officers have the same ranks as those in the Royal
Air Force, and these letters should be added after the name.
They are always addressed by their service rank. Suffixes for
officers of the Reserves and Auxiliaries are respectively
W.R.A.F.R.O. and W.R.Aux.A.F.

BEGINNING OF LETTER

Formal   Dear Madam
Social   Dear Group Captain Smith[1]

These ranks should not be abbreviated. For titled Officers, see
Women's Royal Army Corps.

ENDING OF LETTER

Formal   Yours faithfully (see also p. 2)
Social   Yours sincerely

ENVELOPE

Initials rather than christian name are customarily used:

    Squadron Leader J. K. Brown, W.R.A.F.

Ranks should not be abbreviated.

VERBAL ADDRESS

According to rank, but Flying Officers and Pilot Officers,
W.R.A.F. are usually known by these ranks in place of Miss (or
Mrs.) Jones, in which respect they differ from R.A.F. practice.

DESCRIPTION IN CONVERSATION

According to rank.

[1] For those officers who may be addressed by the rank only, see p. 177.

NON-COMMISSIONED RANKS

Ranks are as for R.A.F., except:

> Senior Aircraftwoman (S.A.C.W.)
> Leading Aircraftwoman (L.A.C.W.)
> Aircraftwoman (A.C.W.)

Warrant Officers, as for R.A.F., with the equivalent alternative Dear Miss (or Mrs.) Smith.
Others according to rank.

Queen Alexandra's Royal Naval Nursing Service

An officer of Queen Alexandra's Royal Naval Nursing Service adds the letters Q.A.R.N.N.S. after her name and any letters signifying Orders, etc.

> The ranks are as follows:
> Matron-in-Chief
> Principal Matron
> Matron
> Superintending Sister
> Senior Nursing Sister
> Nursing Sister

BEGINNING OF LETTER
Formal	(Dear) Madam
Social	Dear Miss (Mrs.) Smith

ENDING OF LETTER
Formal	Yours faithfully (see also p. 2)
Social	Yours sincerely

ENVELOPE
Professional	Miss Rosemary Smith, Matron, Q.A.R.N.N.S.
Private	Miss Rosemary Smith, Q.A.R.N.N.S.

VERBAL ADDRESS
Miss Smith

DESCRIPTION IN CONVERSATION
Miss Smith

SENIOR and JUNIOR RATINGS

The rates of nurses are as follows:

> Head Naval Nurse
> Assistant Naval Head Nurse
> Senior Naval Nurse
> Naval Nurse
> Probationary Naval Nurse

They are all referred to at the beginning of a letter as 'Dear Nurse Smith', but envelopes are addressed to their particular rate, followed by Q.A.R.N.N.S. They are also referred to verbally by their particular rate.

Queen Alexandra's Royal Army Nursing Corps

An officer of Queen Alexandra's Royal Army Nursing Corps adds the letters Q.A.R.A.N.C. after her name and letters signifying Orders, etc.

The ranks are as follows:

Matron-in-Chief and Director of Army Nursing Services	Brigadier
Deputy Director of Army Nursing Sisters	Colonel
Assistant Director of Army Nursing Sisters	Lieutenant-Colonel
Matron, Sister	Major, Captain, Lieutenant

When writing professionally and socially, the appropriate Army rank is used.

Correspondence is as for the Women's Royal Army Corps.

NON-COMMISSIONED RANKS

BEGINNING OF LETTER

Warrant Officers	Dear Madam

Others according to rank, e.g. Dear Corporal Jones

ENVELOPE

As for Women's Royal Army Corps, with the substitution of the letters Q.A.R.A.N.C.

As for Women's Royal Army Corps.

Princess Mary's Royal Air Force Nursing Service

An officer of Princess Mary's Royal Air Force Nursing Service adds the letters P.M.R.A.F.N.S. after her name and letters signifying orders, etc. These ranks are equivalent to those which were formerly used by the Women's Royal Air Force.

The appointments and ranks are as follows:

Matron-in-Chief	Air Commandant
Principal Matron	Group Officer
Senior Matron	Wing Officer (an administrative appointment)
Deputy Matron or Ward Sister	Squadron Officer
Nursing Sister	Flight Officer
	Flying Officer

BEGINNING OF LETTER

Formal	(Dear) Madam
Social	
Professional	Dear Wing Officer Smith (or appropriate rank)
Private	Dear Miss Smith

ENDING OF LETTER

Formal	Yours faithfully (see also p. 2)
Social	Yours sincerely

ENVELOPE

Professional	Squadron Officer Mary Smith, A.R.R.C., P.M.R.A.F.N.S.
Private	Miss Mary Smith, A.R.R.C.

VERBAL ADDRESS

Professional	Squadron Officer Smith
Private	Miss Smith

DESCRIPTION IN CONVERSATION
As for verbal address.

NON-COMMISSIONED RANKS

The non-commissioned element is addressed as Staff Nurse or as Miss before the name. State Enrolled Nurses (S.E.N.) take air women's rank.

Commonwealth Armed Forces

The names and decorations are followed by the abbreviation of the appropriate service for Naval and Air Force Officers.

Royal Australian Navy
> Captain John Brown, R.A.N.

Royal Australian Air Force
> Squadron Leader John Brown, R.A.A.F.

Royal New Zealand Navy
> Commander William Smith, D.S.C., R.N.Z.N.

Royal New Zealand Air Force
> Group Captain John Robinson, D.F.C., R.N.Z.A.F.

CANADA

On 1st February, 1968, the Canadian Armed Forces adopted new rank titles common to all three Services. However, serving members of the former Royal Canadian Navy were allowed to continue using their traditional Naval ranks.

Therefore the ranks and decorations of all personnel are followed by the letters C.F. (Canadian Forces).

The new ranks are as follows:
> General
> Lieutenant-General
> Major-General
> Brigadier-General
> Colonel
> Lieutenant-Colonel
> Major
> Captain
> Lieutenant
> 2nd Lieutenant

Newly enrolled officers will also use traditional Naval ranks when employed in what can be clearly described as 'Navy' jobs, to match the ranks used in most of the world's navies.

Any member of the former Services may elect to be referred to by his traditional rank when not on duty.

Reserves will follow the pattern set by the Regular Force.

The Corporation of Trinity House

The Corporation of Trinity House administers the (British) Lighthouse Service, is the Chief (British) Pilotage Authority, and controls lighthouses, lightships and maintains a fleet of steam and motor vessels. Active Elder Bretheren also sit with the Judges of the Admiralty Division of the High Court of Justice to act as Nautical Assessors in marine cases tried by that Court.

The Active Elder Bretheren of the Corporation of Trinity House are accorded the style and title of Captain, which they retain for life, according to the Royal Warrant issued on 20th December, 1912. On social and ceremonial occasions they have place and precedence next and immediately after the place and precedence accorded to Captains in the Royal Navy.

No person is eligible to fill the office of an Active Elder Brother unless he has served afloat in command of one or more of H.M. Ships for at least two years after having attained the rank of Commander Royal Navy, or unless he has held command in the Mercantile Marine on foreign voyages for at least three years.

An Elder Brother does not have letters after his name to signify his office. The form of address is as for a Captain in the Royal Navy unless he is of more senior naval rank.

The title Captain is also accorded to the Lighthouse Service Superintendents and Pilotage Superintendents. In the case of the former, the description is Captain T.H.S. (Trinity House Service). These letters are placed after his name and decorations (if any) on the envelope.

POLITICAL AND CIVIL SERVICE SECTION

All Cabinet Ministers of the United Kingdom and Northern Ireland Parliaments are members of the Privy Council of either of these two countries. Other Ministers outside the two Cabinets may also be admitted to the Privy Council. They accordingly have the prefix 'The Rt. Hon.' before their names. (N.B.—The Rt. Hon. takes the place of Mrs. or Miss before a lady's name.) See *Privy Council* (p. 78).

All Members of the Houses of Commons of the United Kingdom and Northern Ireland have the letters M.P. following their names. See *Letters After the Name* (p. 96).

There is no special form of address for the wife of either a Privy Counsellor or a Member of Parliament.

There are several junior Ministers of an administration who are not admitted to the Privy Council. Most of these are Members of Parliament, but a few may have seats in the House of Lords.

A member of the Senate of Northern Ireland may be addressed as 'Senator' in correspondence, but this is not usual for a member of the Privy Council. In speech a member of the Senate may be called 'Senator' on an official matter, otherwise as Mr. —— or appropriate rank.

Member of Her Majesty's Government

BEGINNING OF LETTER

He is addressed as for an esquire:

Formal	(Dear) Sir
Social	Dear Mr. Blake, or appropriate rank

If the writer knows the Minister concerned, and the subject of his letter broadly concerns his department, it is permissible to write to him by his appointment, e.g.:

Dear (Mr.) Prime Minister
Dear Lord Chancellor (see p. 209)
Dear Lord Privy Seal
Dear (Mr.) Chancellor
Dear (Mr.) Minister
Dear Lord President [of the Council]
Dear (Mr.) President [of the Board of Trade]
Dear Home/Foreign Secretary, *or* Dear Secretary of State
Dear Solicitor-General
Dear Attorney-General
Dear Lord Advocate
Dear Chief Secretary
Dear Under-Secretary

This form is not used when the name of the appointment is cumbersome.

The inclusion of 'Mr.' before certain officers is now becoming archaic except in very formal correspondence. 'Dear Mr. Secretary' has long passed out of use. 'Dear Secretary of State' is customarily used in the United States, where it is followed by the surname.

The very formal style, viz. 'Sir *or* Madam' is occasionally used officially within the Civil Service and the Armed Forces, but seldom outside.

ENDING OF LETTER

Formal	Yours faithfully (see also p. 2)
Social	Yours sincerely

When writing to a Minister by his appointment (e.g. Dear Minister), the letter is concluded, 'Yours sincerely'.

For a very formal letter, the following is the conclusion:

I have the honour to be,
    Sir,
        Yours faithfully

'Your obedient servant' has become obsolete.

ENVELOPE

Personal Letter

A letter to a Minister sent to his department, normally includes both his name and appointment, e.g.:

The Rt. Hon. Sir Michael Blank, K.B.E., M.P.,
Secretary of State for Foreign Affairs

Ministerial Letter

A letter sent to a Minister as the head of his department is addressed by his appointment only, e.g.:

The Secretary of State for Foreign Affairs

For a minor departmental matter, see *Government Departments* (p. 206).

VERBAL ADDRESS AND DESCRIPTION IN CONVERSATION

By appointment or name.

THE SPEAKER OF THE HOUSE OF COMMONS

The Speaker is usually re-elected, whatever Party is in power. 'Mr. Speaker' is his customary designation on Parliamentary matters, otherwise according to his rank.

GOVERNMENT DEPARTMENTS (CIVIL SERVICE)

BEGINNING OF LETTER

He or she is addressed as for an esquire or the feminine
equivalent:

Formal   Dear Sir *or* Dear Madam
Social   Dear Mr. Byron, Dear Miss Byron, *or*
                         appropriate rank

The alternative style of writing by the appointment is not
normally employed when this is cumbersome, e.g. Dear Permanent Under-Secretary.

The very formal style, viz. 'Sir *or* Madam' is used within the
Civil Service on specific official matters, but only very occasionally
outside.

ENDING OF LETTER

Formal   Yours faithfully (see also p. 2)
Social   Yours sincerely

When writing to a member of the Civil Service by his appointment (e.g. Dear Under-Secretary), the letter is concluded, 'Yours
sincerely'.

For a very formal letter, the following is the conclusion:

     I have the honour to be,

         Sir,

            Yours faithfully

'Your obedient servant' has become obsolete.

ENVELOPE

Personal Letter

A letter to a member of the Civil Service sent to his department,
normally includes both his name and appointment.

Official Letter

This is addressed by appointment only.

If a letter relates only to a minor matter, it is usually addressed
to 'The Secretary' of the appropriate department rather than
to its Ministerial head.

VERBAL ADDRESS AND DESCRIPTION IN CONVERSATION

By appointment or name.

MEMBERS OF COMMONWEALTH PARLIAMENTS

The letters which are placed after the names of Members of

Parliament vary according to the country, state or province and the name of the respective House.

In *Canada* Parliament consists of the Senate and the House of Commons. Members of the latter House place M.P. after the name. Members of the Legislative Assemblies of Canadian Provinces place M.L.A. after the name, except the Province of Quebec, where the appropriate letters are M.P.Q. (Membre du Parlement du Quebec) and Ontario, where the letters are M.P.P. (Member of Provincial Parliament).

In *Australia* Parliament consists of the Senate and the House of Representatives. Members of the latter House place M.P. after the name. Parliament of the Australian States consists of two chambers, apart from Queensland. Members of the Legislative Council (the Upper House) place M.L.C. after the name. In South Australia and Tasmania the Lower House is known as the House of Assembly. In South Australia Members are accorded the letters M.P. and in Tasmania the letters M.H.A. In the other states the Lower House is the Legislative Assembly and Members place M.L.A. after the name.

In *New Zealand* Members of the House of Representatives are designated M.P.

Senators in Canada are described as The Hon. before the name, as appropriate, without the word 'Senator'.

Senators in Australia are addressed as such before the name, e.g. Senator the Hon. John Smith, or Senator John Smith, as applicable.

For the title 'Honourable' before the name in the Commonwealth see below.

MEMBERS OF PARLIAMENT, REPUBLIC OF IRELAND

There are two houses, the House of Representatives (the Dáil) and the Senate. Members of Parliament are entitled to the letters T.D. (Teachta Dala or Deputy of Parliament) after their name. They are sometimes referred to colloquially as Deputies. Senators are addressed as such, both in correspondence and speech.

THE TITLE OF 'HONOURABLE' IN COMMONWEALTH COUNTRIES

Members of Queen's Privy Council for Canada (for life)
Members of Executive Councils of Commonwealth of Australia (for life)

Members of Executive Councils of Victoria and Tasmania (for life)

Members of Executive Councils

Members of Legislative Councils (other than those of Provinces of Canada)

Speaker of Lower House of the Legislatures

Senators of Canada

The following may personally be recommended by the Governor General for Her Majesty's permission to retain the title on retirement:

1. Members of Executive Councils who have served for at least three years as Ministers, or one year as Prime Minister.

2. Presidents of Senates and Legislative Councils, and Speakers of Legislative Assemblies on quitting office after having served three years in their respective offices.

3. Senators and Members of Legislative Councils on retirement or resignation after a continuous service of not less than ten years.

The title is also borne by certain categories of Judges (see *Legal Section*, p. 224), and locally in Associated States and Dependent Territories, as follows.

In Bermuda, British Virgin Islands, Falkland Islands, Gibraltar, and Hong Kong the title is used by Members of the Executive and Legislative Councils. See also the Associated States of the West Indies (below).

In the Cayman Islands and St. Helena the title is used by Members of the Executive Council.

The title is used in other territories as under:

Bahamas	Ministers and Members of the Senate (inside and outside) and Members of House of Assembly (inside the House only).
British Honduras	Senate and House of Representatives (inside and outside).
British Solomon Islands Protectorate	Members of the Executive and Legislative Councils (inside). The only Members of the Executive Council who are addressed 'Honourable' in writing are the Chief Secretary, Financial Secretary and Attorney-General, and those elected Members of the Legislative Council who are appointed Members of the Executive Council.

Gilbert and Ellice Islands Colony	Elected and Appointed Members of Governing Council (inside and outside). The title is attached to office of Ex-officio Members (e.g. The Honourable the Attorney-General).
Montserrat	Official and Elected Members of Executive Council; also other Elected and Nominated Members of the Legislative Council (inside during sessions).
Seychelles	Members of Governing Council.

Associated States
of the West Indies:

Antigua	House of Representatives and Senate.
Dominica	Cabinet and House of Assembly (inside and outside).
St. Vincent	Members of Executive and Legislative Councils.

The title is retained, with The Queen's approval, on *retirement* from membership in Bahamas, Bermuda, and St. Helena, and occasionally in British Honduras and Hong Kong. There have been no cases so far in British Solomon Islands Protectorate, Gibraltar, and Gilbert and Ellice Islands Colony.

LEGAL SECTION

England and Wales

LORD CHANCELLOR

The Lord High Chancellor, colloquially called 'the Lord Chancellor', is the chief judicial officer in England, and receives a peerage on appointment. He is also a member of the Privy Council and of the Cabinet. He is Speaker of the House of Lords where he sits on the Woolsack, President of the House of Lords sitting as the Supreme Court of Appeal, and President of the Court of Appeal and of the High Court. He vacates office with the Government.

A letter concerning his Department should be addressed to The Rt. Hon. the Lord Chancellor.

Correspondence on these matters may be addressed:

Formal	My Lord
Social	Dear Lord Chancellor

Otherwise according to his rank in the peerage.

The letters Q.C. do not appear after his name.

LORD CHIEF JUSTICE OF ENGLAND

He is the head of the judges of the Queen's Bench Division, and takes precedence over all other judges of this Division. He also presides in the Court of Criminal Appeal. He is a Privy Counsellor, and on appointment is raised to the peerage.

A letter concerning his office may be addressed to The Rt. Hon. the Lord Chief Justice of England.

Correspondence may begin:

Formal	My Lord
Social	Dear Lord Chief Justice

Otherwise according to his rank in the peerage.

The letters Q.C. do not appear after his name.

MASTER OF THE ROLLS

The Master of the Rolls sits and presides over the Court of Appeal, and has third place in legal seniority after the Lord Chancellor and the Lord Chief Justice.

He is knighted, and is a member of the Privy Council.

He is addressed according to his judicial rank.

ATTORNEY-GENERAL AND SOLICITOR-GENERAL

They are Law Officers of the Crown, advise the Government on legal matters of importance, and represent the Crown in Court. Both are political appointments.

The Attorney-General is head of the Bar in England, and takes precedence over all barristers. The Solicitor-General is junior in precedence to the Attorney-General, and is a Queen's Counsel. A Solicitor-General is also appointed for Scotland.

(See also p. 204.)

LORD OF APPEAL IN ORDINARY

He is created a life peer so that he may sit in the House of Lords.

The letters Q.C. do not appear after his name.

LORD JUSTICE OF THE COURT OF APPEAL

Five Lord Justices are appointed to sit in the Court of Appeal with the Master of the Rolls. He is admitted to the Privy Council as a member of the Judicial Committee, and normally would have been knighted as a Judge of the High Court of Justice.

The letters Q.C. do not appear after his name.

BEGINNING OF LETTER

Formal	My Lord
Social	Dear Lord Justice

ENDING OF LETTER

Formal	Yours faithfully (see also p. 2)
Social	Yours sincerely

ENVELOPE

The Rt. Hon. the Lord Justice Smith

VERBAL ADDRESS

Formal	My Lord *or* Your Lordship[1]
Social	Lord Justice

DESCRIPTION IN CONVERSATION

Formal and Social	The Lord Justice, *or* Lord Justice Brown
Judicial Matters, especially on the Bench	His Lordship

JUDGE OF HIGH COURT

The High Court of Justice is that part of the Supreme Court of Judicature which does not comprise the Court of Appeal, and is divided into three Divisions, Queen's Bench, Chancery, and Probate, Divorce and Admiralty. High Court Judges, i.e. those styled 'The Hon. Mr. Justice', and below the rank of Lord Justice, are known as Puisne Judges, which literally means 'younger'.

A Judge of the High Court is knighted on appointment. The letters Q.C. do not appear after his name.

See also *Judge of High Court (Lady)*.

[1] See p. 32, note [1].

BEGINNING OF LETTER

Formal	(Dear) Sir,
Judicial Matters	My Lord
Social	Dear Judge (excluding the surname)

ENDING OF LETTER

Formal	Yours faithfully (see also p. 2)
Social	Yours sincerely

ENVELOPE

Formal and Judicial Matters	The Hon. Mr. Justice Smith (excluding the christian name). If more than one Judge of the High Court with the same surname are assembled together the christian name may be added in brackets
Social	Sir John Smith ('The Honourable' is not used in conjunction with 'Sir John Smith')

VERBAL ADDRESS

Formal	Sir
Judicial Matters and on the Bench	My Lord *or* Your Lordship[1]
Social	Judge (excluding the surname) *or* Sir John (Smith), e.g. Sir John and Lady Smith

DESCRIPTION IN CONVERSATION

Formal and Social	The Judge, *or* Mr. Justice Smith, *or* Sir John (Smith), e.g. Sir John and Lady Smith
Judicial Matters especially on the Bench	His Lordship

JUDGE OF HIGH COURT (LADY)

She is created a Dame just as her male counterpart receives a knighthood. The letters Q.C. do not appear after her name.

[1] See p. 32, note [1].

BEGINNING OF LETTER

Formal	(Dear) Madam
Social	Dear Lady Lane

ENDING OF LETTER

Formal	Yours faithfully (see also p. 2)
Social	Yours sincerely

ENVELOPE

Formal	The Hon. Mrs. Justice Lane
Social	Dame Elizabeth Lane ('The Honourable' is not used in conjunction with 'Dame Elizabeth')

VERBAL ADDRESS

Formal	Madam
Judicial Matters and on the Bench	My Lady *or* Your Ladyship[1]
Social	Judge *or privately* Dame Elizabeth (Lane)

DESCRIPTION IN CONVERSATION

Formal and Social	The Judge *or* Mrs. Justice Lane, *or privately*, 'Dame Elizabeth'
Judicial Matters, especially on the Bench	Her Ladyship

JUDGE OF HIGH COURT (RETIRED)

Since the passing of the Judicial Pensions Act 1959, High Court Judges retire at the age of 75 years. Those appointed before the passing of the Act retire according to their wishes.

The prefix 'The Hon. Mr. Justice' is dropped on retirement.

BEGINNING OF LETTER

Formal	(Dear) Sir
Social	Dear Judge (excluding the surname)[1] *or* Dear Sir John
	Dear Sir John Brown (if of slight acquaintance)

[1] See p. 36, note [2].

ENDING OF LETTER

Formal	Yours faithfully (see also p. 2)
Social	Yours sincerely

ENVELOPE

Formal and Social	Sir John Brown

VERBAL ADDRESS

Formal	Sir
Social	Judge (excluding the surname)[1] *or* Sir John (Brown)

DESCRIPTION IN CONVERSATION

Formal and Social	The Judge[1] *or* Sir John (adding the surname if necessary)

JUDGE OF COUNTY COURT

Q.C. appears after his (or her) name in correspondence.

BEGINNING OF LETTER

Formal and Judicial *Matters*	(Dear) Sir *or* (Dear) Madam
Social	Dear Judge

ENDING OF LETTER

Formal	Yours faithfully (see also p. 2)
Social	Yours sincerely

ENVELOPE

Formal and Social	His (*or* Her) Honour Judge Smith (excluding the christian name). If more than one Judge of the County Court of the same surname are assembled together at the same address, the christian name may be added in brackets

If a Knight:

Formal	His Honour Judge Smith (excluding the christian name)
Social	Sir John Smith

[1] Retained only by courtesy.

VERBAL ADDRESS

Formal	Sir (or Madam)
Judicial Matters and on the Bench	Your Honour. If he is a Special Commissioner in High Court Divorce cases he is referred to on the Bench as 'My Lord' *or* 'Your Lordship'[1]
Social	Judge (excluding the surname). If he is a Knight, he may also be called privately, Sir John (Smith), e.g. Sir John and Lady Smith

DESCRIPTION IN CONVERSATION

Formal and Social	The Judge, *or* Judge Smith
Judicial Matters and on the Bench	His (*or* Her) Honour

JUDGE OF COUNTY COURT (RETIRED)

The prefix 'His (or Her) Honour' is retained on retirement from office, but 'Judge' is dropped.[2]

BEGINNING OF LETTER

Formal	(Dear) Sir (or Madam)
Social	Dear Judge[3] *or*
	Dear Mr. *or* Mrs. Brown

ENDING OF LETTER

Formal	Yours faithfully (see also p. 2)
Social	Yours sincerely

ENVELOPE

Formal and Social	His Honour John Brown *or*
	Her Honour Mary Brown
If a Knight	His Honour Sir John Brown

VERBAL ADDRESS

Formal	Sir (or Madam)
Social	Judge (excluding the surname)[3] *or*
	Mr. Brown, Mrs. Brown, Miss Brown

[1] See p. 32, note 1.
[2] There is no retired lady County Court Judge in England and Wales at the time of going to press.
[3] Retained only by courtesy.

If a knight, he is officially called Sir John (Brown)

Formal and Social   The Judge, *or* Judge Brown *or*
                          Mr. Brown

Where a retired County Court Judge retains his Service rank, this should follow 'His Honour'. Since in the Tables of General Precedence, Judges of County Courts in England and Wales are mentioned specifically but members of the Armed Forces are not, the legal rank takes precedence. It has also been pointed out that the legal style precedes Service rank because the former (His *Honour*) is a noun, and is therefore not analogous with 'The Honourable' which is adjectival, i.e. 'His Honour Commander John Brown, R.N.' but 'Commander the Hon. John Brown, R.N.'

OFFICIAL REFEREES OF THE SUPREME COURT

They are styled as Judges of the County Court.

ADDITIONAL JUDGES OF THE CENTRAL CRIMINAL COURT

By Royal Warrant of 31st July, 1969, they are accorded the same style as County Court Judges.

CHAIRMEN OF COURTS OF QUARTER SESSIONS

By Royal Warrant of 31st July, 1969, salaried whole-time Chairmen of Courts of Quarter Sessions are accorded the same style as County Court Judges.

Other Chairmen are referred to as Esquires. There is no uniform style of referring to them on the Bench.

DEPUTY CHAIRMAN OF COURTS OF QUARTER SESSIONS

By Royal Warrant of 31st July, 1969, salaried whole-time Deputy Chairmen of Courts of Quarter Sessions are accorded the same style as County Court Judges.

RECORDERS

(For *The Recorders of Liverpool and Manchester*, see p. 217.)

BEGINNING OF LETTER
Formal   (Dear) Sir
Official Business Dear Mr. Recorder
                    (Note.—In this instance 'Mr.' is always
                    included)
Social   As for an Esquire, or applicable rank

ENDING OF LETTER
Formal   Yours faithfully (see also p. 2)
Social   Yours sincerely

ENVELOPE
Formal   As for an Esquire
Official Business John Jones, Esq., Q.C., Recorder of
                    Littletown *or*
                    The Recorder of Littletown, John Jones,
                    Esq., Q.C.
Social   As for an Esquire

Otherwise as for an Esquire, but whilst on the Bench he is
addressed as 'Your Honour' and referred to as 'His Honour'.

THE RECORDERS OF LIVERPOOL AND MANCHESTER

The Recorders of Liverpool and Manchester sit as Judges of The
Crown Court at these two cities by virtue of a Royal Commission.
The Crown Court has Assize status.

The Recorder is addressed as Judge before his surname in the
commencement of a letter, and on the Bench he is addressed as
'My Lord' or 'Your Lordship'. This also applies to any other
County Court Judge and Queen's Counsel sitting temporarily as
Judges of the Crown Court.

QUEEN'S COUNSEL

Barristers are divided into Queen's Counsel and Junior Counsel.
When a Barrister becomes a Q.C., he is said to 'take silk' from the
silk gown that he will wear.

The letters Q.C. are placed after the name, including County
Court Judges, but excluding High Court Judges and higher legal
appointments. Those who were appointed King's Counsel
changed their letters K.C. to Q.C. in the present reign.

For the position of the letters see *Letters After the Name*, p.
96.

JUSTICE OF THE PEACE AND MAGISTRATE

Justices of the Peace are appointed by the Crown for every county and for those boroughs to which separate Commissions of the Peace have been granted.

While on the Bench he or she is addressed as 'Your Worship' and described as 'His *or* Her Worship'. Otherwise as an Esquire or feminine equivalent. He or she may use the letters 'J.P.' after the name, but this is not obligatory. The letters J.P. precede D.L. as the former is a Crown appointment, and the latter a Lord Lieutenant's appointment. See also *Letters After the Name*, p. 96.

If a Justice of the Peace has been transferred to the Supplemental List at the age of 75, he may still have the letters J.P. placed after his or her name.

STIPENDIARY MAGISTRATE

These are whole time paid appointments, held by barristers.

While on the Bench he or she is addressed as a Magistrate, otherwise as an Esquire, followed by the appointment. A Stipendiary Magistrate is not accorded J.P. after his name.

CORONER

His is addressed as an Esquire, and is known as 'Sir' in court.

LORD LIEUTENANT (see p. 248)

VICE-LIEUTENANT (see p. 249)

DEPUTY LIEUTENANT (see p. 249)

HIGH SHERIFF (see p. 249)

DIOCESAN CHANCELLOR

The Diocesan Chancellor is usually appointed for life by the Bishop of his Diocese. He acts as the legal adviser to the Bishop and is Judge of the Consistory Court.

The following instructions are for writing to the Diocesan Chancellor in his official capacity only.

BEGINNING OF LETTER

Formal	Dear Mr. Chancellor *or* Dear Sir
Social	Dear Chancellor

ENDING OF LETTER

Formal   Yours faithfully (see also p. 2)
Social   Yours sincerely

ENVELOPE

The Worshipful Chancellor Peter (or P.) Smith

VERBAL ADDRESS

Formal   Mr. Chancellor
Social   Chancellor
In Court   Sir *or* Worshipful Sir (*not* Your Worship)

DESCRIPTION IN CONVERSATION

The Chancellor (*or if necessary* The Diocesan Chancellor)

DIOCESAN CHANCELLOR (LADY)[1]

As above, with the following exceptions

BEGINNING OF LETTER

Formal   Dear Madam Chancellor *or* Dear Madam
Social   Dear Chancellor

ENVELOPE

The Worshipful Chancellor Miss Sheila Cameron

VERBAL ADDRESS

Formal   Madam Chancellor
Social   Chancellor
In Court   Madam, *or* Worshipful Madam, (*not* Your
                           Worship)

Scotland

LORD JUSTICE-GENERAL

On taking his seat on the bench he receives a Judicial title (see *Lord of Session*, p. 221) but is always described by his office. He is invariably a Privy Counsellor.

[1] In 1970 a lady was appointed Chancellor of the Diocese of Colchester.

BEGINNING OF LETTER

Formal	My Lord
Social	Dear Lord Justice-General

ENDING OF LETTER

Formal	Yours faithfully (see also p. 2)
Social	Yours sincerely

ENVELOPE

The Rt. Hon. the Lord Justice-General

VERBAL ADDRESS

Formal	My Lord
Social	Lord Justice-General

DESCRIPTION IN CONVERSATION

Lord Justice-General

RETIREMENT

On retirement from office, he is known by his Judicial title, with the prefix 'The Right Honourable'.

WIFE OR WIDOW OF LORD JUSTICE-GENERAL

As for the wife or widow of a Lord of Session.
(See p. 222.)

LORD JUSTICE-CLERK

On taking his seat on the bench he receives a Judicial Title (see *Lord of Session*, p. 221), but is always described by his office.

BEGINNING OF LETTER

Formal	My Lord
Social	Dear Lord Justice-Clerk

ENDING OF LETTER

Formal	Yours faithfully (see also p. 2)
Social	Yours sincerely

ENVELOPE

The Rt. Hon. the Lord Justice-Clerk if a Privy Counsellor, otherwise The Hon. the Lord Justice-Clerk

VERBAL ADDRESS

Formal	My Lord
Social	Lord Justice-Clerk

DESCRIPTION IN CONVERSATION

Lord Justice-Clerk

RETIREMENT

If he retires from office he will be known by his Judicial title, with the prefix 'The Right Hon.', if a Privy Councillor, otherwise 'The Hon.'.

WIFE OR WIDOW OF LORD JUSTICE-CLERK

As for the wife or widow of a Lord of Session. (See p. 222.)

LORD OF SESSION

A Senator (Judge) of the College of Justice in Scotland is known as a Lord of Session. On taking his seat on the bench he is given a Judicial title by which he is known both in office and on retirement. The Lord Justice-General and the Lord Justice-Clerk are addressed for all purposes by their appointments and not by the Judicial Titles with which they take their seats on the bench (see *Lord Justice-Clerk* or *Lord Justice-General*).

COMMENCEMENT OF LETTER

Formal	My Lord
Social	Dear Lord Cameron

CONCLUSION OF LETTER

Formal	Yours faithfully (see also p. 2)
Social	Yours sincerely

ENVELOPE

The Hon. Lord Cameron
If a Privy Counsellor, The Rt. Hon. Lord Milligan.

VERBAL ADDRESS

Formal	My Lord
Social	Lord Cameron

By their Judicial title, e.g. Lord Cameron, The Lord Justice-General and The Lord Justice-Clerk are known by their appointments.

RETIREMENT
As in office.

CHAIRMAN OF SCOTTISH LAND COURT

On appointment as Chairman he receives a Judicial title by which he is always known, both in office and on retirement. He is treated as a Lord of Session (see *Lord of Session*).

WIFE OR WIDOW OF A LORD OF SESSION AND THE CHAIRMAN OF SCOTTISH LAND COURT

A wife or widow of a Lord of Session (including Lord Justice-General and Lord Justice-Clerk) and the Chairman of the Scottish Land Court is addressed by her husband's Judicial title preceded by 'Lady'.

She has no prefix before 'Lady', but in other respects she is addressed as the wife of a Baron.

CHILDREN OF A LORD OF SESSION AND CHAIRMAN OF SCOTTISH LAND COURT

They receive no courtesy rank or style.

LORD ADVOCATE

The Lord Advocate is the principal Law Officer of the Crown in Scotland, corresponding to the Attorney General in England. He is one of the four Law Officers of the Crown, and as such a Minister of the Crown. He may be either a Member of Parliament or a member of the House of Lords, but need not necessarily be either. He is invariably admitted to the Privy Council on taking office as he is a member of the Scottish Universities Committee of the Council.

BEGINNING OF LETTER
Formal
If a Peer	My Lord
Otherwise	(Dear) Sir

Social   By name, but if connected with his department, 'Dear Lord Advocate'

ENDING OF LETTER
Formal   Yours faithfully (see also p. 2)
Social   Yours sincerely

ENVELOPE
The Rt. Hon. the Lord Advocate, Q.C. (M.P.)
The Rt. Hon. John Smith, Q.C. (M.P.)

SHERIFF, SCOTLAND

The office of Sheriff in Scotland is now principally a judicial office. The Sheriff Courts have a very wide criminal and civil jurisdiction—considerably wider than the jurisdiction of Quarter Sessions and the County Courts in England.

The holder of the office of Sheriff is, however, the direct descendant of the King's peace-keeping officer of feudal times and continues to exercise administrative and executive functions within his Sheriffdom.

Scotland is divided into twelve Sheriffdoms, each having its own Sheriff. Each Sheriffdom is further divided into two or more Sheriff Court districts, each having one or more Sheriffs-Substitute. The term 'Sheriff Principal' is sometimes used to describe the Sheriff in order to distinguish him from his Substitutes. Within his own Sheriffdom, the Sheriff takes precedence immediately after the Lord Lieutenant.

The Sheriffs are all senior Queen's Counsel. Of these, the Sheriffs of the Lothians and Lanarkshire are appointed on a full-time basis, while the remaining ten Sheriffs are appointed on a part-time basis and are usually in active practice at the Scottish Bar. All the Sheriffs-Substitute are either Advocates or Solicitors and are appointed on a full-time basis.

All Sheriffs and Sheriffs-Substitute are addressed as 'My Lord' *or* 'My Lady', on the bench, and as 'Sheriff Smith' formally and socially. The Sheriffs (i.e., the Sheriffs Principal) are sometimes referred to by abbreviations of their territorial titles, e.g. 'Sheriff of Inverness', 'Sheriff of Zetland', 'Sheriff of Argyll'.

Northern Ireland

The Judiciary are addressed as in England and Wales.

Canada

The Chief Justice of Canada is styled 'The Right Honourable' for life.

The following Judges are styled 'The Honourable' during tenure of office, and on retirement, if approval is given.

Judges of the Supreme and Exchequer Courts of Canada. Chief Justices and Judges of the following Courts:

Alberta British Columbia Newfoundland New Brunswick Nova Scotia Ontario Prince Edward Island	The Supreme Court
Quebec	The Court of Queen's Bench, and the Superior Court
Manitoba Saskatchewan	The Court of Appeal, and the Court of Queen's Bench
Northwest Territories Yukon Territory	The Territorial Court

N.B. The spellings of 'Honourable' and 'Honour' are officially adopted in Canada, but 'Honorable' and 'Honor' are sometimes used.

THE CHIEF JUSTICE OF CANADA

BEGINNING OF LETTER

Formal	(Dear) Sir
Social	Dear Chief Justice
Envelope	The Rt. Hon. the Chief Justice of Canada *or* The Rt. Hon. (followed by his name), The Chief Justice of Canada

THE CHIEF JUSTICE OF SUPREME COURTS AND OTHER HIGH COURTS

ENDING OF LETTER

Formal	(Dear) Sir
Social	Dear Chief Justice

ENVELOPE

The Hon. the Chief Justice of . . .
The Rt. Hon. the Chief Justice of . . . (if a Member of the Privy Council) *or*
The Hon John Smith
The Chief Justice of . . .

JUDGES OF SUPREME COURTS AND OTHER HIGH COURTS

The Hon. Mr. Justice (surname)
see High Court Judges
On the bench Judges are referred to as 'Your Lordship'.

JUDGES OF LOWER COURTS

Judges of County and District Courts in Canadian Provinces are referred to and addressed 'His Honour'.

Australia

The highest court is the High Court of Australia. Each State in Australia has its own Supreme Court. The High Court sits on appeals from the Supreme Courts of the States. The members of the High Court are referred to as Justices and not Judges.

The following Justices and Judges are styled 'The Honourable' during tenure of office, and may be permitted to retain the style on retirement if approval is given:

The Chief Justice of Australia
Justices of the High Court of Australia
Chief Judge and Judges of the Commonwealth Court of Conciliation and Arbitration
Judge of the Federal Court of Bankruptcy
The Chief Justice, President of Court of Appeal, Judges of Appeal and Puisne Judges of Supreme Court, New South Wales

The Chief Justice and Puisne Judges of Supreme Courts of:
Victoria
Queensland
South Australia
Western Australia
Tasmania
Judge of Supreme Court of Australian Capital Territory and Northern Territory

N.B. The spellings of 'Honourable' and 'Honour' are officially adopted in Australia (e.g. *The Commonwealth Directory*), but 'Honorable' and 'Honor' are sometimes used (e.g. *The Parliamentary Handbook*).

THE CHIEF JUSTICE OF AUSTRALIA

He is addressed as for The Chief Justice of Canada (above).

HIGH COURT OF AUSTRALIA

Judges of the High Court are normally knighted and admitted to the Privy Council. They are known both officially and colloquially as *Justices*.

The forms of address are as follows:

BEGINNING OF LETTER

Formal	(Dear) Sir
Social	Dear Justice

ENVELOPE

The Rt. Hon. Mr. Justice Smith
If a Justice has not yet
been admitted to the
Privy Council   The Hon. Mr. Justice Smith

Socially the following may be used for other Justices:
The Rt. Hon. Sir John Smith, K.B.E.
The Hon. Sir John Smith, K.B.E. (if not yet admitted to the Privy Council)
On the bench he is referred to as 'Your Honour'.

SUPREME COURT

BEGINNING OF LETTER

Formal   (Dear) Sir

Social	Dear Judge
If the Chief Justice	Dear Chief Justice

ENDING OF LETTER

Formal	Yours faithfully (see also p. 2)
Social	Yours sincerely

ENVELOPE

	The Hon. Mr. Justice Smith
If the Chief Justice	The Chief Justice of the Supreme Court of (New South Wales), the Hon. . . .

Socially the following may be used for other Judges, if knighted:
The Hon. Sir John Smith

If a lady:
The Hon. Justice Mary Smith
On the bench he or she is referred to as 'Your Honour'.

OTHER COURTS

As for Supreme Court Judge, except the Chief Judge of the Commonwealth Court of Conciliation and Arbitration and the Industrial Court is addressed as:
Dear Chief Judge

LOWER COURTS

Judges of County and District Courts in the States of Australia are addressed as 'His Honour' and he is referred to on the Bench as 'Your Honour'. See *County Court Judge* (p. 214).

New Zealand

The Chief Justice of New Zealand and the President and the two other Judges of the Court of Appeal are normally admitted to the Privy Council, and as such are styled 'The Right Honourable' during tenure of office and during retirement. It is usual for the Chief Justice, and for the President and Judges of the Court of Appeal, to be knighted.

The Puisne Judges of the Supreme Court are styled 'The Honourable' during tenure of office, and may be permitted to retain that style during retirement if approval is given. The Senior

Puisne Judge is normally knighted. Judges of the Court of Arbitration, of the Compensation Court, and of the Maori Land Court are styled 'Judge' during tenure of office, with the exception of the Chief Judge of the Maori Land Court who is styled 'Chief Judge'.

Judges of the Court of Appeal and of the Supreme Court in New Zealand are referred to and addressed in the same way as High Court Judges in the United Kingdom, i.e. (Dear) Sir, *or* Dear Judge. The envelope is addressed 'The Hon. Mr. Justice Smith', *or* 'The Rt. Hon. Mr. Justice Smith' if admitted to the Privy Council.

A letter to the Chief Justice is addressed 'The Rt. Hon. the Chief Justice', or 'The Rt. Hon. Sir . . ., Chief Justice of New Zealand'.

The commencement of the letter is:

'(Dear) Sir', *or*
'Dear Chief Justice'.

There are no Courts in New Zealand which correspond to the British County Courts.

Other Commonwealth Countries

Chief Justices, Judges of the Courts of Appeal and Puisne Judges of the Supreme and High Courts, including Dependent Territories, during office are addressed as The Hon. Mr. Justice before the surname, including Knights. Forms of address are as for Judges of the High Court of England and Wales.

Deemsters of the Isle of Man are accorded 'The Hon.' before the name, and referred to as 'Deemster' in place of 'Judge'. Bailiffs in Jersey and Guernsey have no Judicial prefix, and are addressed either by office (Dear Bailiff) or name.

MEDICAL SECTION

There are two distinct forms of address, for the broad disciplines of Medicine and Surgery.

MEDICINE (INCLUDING GENERAL PRACTICE)

A Doctor of Medicine who practises *medicine* is known as 'Doctor'.

A Physician who holds other medical degrees or diplomas (including those which are both medical and surgical, e.g. M.R.C.S., L.R.C.P., M.B., B.S.) is known by courtesy as 'doctor' in speech.

Where one has qualifications in more than one discipline he (or she) is usually addressed according to that which he (or she) practises.

Where one progresses in the same degree, qualification, etc., only the higher is shown, i.e. if a Bachelor of Medicine becomes a Doctor of Medicine he is shown only as M.D. *or* D.M. (according to the University); similarly if a M.R.C.P. becomes a F.R.C.P. only the latter is shown.

An Anaesthetist (F.F.A., R.C.S.), a Pathologist (F.R.C. Path.), and a Radiologist (F.F.R.) are all called 'Doctor'.

BEGINNING OF LETTER

Formal	Dear Sir
Social	Dear Doctor Smith

ENDING OF LETTER

Formal	Yours faithfully (see also p. 2)
Social	Yours sincerely

ENVELOPE

John Smith, Esq., M.D., F.R.C.P. *or* Dr. John Smith, M.D., F.R.C.P.

John Brown, Esq., B.M., B.S. *or* Dr. John Brown

William Robinson, Esq., M.R.C.S., L.R.C.P. *or* Dr. William Robinson

Note.—Those with doctorates, masterships and fellowships should be addressed on the envelope with the appropriate letters. Others who practise medicine, as in the second and third examples, may be addressed on the envelope as Dr. William Robinson if the exact qualifying diplomas (e.g. M.B. or B.M., B.S., B.Chir. or Ch.B.) are not known. See *Letters After the Name, below.*

VERBAL ADDRESS AND DESCRIPTION IN CONVERSATION

Dr. Smith

SURGERY (INCLUDING GYNAECOLOGY)

A Surgeon (usually with a Mastership or Fellowship in Surgery) is known as 'Mr. Smith' in speech.

A Doctor of Medicine who practises surgery is known as 'Mr. Smith' in speech.

Where a doctor has qualifications in more than one discipline, it is usual for him (or her) to be addressed according to that which he (or she) practises. See *Letters After the Name, below.*

BEGINNING OF LETTER

Formal	Dear Sir,
Social	Dear Mr. Smith

ENDING OF LETTER

Formal	Yours faithfully (see also p. 2)
Social	Yours sincerely

ENVELOPE

John Smith, Esq., M.S., F.R.C.S.
William Jones, Esq., D.M., M.S., F.R.C.S.

An Obstetrician and Gynaecologist (usually M.R.C.O.G. or F.R.C.O.G.) is addressed as a Surgeon in England and Wales. Elsewhere, including Scotland, Ireland, Australia, Canada, New Zealand, South Africa and the U.S.A., it is the custom for him (or her) to be called 'Doctor'.

VERBAL ADDRESS AND DESCRIPTION IN CONVERSATION

Mr. Smith

DENTAL PRACTITIONER

If a Dental Surgeon, he is referred to as a Surgeon, i.e. Mr. John Jones, with the appropriate letters signifying his degrees or qualifications.

In general practice he may be referred to as a Doctor if he has a medical degree or qualification in addition to a dental qualification, but not otherwise.

LETTERS AFTER THE NAME

By custom those denoting medicine follow those of Orders, Decorations, and Medals bestowed by the Crown.

They are usually placed in the following order:

Doctorates

Masterships

Baccalaureates (degrees of Bachelor)

Postgraduate Diplomas (e.g. Fellowships and Memberships except M.R.C.S.)

Qualifying Diplomas (M.R.C.S., L.R.C.P., etc.)

It is the custom for letters indicating Doctorates, Masterships, and Fellowships to be given in correspondence. Baccalaureates, Memberships, and Qualifying Diplomas may be shown if no higher qualifications are held.

It is sufficient for a maximum of three series of letters to be shown.

If required for formal lists, the following is the complete list of letters commonly used in medicine in the British Isles.

DOCTORATES

D.M.—Doctor of Medicine

M.D.—Doctor of Medicine

D.Ch.—Doctor of Surgery

MASTERSHIPS

M.Ch.—Master of Surgery

M.Chir.—Master of Surgery

M.S.—Master of Surgery

Ch.M.—Master of Surgery

M.D.S.—Master of Dental Surgery

M.A.O.—Master of the Art of Obstetrics

BACCALAUREATES

B.M.—Bachelor of Medicine

M.B.—Bachelor of Medicine

B.Ch.—Bachelor of Surgery

B.Chir.—Bachelor of Surgery

B.S.—Bachelor of Surgery

Ch.B.—Bachelor of Surgery

B.D.S.—Bachelor of Dental Surgery

B.A.O.—Bachelor of the Art of Obstetrics

POSTGRADUATE DIPLOMAS (Fellowships and Memberships except M.R.C.S.)

F.R.C.P.—Fellow of the Royal College of Physicians

F.R.C.P. Ed.—Fellow of the Royal College of Physicians of Edinburgh

F.R.C.P.I.—Fellow of the Royal College of Physicians of Ireland

F.R.C.P. (Glasg.)—Fellow (*qua* physician) of the Royal College of Physicians and Surgeons of Glasgow

M.R.C.P.—Member of the Royal College of Physicians

M.R.C.P. Ed.—Member of the Royal College of Physicians of Edinburgh

M.R.C.P.I.—Member of the Royal College of Physicians of Ireland

M.R.C.P. (Glasg.)—Member of the Royal College of Physicians and Surgeons of Glasgow

F.R.C.S.—Fellow of the Royal College of Surgeons

F.R.C.S. Ed.—Fellow of the Royal College of Surgeons of Edinburgh

F.R.C.S.I.—Fellow of the Royal College of Surgeons in Ireland

F.R.C.S. (Glasg.)—Fellow (*qua* surgeon) of the Royal College of Physicians and Surgeons of Glasgow

F.R.C.O.G.—Fellow of the Royal College of Obstetricians and Gynaecologists

M.R.C.O.G.—Member of the Royal College of Obstetricians and Gynaecologists

F.R.C.G.P.—Fellow of the Royal College of General Practitioners

M.R.C.G.P.—Member of the Royal College of General Practitioners

F.R.C.Path.—Fellow of the Royal College of Pathologists

M.R.C.Path.—Member of the Royal College of Pathologists

F.F.R.—Fellow of the Faculty of Radiologists

F.F.A., R.C.S.—Fellow of the Faculty of Anaesthetists, the Royal College of Surgeons

F.D.S., R.C.S.—Fellow in Dental Surgery, the Royal College of Surgeons

QUALIFYING DIPLOMAS

M.R.C.S., L.R.C.P.—Member of the Royal College of Surgeons; Licentiate of the Royal College of Physicians

L.R.C.P., L.R.C.S., L.R.F.P.S.—Licentiate of the Royal College of Physicians of Edinburgh, of the Royal College of Surgeons of Edinburgh, and of the Royal Faculty of Physicians and Surgeons of Glasgow[1]

L.R.C.P., L.R.C.S., L.R.C.P.S.—Licentiate of the first two Royal Colleges, and of the Royal College of Physicians and Surgeons of Glasgow[1]

L.R.C.P.I. and L.M.—Licentiate of the Royal College of Physicians of Ireland, and Licentiate in Midwifery

L.R.C.S.I. and L.M.—Licentiate of the Royal College of Surgeons in Ireland, and Licentiate in Midwifery

L.S.A.—Licentiate of the Society of Apothecaries

L.M.S.S.A.—Licentiate in Medicine and Surgery, the Society of Apothecaries

L.A.H.—Licentiate of the Apothecaries' Hall, Dublin

OTHER POSTGRADUATE DIPLOMAS

M.M.S.A.—Master of Midwifery, Society of Apothecaries

D.P.H.—Diploma in Public Health

D.O.—Diploma in Ophthalmology

D.O.M.S.—Diploma in Ophthalmic Medicine and Surgery

D.P.M.—Diploma in Psychological Medicine

D.C.P.—Diploma in Clinical Pathology

Dip. Bact.—Diploma in Bacteriology

D.M.R.D.—Diploma in Medical Radio-Diagnosis

D.M.R.T.—Diploma in Medical Radio-Therapy

D.M.R.E.—Diploma in Medical Radiology and Electrology

D.Phys.Med.—Diploma in Physical Medicine

D.A.—Diploma in Anaesthesia

D.C.H.—Diploma in Child Health

D.I.H.—Diploma in Industrial Health

D.L.O.—Diploma in Laryngology and Orology

D.Obst.R.C.O.G.—Diploma in Obstetrics, the Royal College of Obstetricians and Gynaecologists

D.T.M. and H.—Diploma in Tropical Medicine and Hygiene

D.M.J.—Diploma in Medical Jurisprudence

Dip.Soc.Med. Edin.—Diploma in Social Medicine of the University of Edinburgh

[1] The Royal Faculty of Physicians and Surgeons of Glasgow has recently become a Royal College, but those who qualified in the former letters (L.R.F.P.S.), retain them.

NURSING SECTION

According to the recommendations of the Salmon Committee on Senior Nursing Staff Structure 1966, the following appointments will be implemented in the Nursing Service, where possible, by the end of 1971:

Chief Nursing Officer
Principal Nursing Officer
Senior Nursing Officer
Nursing Officer
Charge Nurse (ladies who were previously known as Sisters may retain this title or adopt the newer one of Charge Nurse)
Staff Nurse

This will apply to all nurses working in hospitals within the National Health Service although the old titles (Matron, Sister, etc.) will probably continue to be used both in N.H.S. hospitals and in other hospitals and nursing homes.

The term 'Nurse' is protected by Act of Parliament, and the following are entitled to be so called in England and Wales:

State Registered Nurse (S.R.N.)
Registered Mental Nurse (R.M.N.)
Registered Nurse for the Mentally Sub-Normal (R.N.M.S.)
Registered Sick Children's Nurse (R.S.C.N.)
Student Nurses training for the Register
State Enrolled Nurse (S.E.N.)
Pupil Nurses training for the Roll

These titles are different in Scotland, e.g. the equivalent of a State Registered Nurse is Registered General Nurse (R.G.N.).

It is now the custom to write to all the above by his or her name. The appointment may follow, if required (e.g. Miss Marion Smith, Chief Nursing Officer, West Blankshire Hospital). If the name or terminology of the senior appointment is not known (e.g. Chief Nursing Officer or Matron) correspondence may be addressed to 'Head of the Nursing Services'.

MIDWIFE

The term 'Midwife' is protected by Act of Parliament.

It is customary to write to a State Certified Midwife (S.C.M.) or a Pupil Midwife training for certification by her name.

NURSING CORPS AND SERVICES

(See *Queen Alexandra's Royal Naval Nursing Service,* p. 199;
Queen Alexandra's Royal Army Nursing Corps, p. 200; *Princess
Mary's Royal Air Force Nursing Service,* p. 201.)

CIVIC SECTION

LORD MAYOR

The Lord Mayors of London and York have since time
immemorial been accorded the privilege of being styled 'The
Right Honourable'.

Other Lord Mayors are only styled 'The Right Honourable'
where this privilege has been granted by The Queen. These are:

Northern Ireland : Belfast

Wales : Cardiff

Australia : The state capitals of Sydney, Melbourne, Adelaide,
Perth, Brisbane, Hobart.

Dublin and Cork were also accorded this privilege when all
Ireland formed part of the United Kingdom. This style has been
continued since the formation of the Republic of Ireland.

Lord Mayors of other cities are styled 'The Right Worshipful'.
In England and Wales they are:

Birmingham	Newcastle upon Tyne
Bradford	Norwich
Bristol[1]	Nottingham
Coventry	Oxford
Kingston upon Hull	Plymouth
Leeds	Portsmouth
Leicester	Sheffield
Liverpool	Stoke on Trent
Manchester	Westminster

There is no difference in the form of address for a Lord Mayor
who is a lady.

BEGINNING OF LETTER

Formal	My Lord Mayor
Social	Dear Lord Mayor *or* by name

[1] The Lord Mayor of Bristol is sometimes styled 'The Right Honourable' but there is no official authority for this.

ENDING OF LETTER

Formal	Yours faithfully (see also p. 2)
Social	Yours sincerely

ENVELOPE

Formal The Right Honourable the Lord Mayor of Cardiff

The Right Worshipful the Lord Mayor of Birmingham

(as applicable, see above)

If desired, the name, preceded by Alderman or Councillor, may follow the office,[1] but 'The Right Honourable' or 'The Right Worshipful' (as applicable) should always be placed immediately before 'the Lord Mayor'.

Social As above *or* by name

VERBAL ADDRESS

My Lord Mayor, *or*
Lord Mayor

DESCRIPTION IN CONVERSATION

The Lord Mayor *or*
The Lord Mayor of . . .

DEPUTY LORD MAYOR AND DEPUTY MAYOR

There is no Deputy Lord Mayor of London.

In other cities the Lord Mayor's deputy is in some cases styled 'Deputy Lord Mayor', in others 'Deputy Mayor'. In neither case is he styled 'The Right Honourable' or 'The Right Worshipful'. In all other respects the above rules apply.

LADY MAYORESS

A Lady Mayoress is not accorded the style of 'The Right Honourable' or 'The Right Worshipful'.

BEGINNING OF LETTER

Formal	My Lady Mayoress
Social	Dear Lady Mayoress, *or* by name

[1] Not applicable to the Lord Mayor of London.

ENDING OF LETTER

Formal   Yours faithfully (see also p. 2)
Social   Yours sincerely

ENVELOPE

Formal   The Lady Mayoress of Portsmouth
   If desired, the name, preceded by Alderman or Councillor
where applicable, may follow the office.
Social   As above, *or* by name

VERBAL ADDRESS

   My Lady Mayoress *or*
   Lady Mayoress

DESCRIPTION IN CONVERSATION

   The Lady Mayoress *or*
   The Lady Mayoress of . . .

DEPUTY LADY MAYORESS AND DEPUTY MAYORESS

There is no Deputy Lady Mayoress of London. In other cities
the Lady Mayoress's deputy is in some cases styled 'Deputy Lady
Mayoress', in others 'Deputy Mayoress'.

MAYOR OF A CITY

If a city has no Lord Mayor, the Mayor is styled 'The Right
Worshipful'.

   The cities in England and Wales[1] with Mayors so styled are:

Bath	Hereford	Salisbury
Cambridge	Lancaster	Southampton
Canterbury	Lichfield	Swansea
Carlisle	Lincoln	Truro
Chester	Peterborough	Wakefield
Chichester	Ripon	Wells
Durham	Rochester	Winchester
Exeter	St. Albans	Worcester
Gloucester	Salford	

   For Bangor, North Wales, see *Mayor of a Borough*.

[1] The status of City, which once denoted a cathedral see, is now conferred by The Queen.

The Cities of Ely and St. Davids have no Mayors. The former is administered by an Urban District Council, and the latter by a Parish Council.

BEGINNING OF LETTER

Formal	Mr. Mayor[1]
Social	Dear Mr. Mayor,[1] *or* by name

The form of address 'Mr. Mayor' is properly used even though the Mayor be a lady, but some lady Mayors prefer the form 'Madam Mayor'.

ENDING OF LETTER

Formal	Yours faithfully (see also p. 2)
Social	Yours sincerely

ENVELOPE

Formal   The Right Worshipful the Mayor of Bath.

If desired, the Mayor's name, preceded by Alderman or Councillor, may follow the office, but 'The Right Worshipful' should always precede 'the Mayor'.

Social   As above, or by name

DESCRIPTION IN CONVERSATION

The Mayor *or*
The Mayor of . . .

VERBAL ADDRESS

Mr. Mayor

The use of 'Your Worship' is archaic, except when the Mayor is sitting as a magistrate.[2] If, however, more than one Mayor is present, the term 'Your Worships' is used, since there is no other acceptable plural term.

DEPUTY MAYOR

The Mayor's deputy is styled 'Deputy Mayor'. He is not styled 'The Right Worshipful'. Otherwise the above rules apply.

[1] This applies even though the Mayor be a peer of the realm.
[2] Only applicable when the Mayor is a Justice of the Peace. (All Mayors used to be Justices of the Peace *ex-officio*, but this privilege was abolished in 1969.)

MAYOR OF A CINQUE PORT

The Mayors of the Cinque Ports, i.e.:

Dover	Rye
Hastings	Sandwich
Hythe	Winchelsea
New Romney	

are also accorded the style 'The Right Worshipful', the form of address being as for the Mayor of a City.

There were originally the five 'Head Ports' of Hastings, Romney Hythe, Dover, and Sandwich. At various times between the ninth and thirteenth centuries, no fewer than thirty ports were included in the 'Confederation'. Rye and Winchelsea were included as 'Head Ports' during this period, although silting ultimately brought an end to their function as proper ports. Nevertheless, Rye and Winchelsea remain as two of the seven 'Cinque Ports' acknowledged today.

All, save Winchelsea, remain as local authorities. Winchelsea has no elected Parish Council, and is administered by Icklesham Parish Council for local government purposes. Despite this, the Parish of Winchelsea has twelve Jurats, one of whom is elected Mayor each year.

MAYOR OF A BOROUGH

Mayors of English and Welsh boroughs are styled 'The Worshipful the Mayor'.

This includes the City of Bangor, North Wales, and the following boroughs which have a cathedral but which have not been accorded the status of city:

Brecon	Guildford
Blackburn	Newport (Diocese of Monmouth)
Bradford	Southwark
Bury St. Edmunds	

The following are styled 'The Worshipful the Mayor of the Royal Borough of . . .'

Caernarvon
Kensington and Chelsea
Kingston upon Thames
New Windsor

All Mayors in Ireland are styled 'The Worshipful'.

BEGINNING OF LETTER
As for the Mayor of a city.

ENDING OF LETTER
As for the Mayor of a city.

ENVELOPE
As for the Mayor of a city, omitting 'Right' before 'Worshipful'.

VERBAL ADDRESS
As for the Mayor of a city.

DESCRIPTION IN CONVERSATION
As for the Mayor of a city.

VERBAL ADDRESS
As for the Mayor of a city.

DEPUTY MAYOR

The Mayor's deputy is styled 'Deputy Mayor'. He is not styled 'The Worshipful'. Otherwise the above rules apply.

MAYORESS

A Mayoress is not accorded the style of 'The Right Worshipful or 'The Worshipful'.

BEGINNING OF LETTER

Formal	Madam Mayoress[1]
Social	Dear Mayoress[1], *or* by name

ENDING OF LETTER

Formal	Yours faithfully (see also p. 2)
Social	Yours sincerely

ENVELOPE

Formal	The Mayoress of Worthing

[1] This applies even though the Mayoress be a peeress.

If desired, the name, preceded by Alderman or Councillor where applicable, may follow the office.
Social   As above, *or* by name

VERBAL ADDRESS
    Mayoress

DESCRIPTION IN CONVERSATION
    The Mayoress *or*
    The Mayoress of . . .

DEPUTY MAYORESS

As above, with the addition of 'Deputy'.

City of London

There are two Sheriffs elected for the City of London. It is customary for Common Hall to elect an Alderman who has not served the office of Lord Mayor as one, who is known as the Aldermanic Sheriff; the other Sheriff elected, if he is not an Alderman, is known as the Lay Sheriff.

ALDERMANIC SHERIFF

He is addressed according to his rank, *or simply* as Mr. Sheriff, but in writing to him in his official capacity the following form may be used.

BEGINNING OF LETTER
    Dear Alderman and Sheriff (omitting the name)

ENVELOPE
    Mr. Alderman and Sheriff . . . (followed by his name)
    Alderman and Sheriff Sir . . . (followed by his name, in the
        case of a baronet or knight)
    Alderman and Sheriff the Rt. Hon. Lord . . . (followed by
        his title, in the case of a peer)
    Lieutenant-Colonel, Alderman and Sheriff . . . (followed by
        his name)

ALDERMAN

As above, but omitting all reference to Sheriff.

LAY SHERIFF

As above, but omitting all reference to Alderman (e.g. commencement of letter, Dear Sheriff, and envelope, Mr. Sheriff, followed by his name *or*, if applicable, Colonel and Sheriff, followed by his name).

COMMON COUNCILMAN

As for an Esquire or appropriate rank. On the envelope the letters C.C. (denoting Common Councilman) should follow the name, after any orders or decorations.

Members of the Court of Common Council are not styled 'Councillor'.

DEPUTY

The Senior Common Councilman in each Ward is appointed Deputy to the Alderman of his Ward. He is addressed at the commencement of a letter as 'Dear Deputy'; and on the envelope as for an Esquire, or appropriate rank, followed by the word 'Deputy'.

OTHER OFFICERS OF THE CITY OF LONDON

Officers of the Corporation are normally addressed by their appointment (e.g. at the commencement of a letter 'Dear Mr. Town Clerk', and on the envelope, 'The Town Clerk'; similarly, 'Dear Mr. Chamberlain', 'Dear Mr. City Solicitor', 'Dear Mr. Remembrancer').

Sheriffs, other than those elected for the City of London

Sheriffs of cities and boroughs are not to be confused with High Sheriffs of Counties (p. 249).

The following boroughs which were anciently counties in

themselves, or were 'counties corporate', are entitled to appoint Sheriffs:

Berwick-upon-Tweed	Lichfield
Bristol	Lincoln
Canterbury	Newcastle upon Tyne
Carmarthen	Norwich
Chester	Nottingham
Durham	Poole
Exeter	Southampton
Gloucester	Worcester
Haverfordwest	York
Kingston-upon-Hull	

The City of Oxford also has this right.

There is no special form of address for these Sheriffs, although the appointment may follow the name in official correspondence.

Alderman of a City, County Borough, or Borough, other than of the City of London

BEGINNING OF LETTER

Formal   My Lord, (Dear) Sir, (Dear) Madam *or*
Dear Mr. Alderman (Dear Alderman if holder of a title) *or*
Dear Alderman Lord Smith,[1] Sir John Smith, Colonel Smith, Smith, Lady Smith, Mrs. Smith, Miss Smith

Social   Dear Alderman, *or* by name

ENDING OF LETTER

Formal   Yours faithfully (see also p. 2)
Social   Yours sincerely

ENVELOPE

The general practice is to omit 'Alderman', but when included this precedes other styles, e.g. Alderman Colonel Smith.

VERBAL ADDRESS

Formal   Alderman (Lord Smith, Sir John Smith, Colonel Smith, Mrs. Smith, Miss Smith)

[1] See p. 71. Style from sources other than the Crown.

<table>
<tr><td>*Informal*</td><td>Mr. Alderman (not to a holder of a title), *or* Alderman, *or* by rank and name (Sir John, Colonel Smith,[1] Mr. Smith, Mrs. Smith, Miss Smith)</td></tr>
</table>

DESCRIPTION IN CONVERSATION

Alderman (Lord Smith, Sir John Smith, Colonel Smith,[1] Smith, Mrs. Smith, Miss Smith), or by rank and name

Councillor of a City, County Borough, or Borough, other than of the City of London

As for an alderman of a city, county borough, or borough, substituting 'Councillor' for 'Alderman'.

County, Urban, and Rural District Council

The Chairman of the Greater London Council has been granted the style 'The Right Honourable' by The Queen. For all other councils the style is 'Chairman'.

BEGINNING OF LETTER

Dear Mr. Chairman (even though the office is held by a lady)

ENDING OF LETTER

Formal	Yours faithfully (see also p. 2)
Social	Yours sincerely

ENVELOPE

Formal	The Right Honourable the Chairman of the Greater London Council
	The Chairman of the . . . County Council/Urban District Council/Rural District Council
Social	By name

VERBAL ADDRESS

Mr. Chairman (even though the office is held by a lady), *or* by name

[1] See p. 71. Style from sources other than the Crown.

DESCRIPTION IN CONVERSATION
    The Chairman, *or* by name

VICE-CHAIRMAN/DEPUTY CHAIRMAN

The above rules apply, except for the omission of 'The Right Honourable' in the case of the Greater London Council.

County Alderman, County Councillor, Member of Urban District Council and Member of Rural District Council.

These are not styled 'Alderman' or 'Councillor'. Some members of the Greater London Council use the suffix 'G.L.C.' after their names, but there is no official authority for this, neither have the abbreviations C.A. and C.C., for County Aldermen and Councillors of other county councils any official standing.

Other Municipal officers

As for an esquire or appropriate rank. The appointment may precede or follow the name, if desired.
    For an official letter the appointment only is sufficient, e.g.:
    The Town Clerk (of . . .)
    The City Engineer,
    Westminster City Hall
    A formal letter to the Town Clerk should begin 'Dear (Mr.) Town Clerk'. Formal letters to other officers should begin 'Dear Sir'.

Scotland

LORD PROVOST

The following Scottish cities and royal burghs have Lord Provosts corresponding to a Lord Mayor in England, Northern Ireland, and Wales[1]:

Edinburgh	Dundee
Glasgow	Aberdeen
Perth	

    The Lord Provosts of Edinburgh and Glasgow are entitled to 'The Right Hon.' as a prefix. According to precedent, The Lord Provost of Edinburgh uses this style before his actual name.

[1] The City of Elgin is sometimes included but there is no official authority for the appointment of a Lord Provost of that Royal Burgh.

BEGINNING OF LETTER

Formal	My Lord Provost
Social	Dear Lord Provost

ENDING OF LETTER

Formal	Yours faithfully (see also p. 2)
Social	Yours sincerely

ENVELOPE

The Rt. Hon. John Smith
Lord Provost of Edinburgh
The Rt. Hon. The Lord Provost of Glasgow[1]
The Lord Provost of Perth, Dundee or Aberdeen[1]

VERBAL ADDRESS

Formal	My Lord Provost
Social	The Lord Provost

DESCRIPTION IN CONVERSATION

The Lord Provost

WIFE OF A LORD PROVOST

She has no special style.

PROVOST

Each Scottish royal burgh and other burghs has a Provost (except cities and royal burghs with a Lord Provost).

BEGINNING OF LETTER

Formal	Dear Provost
Social	By name

CONCLUSION OF LETTER

Formal	Yours faithfully (see also p. 2)
Social	Yours sincerely

[1] The order of precedence by which Lord Provosts entered the old Scottish Parliament was Edinburgh, Perth, Dundee, Aberdeen, and Glasgow. Whereas Perth is recognized in second place, the order of the remaining cities is still a subject of discussion.

ENVELOPE
> John Smith, Esq.
> Provost of Bathgate

VERBAL ADDRESS
> Provost

DESCRIPTION IN CONVERSATION
> The Provost

WIFE OF A PROVOST

> She has no special style.

BAILIE

A Bailie of a burgh is the Scottish counterpart of an Alderman.

BEGINNING OF LETTER

Formal	(Dear) Sir
Social	Dear Bailie Smith

ENDING OF LETTER

Formal	Yours faithfully (see also p. 2)
Social	Yours sincerely

ENVELOPE
> Bailie Kenneth Smith
> The word 'Bailie' precedes other styles (e.g. Bailie Major W. J.
Smith).

VERBAL ADDRESS
> Bailie Smith

DESCRIPTION IN CONVERSATION
> Bailie Smith

COUNCILLOR

The form of address follows English practice.

COUNTY SECTION

LORD LIEUTENANT

England and Wales

A Lord Lieutenant is appointed by the Crown for each county, and for the three ridings of Yorkshire. In addition, he is usually appointed Custos Rotulorum (Custodian of the County Records). He is the Sovereign's representative in a county.

By Royal Warrant in 1904 he was given precedence before the High Sheriff of the county. This is a personal precedence, and does not apply when a Vice-Lieutenant or Deputy Lieutenant represents the Lord Lieutenant.

Officially he is appointed 'Her Majesty's Lieutenant of and in the County of . . .' and so is formally described as 'H.M. Lieutenant of Blankshire', but he is usually known by old established practice as 'The Lord Lieutenant of Blankshire'.

Scotland

A Lord Lieutenant is appointed for each county. Note, a Lord Lieutenant is appointed for the county of Zetland, not Shetland.

Northern Ireland

A Lieutenant is appointed for each county. Here he is never known as the *Lord* Lieutenant, because the Crown formerly appointed the Lord Lieutenant of Ireland, and this practice has been continued for Lieutenants of counties.

Form of Address. There is no specific form of address for a Lord Lieutenant, and no letters are appended after his name, except for Northern Ireland, but if correspondence is on an official matter the appointment is included after the name, e.g.:

Very Formally	Colonel Sir John Brown, K.C.B., D.S.O., H.M. Lieutenant of Blankshire
Otherwise	Colonel Sir John Brown, K.C.B., D.S.O., Lord Lieutenant of Blankshire

A Lord Lieutenant is formally called in speech as 'My Lord Lieutenant'. The plural form is 'Lord Lieutenants'.

In Northern Ireland the Lieutenant of a county has the letters H.M.L. appended after his name. He is formally called in speech 'Her Majesty's Lieutenant'.

VICE-LIEUTENANT

A Lord Lieutenant appoints a Vice-Lieutenant for his period of office. There is no recognized abbreviation, V.L. As a Vice-Lieutenant is also a Deputy Lieutenant he continues to use the letters D.L. after his name, as for other Deputy Lieutenants. When corresponding with a Vice-Lieutenant on an official matter his appointment may be placed after his name:

John Smith, Esq., D.L.,
Vice-Lieutenant of Blankshire

In addition, the Lord Lieutenant of Greater London may appoint four Assistant Lieutenants, but at the time of going to press these appointments have not been filled.

DEPUTY LIEUTENANT

Several Deputy Lieutenants are appointed by the Lord Lieutenant of a county. The appointment is held for life. The letters D.L. are placed after his name, but in practice they are sometimes omitted in social correspondence. If included, D.L. follows J.P. See *Position of Letters After the Name*, p. 101.

HIGH SHERIFF

A High Sheriff is appointed annually in March for each county in England (including the three ridings of Yorkshire and Hallamshire), Wales and Northern Ireland.

He is responsible for the administration of justice within his county. A warrant of appointment has the phrase: '. . . require you to take the Custody and Charge of the said County . . .', but by Royal Warrant of 1904, after centuries of uncertainty, his precedence was placed after the Lord Lieutenant. This is a personal precedence, and does not apply when the Deputy Sheriff represents the High Sheriff. Within his (or her) city or borough the Lord Mayor or Mayor takes precedence of the High Sheriff, except on 'County' occasions.

Though the wording of the Warrant and the Declaration does not contain the word 'High', it is an old established practice for Sheriffs appointed by Her Majesty in Council to be referred to as High Sheriff. Like 'Lord' before the Lieutenant, 'High' before Sheriff signifies a senior Crown appointment, e.g. High Commissioner. It also distinguishes a High Sheriff from the Sheriff of a city, town or borough (p. 242).

There is no specific form of address for a High Sheriff, but if corresponding on an official matter the appointment may be included after the name, e.g.:

Brigadier John Jones, C.B.E.,
High Sheriff of Hertfordshire

A lady may be appointed as a High Sheriff.

A High Sheriff is formally called in speech 'High Sheriff', *not* Mr. High Sheriff.

UNDER SHERIFF

One (or occasionally more) Under Sheriff is appointed by the High Sheriff to assist him, or to act for him in his absence. He is generally a practising solicitor. There is no specific form of address, but if correspondence is on an official matter, the appointment is included after the name, e.g.:

Brigadier John Jones, C.B.E.,
Under Sheriff of Hertfordshire

SHERIFF, SCOTLAND

(See *Legal Section*, p. 223.)

JUSTICE OF THE PEACE

(See *Legal Section*, p. 218.)

CHAIRMAN OF A COUNTY COUNCIL

(See *Civic Section,* p. 244.)

CONVENER OF A COUNTY COUNCIL

This is the Scottish equivalent of a Chairman of a County Council. A man or woman is addressed 'Dear Convener'. The envelope is addressed formally 'The Convener of . . .' and socially by name.

ALDERMAN OF A COUNTY COUNCIL

(See *Civic Section*, p. 245.)

COUNCILLOR OF A COUNTY COUNCIL

(See *Civic Section*, p. 245.)

POLICE SECTION

Metropolitan Police and City of London Police

COMMISSIONER

BEGINNING OF LETTER

Formal	(Dear) Sir
Social	
If a Knight	Dear Sir John (Smith)
Otherwise	Dear Mr. Smith *or* Commissioner

ENDING OF LETTER

Formal	Yours faithfully (see also p. 2)
Social	Yours sincerely

ENVELOPE

Sir John Jones (followed by Decorations)
John Jones, Esq. (followed by Decorations)
Commissioner of Police of the Metropolis, *or* for the City of London

VERBAL ADDRESS

Commissioner, *or* by name

DEPUTY OR ASSISTANT COMMISSIONER

BEGINNING OF LETTER

As for Commissioner, but if by his appointment, Dear Deputy Commissioner (*or* Assistant Commissioner).

ENVELOPE

Sir John Smith (followed by Decorations)
or John Smith, Esq. (followed by Decorations)
Deputy Commissioner of Police } of the Metropolis, *or*
or Assistant Commissioner of Police } for the City of London

VERBAL ADDRESS

By appointment *or* by name.

DEPUTY ASSISTANT COMMISSIONER

Formal   (Dear) Sir
Social   Dear Mr. Smith *or*
       Dear Deputy Assistant Commissioner

ENVELOPE

John Smith Esq. (followed by Decorations)
Deputy Assistant Commissioner, Metropolitan Police

VERBAL ADDRESS

By appointment *or* by name.

COMMANDER OR CHIEF SUPERINTENDENT

Note: The rank of Superintendent is vacant in the Metropolitan Police and City of London Police.

BEGINNING OF LETTER

Formal   (Dear) Sir (*or* Madam)
Social   Dear Commander Smith (*or* appropriate
       rank)
       or Dear Mr./Mrs./Miss Smith

ENVELOPE

(Men) With his rank before his name, followed by 'Metropolitan Police' *or* 'City of London Police', e.g.
     Chief Superintendent J. W. Johnson, M.B.E., Metropolitan Police
    or by his name, followed by his appointment, e.g.
     John W. Johnson, Esq., M.B.E., Chief Superintendent, Metropolitan Police.
(Women) With her rank before her name, as above, e.g.
     Chief Superintendent Mrs./Miss J. W. Smith, M.B.E., City of London Police.
    or by her name, followed by her appointment, e.g.
     Miss Julia W. Smith, M.B.E., Chief Superintendent, City of London Police.
(C.I.D.) 'Detective' is added before Chief Superintendent.

By the appointment, *or* by name.

CHIEF INSPECTOR, INSPECTOR, POLICE SERGEANT AND POLICE CONSTABLE

At the beginning of a letter the appropriate rank is placed before the name, i.e. Dear Chief Inspector (Inspector, Sergeant or Constable) Smith, with the prefix 'Detective' if a member of C.I.D.

The rank is placed on the envelope before the name. Police Sergeant is often abbreviated to P.S., Police Constable to P.C., Detective Sergeant to D.S. and Detective Constable to D.C.

On the envelope a woman Chief Inspector or Inspector is addressed Chief Inspector (or Inspector) Mrs. or Miss Smith, though in the City of London Police the form W/Chief Inspector or W/Inspector Smith is used. A woman Police Sergeant is often abbreviated to W.P.S., Police Constable to W.P.C., Detective Sergeant to W.D.S. and Detective Constable to W.D.C., which are placed before the name.

'Metropolitan Police' *or* 'City of London Police' follows the name.

Other Police Forces

CHIEF CONSTABLE

BEGINNING OF LETTER
By name, *or* 'Dear Chief Constable'.

ENVELOPE
  Sir John Smith *or* John Smith Esq., as appropriate (followed by Decorations)
  Chief Constable, Blankshire Constabulary

VERBAL ADDRESS
  Chief Constable, *or* by name

DESCRIPTION IN CONVERSATION
  The Chief Constable, *or* by name

DEPUTY OR ASSISTANT CHIEF CONSTABLE

As for Chief Constable, with the substitution of the appropriate appointment.

CHIEF SUPERINTENDENT

As for Metropolitan Police, with the substitution of the appropriate Force.

SUPERINTENDENT

As for Chief Superintendent, with the deletion of 'Chief'.

CHIEF INSPECTOR AND OTHER RANKS

Chief Inspector, Inspector, Police Sergeant and Police Constable as for Metropolitan Police with the substitution of the appropriate Force.

MERCHANT NAVY AND AIRLINE OFFICERS SECTION

MERCHANT NAVY

Officer ranks in the Merchant Navy, of which the old name was the Mercantile Marine, vary from company to company.

The Master of the ship always ranks as Captain (i.e. he holds a Master's Certificate and commands, or has commanded a ship). In some companies the senior Captain holds the rank of Commodore, of which there is one per company.

In large ships (mostly passenger) there is a Staff Captain, in addition to the Captain. Other deck officers are as follows:

> Chief Officer
> Second Officer
> Third Officer
> Fourth Officer[1]

The old names of First Mate (for Chief Officer), Second Mate (for Second Officer), etc., are still used, mostly in coastal ships.

In the engineering department, the Chief Engineer is sometimes known as Commodore Chief Engineer, otherwise Chief

[1] Some ships carry a Junior Chief Officer. In large ships there can be as many as three First Officers, three Second Officers and three Third Officers. In this case each is known as 'Senior', 'Intermediate', and 'Junior'.

Engineer. The other ranks are Second Engineer Officer, Third Engineer Officer, etc., occasionally down to Eighth Engineer Officer.[1]

Other ship's officers include the Surgeon, Purser, Assistant Purser, Catering Officer (and occasionally Assistant Catering Officer), and Radio Officer.

FORMS OF ADDRESS

The Commodore and Captain are addressed and referred to by these ranks.

The Staff Captain is addressed and referred to as Captain Jones.

All other officers (including the Commodore Chief Engineer), are referred to as Mr. Jones, except the Surgeon, who is known by his medical status, e.g. Dr. Johnson.

BEGINNING OF LETTER

Formal	Dear Sir
Social	Dear Commodore Jones
	Dear Captain Brown
	Dear Mr. Smith

ENDING OF LETTER

Formal	Yours faithfully (see also p. 2)
Social	Yours sincerely

ENVELOPE

Letters signifying Orders, etc., are followed by those indicating the Service (e.g. R.N.R.).

Commodore John Jones, O.B.E., R.N.R.

Captain William Smith, M.B.E.

Captain William Brown
 Staff Captain, S.S. Bengal

John Robinson, Esq.
 Third Officer, S.S. Bengal

Edward Black, Esq.
 Second Engineer Officer, S.S. Bengal

---

[1] As with the deck officers, in large ships there can also be more than one Second Engineer Officer, Third Engineer Officer, etc.

    Commodore Jones
    Captain Smith
    Mr. Robinson

DESCRIPTION IN CONVERSATION
As for verbal address.

AIR LINE OFFICERS

The Captain is referred to as Captain Smith, and addressed as Captain John (or J.) Smith.

Other officers vary according to the company, but in the main they are Senior First Officer, First Officer, and Second Officer. They are addressed as John Jones, Esq., and referred to as Mr. Jones.

ACADEMIC SECTION

CHANCELLOR OF A UNIVERSITY

The Chancellor of a University is addressed according to his rank and name, for which see the applicable section, but if a letter concerns his university, the style 'Dear Chancellor' may be used both formally and socially.

The old style of 'Dear Mr. Chancellor' is becoming archaic, but is still sometimes used in the Universities of Oxford and Cambridge.

In the main, 'Mr. Chancellor' is restricted to formal documents and verbally to formal occasions, such as at an official function.

The following is the form of address used on matters pertaining to his university.

BEGINNING OF LETTER

Formal	My Lord *or* (Dear) Sir (as applicable) *or* Dear Chancellor
Social	Dear Lord Blank, Dear Sir Henry (Smith) *or* Dear Dr. (Mr.) Jones (as applicable) *or* Dear Chancellor—this is a more distant style than by his name.

ENDING OF LETTER

Formal	Yours faithfully (see also p. 2)
Social	Yours sincerely

ENVELOPE

Formal	The Chancellor of the University of Huntingdon
Social	Sir John Jones, C.H., K.B.E., LL.D., Chancellor of the University of Huntingdon

VERBAL ADDRESS

Formal	Mr. Chancellor (on a platform, otherwise according to his rank or name, 'My Lord', 'Sir Henry', etc.)
Social	By name, *or* Chancellor

DESCRIPTION IN CONVERSATION

The Chancellor, *or* by name

HIGH STEWARD OF THE UNIVERSITIES OF OXFORD AND CAMBRIDGE

The High Steward is addressed according to his rank and name. For formal and social correspondence, see the applicable section, but if the subject of the letters concerns his university, the style of 'Dear High Steward' may be used, both in formal and social correspondence.

ENVELOPE

Formal	The High Steward of the University of Oxford *or* The Rt. Hon. the Viscount Blank, High Steward of the University of Oxford
Social	The High Steward of the University of Oxford *or* The Viscount Blank, High Steward of the University of Oxford

DEPUTY HIGH STEWARD OF THE UNIVERSITY OF CAMBRIDGE

The Deputy High Steward is addressed according to his rank and name. If the subject of the letter concerns his university, the form of address is as for the High Steward, with the addition of the word 'Deputy'.

VICE-CHANCELLOR OF A UNIVERSITY

The Vice-Chancellor of a university is addressed according to his rank and name, but if the subject of the letter concerns his university, the formal and social style of 'Dear Vice-Chancellor' may be used. In the newer universities it is more usual to write to him by his name.

The old style of Mr. Vice-Chancellor is becoming archaic, but is sometimes used in the Universities of Oxford and Cambridge.

The tenure of office for the Vice-Chancellor of the Federal Universities of Oxford, Cambridge, London and Wales, is limited to a specific period.

For Scottish universities, some of which have the joint appointment of Vice-Chancellor and Principal, see *Executive Head of a University*.

BEGINNING OF LETTER

Formal	(Dear) Sir (*or* according to rank) *or* Dear Vice-Chancellor (on a matter concerning his university)
Social	Dear Sir Henry (Jones) Dear Dr. Jones, etc. *or* Dear Vice-Chancellor (on a matter concerning his university; this is a more distant style than by name)

ENDING OF LETTER

Formal	Yours faithfully (see also p. 2)
Social	Yours sincerely

ENVELOPE

Formal	The Vice-Chancellor,
	The University of Milton Keynes
Social	Sir Philip Jones, C.B.E., LL.D.,
	Vice-Chancellor,
	The University of Milton Keynes[1]

For the Universities of Oxford and Cambridge the designations of the Vice-Chancellor are:

The Reverend the Vice-Chancellor of the University of Oxford (irrespective of whether he is in Holy Orders)

The Right Worshipful the Vice-Chancellor of the University of Cambridge

VERBAL ADDRESS

Formal	Mr. Vice-Chancellor (on a platform, etc.)
	Vice-Chancellor, *or* by name
	Sir Henry, etc.
Social	Vice-Chancellor, *or* by name

DESCRIPTION IN CONVERSATION

The Vice-Chancellor, *or* by name

DEPUTY CHANCELLOR, PRO-CHANCELLOR, DEPUTY VICE-CHANCELLOR, OR PRO-VICE-CHANCELLOR

The holders of these appointments are addressed by name, but for correspondence on university matters the envelope should include the appointment.

EXECUTIVE HEAD OF A UNIVERSITY

The Executive Head of a Scottish University is sometimes jointly appointed Vice-Chancellor and Principal. He is then addressed as Principal.

For the form of address to a Principal, see a *University Head of College*.

Broadly speaking, for other universities whose executive head

[1] Or Vice-Chancellor of The University of . . .

is jointly Vice-Chancellor and Principal, e.g. The University of Birmingham, he is addressed as Vice-Chancellor.

(See also *Commonwealth Universities*.)

COMMONWEALTH UNIVERSITIES

It is not possible to formulate any uniform system for the appointments and forms of address within the various universities of the Commonwealth, since there are no generally accepted rules. Reference should be made to the 'Commonwealth Universities Yearbook' for lists of academic and administrative offices, but the following information is given of a general nature.

For those who hold the joint appointment of Vice-Chancellor and Principal see *Executive Head of a University*, above.

CANADA

In the main there are three names for the executive heads of Canadian Universities, viz.:

Vice-Chancellor
Principal
President

In French Canadian universities the executive head is usually a Rector. The heads of various faculties in a university are usually Deans.

A President or Dean is addressed with the addition of his surname, e.g.:

Dear President Jones
Dear Dean Smith

A Vice-Chancellor or Principal is addressed as in Britain.

MALTA

The Executive Head of the University is termed Rector Magnificus.

OTHER COMMONWEALTH COUNTRIES

In Australia, New Zealand, and most other Commonwealth countries the form of address is usually based upon the British system.

HEAD OF A UNIVERSITY COLLEGE

The title of the Head varies from college to college. The following shows the principal titles adopted, together with some examples of colleges, etc. under each appropriate appointment.

Dean

      Christ Church, Oxford[1]
      King's College, Theological Dept., University of London
      School of Pharmacy, University of London
      London School of Hygiene and Tropical Medicine
The Heads of the Medical Schools and Colleges of the University of London.
The Heads of the Institutes of the British Postgraduate Medical Federation.

Director

      London School of Economics and Political Science, University of London
      School of Oriental and African Studies, University of London
      British Postgraduate Medical Federation
      Lister Institute of Preventive Medicine and of Postgraduate Institutes and Institute of Education.

Master

      Balliol College, Oxford
      Pembroke College, Oxford
      University College, Oxford
      St. Catherine's College, Oxford
      St. Cross College, Oxford
      St. Peter's College, Oxford
      St. Benet's Hall, Oxford[2]
      Campion Hall, Oxford[2]
      The Colleges of the University of Cambridge *except* King's, Queens' and the Colleges for women.
      Birkbeck College, University of London

Mistress

      Girton College, Cambridge

[1] He is also Dean of Oxford, and has the ecclesiastical title 'The Very Reverend', see p. 131.
[2] He is invariably a clergyman, and is addressed 'The Reverend the Master'.

President

> Corpus Christi College, Oxford
> Magdalen College, Oxford
> St. John's College, Oxford
> Trinity College, Oxford
> Wolfson College, Oxford
> Lucy Cavendish Collegiate Society, Cambridge
> New Hall, Cambridge
> Queens' College, Cambridge
> University College, Cambridge
> University Colleges of Dublin, Cork and Galway
> Queen's University of Belfast
> Magee University College, Londonderry

Principal

> Brasenose College, Oxford
> Hertford College, Oxford
> Jesus College, Oxford
> St. Edmund Hall, Oxford
> Ruskin College, Oxford
> Linacre College
> Mansfield College
> Regent's Park College
> The Colleges for women, University of Oxford
> Newnham College, Cambridge
> The following Schools, University of London:
>> Bedford College
>> Chelsea College of Science and Technology
>> King's College
>> New College
>> Queen Elizabeth College
>> Queen Mary College
>> Richmond College
>> Royal Holloway College
>> Royal Veterinary College (*Principal and Dean*)
>> Westfield College
>> Wye College
> The Colleges of the University of Durham *except* University and Hatfield
> The Colleges of the University of Wales

Provost

Oriel College, Oxford
Queen's College, Oxford
Worcester College, Oxford
King's College, Cambridge
Trinity College, Dublin
University College, London

Rector

Exeter College, Oxford
Lincoln College, Oxford
Imperial College of Science and Technology, University of
London

In a Scottish university a Rector has a unique meaning as the students' representative.

Warden

All Souls College, Oxford
Greyfriars Hall, Oxford[1]
Keble College, Oxford
Merton College, Oxford
New College, Oxford
Nuffield College, Oxford
St. Anthony's College, Oxford
Wadham College, Oxford
Goldsmith's College[2]

BEGINNING OF LETTER

Formal	(Dear) Sir *or* Madam
Social	By name (Dear Dr. Smith, etc.), *or* by appointment
	Dear Dean, Director, Master, Mistress, President, Principal, Provost, Warden

The old style of placing 'Mr.' before the following appointments: Dean, President, Provost, Warden, is becoming archaic, but is still sometimes used within the Universities of Oxford and Cambridge.

[1] He is invariably a clergyman, and is addressed as 'The Very Reverend the Warden'.
[2] An institution with recognized teachers of the University of London. The Heads of the other similar institutions are Principals, but the head of the Royal College of Music is Director.

'Mr. Dean' is also used when a Dean of a college has that ecclesiastical rank, although it is not included in the new form of address used by the Church of England. (See p. 131.)

ENDING OF LETTER

Formal	Yours faithfully (see also p. 2)
Social	Yours sincerely

ENVELOPE

Formal
The Master,
Pepys' College,
Cambridge

Social
Sir James Smith, Ph.D.,
Master of Pepys' College,
Cambridge

Clergymen

When the head of a college is a clergyman, his ecclesiastical rank is shown before his name or appointment, e.g.:

The Very Reverend the Dean,
Christ Church *or*
The Very Reverend John Smith, D.D.,
Dean of Blank Hall

VERBAL ADDRESS

Formally (at a function) (for Universities of Oxford and Cambridge) 'Mr. Dean', 'Mr. President', 'Mr. Provost', and 'Mr. Warden', (note that this form is inappropriate for Master, Principal, or Rector), otherwise, Sir *or* Madam, Dean, President, Master, Provost, Warden, etc., *or* by name.

DESCRIPTION IN CONVERSATION

By his appointment, i.e. The Master (of Blank College), *or* by name.

PROFESSOR

A Professor is addressed by name, e.g. Professor John Jones. Though he may also hold a doctorate he continues to be addressed as a Professor while he has a chair.

Should a Professor be in Holy Orders he is addressed as the Reverend Professor John Smith and known verbally as Professor Smith.

Should a Professor be a Canon (or have higher ecclesiastical rank) he is sometimes known as Professor Smith, but strictly speaking the ecclesiastical rank supersedes the academic. Thus, a canon should be known as Canon Smith rather than as Professor Smith, but in practice this is a matter of personal choice. The academic style is used more often within a university, and the ecclesiastical style outside.

On the Continent, the style Professor the Reverend . . . is sometimes adopted.

When a Professor retires from his (or her) chair at a university and emeritus rank is conferred, the Professor Emeritus or Emeritus Professor[1] continues to be addressed as previously in correspondence. On the Continent the word 'Emeritus' is sometimes used after Professor.

For the use of the term Professor in America, see p. 120.

BEGINNING OF LETTER

Formal	Dear Sir *or* Madam
Social	Dear Professor Jones (should he be a peer, Dear Lord Kirkcudbright, *or* a knight, Dear Sir Henry (Jones))

ENDING OF LETTER

Formal	Yours faithfully (see also p. 2)
Social	Yours sincerely

ENVELOPE

Professor John Smith

'Professor' precedes any title held, e.g. Professor Lord Blank,[2] or Professor Sir Henry Smith,[2] Professor Dame Mary Smith[2] or Professor the Hon. John Robinson.[2]

Should he be in Holy Orders, the ecclesiastical rank precedes the academic, i.e. The Reverend Professor John Jones.

If a Canon: The Reverend Canon Edward Jones, or The

---

[1] University of London usage.
[2] It is not customary in *formal* usage to combine the style emanating from other sources, i.e. Professor, with titles conferred by the Sovereign. In social usage this is not uncommon, though deprecated by purists.

Reverend Professor Edward Jones, as desired (usually on a university matter the latter is used, otherwise the former).

The form 'The Reverend Canon Professor Edward Jones' is never used as it is too cumbersome.

VERBAL ADDRESS

Professor Jones

Should he possess a title, he is known as Lord Blank, or Sir John Jones.

If a Canon, Canon Jones or Professor Jones, as desired (see also Envelope).

DESCRIPTION IN CONVERSATION

As for Verbal Address.

DOCTOR

The recipient of a doctorate conferred by a university or other body, such as The Council for National Academic Awards, is entitled to be addressed as 'Doctor'. See *University Degrees* (p. 269).

The exception to the above is a surgeon (also in England and Wales, a gynæcologist) who is known as 'Mr.'. See *Medical Section* (p. 230).

The recipient of an honorary doctorate is entitled to the style of 'Doctor', In practice, when a well-known figure outside the academic world receives an honorary doctorate (or doctorates) the recipient does not always use this style if he has other prefixes, e.g. a peer, a high-ranking Service officer, a judge, etc. This, however, is a matter of the recipient's choice.

BEGINNING OF LETTER

Formal	Dear Sir
Social	Dear Doctor Jones
If a peer	Dear Lord Blank
Or a baronet or knight	Dear Sir Henry (Jones)

ENDING OF LETTER

Formal	Yours faithfully (see also p. 2)
Social	Yours sincerely

It is a matter of choice whether the appropriate degree(s) should be placed after his (or her) name or to address the doctor as Dr. John *or* Dr. Mary Smith, though by custom, a Doctor of Divinity always has the letters D.D. appended after his name. This arises because many recipients, such as an archbishop or bishop, are not normally addressed as Dear Doctor Blank. See also Medical Section, p. 228.

In the University of Oxford the appropriate letters are usually omitted, and the envelope is addressed 'Dr. John Smith', irrespective of the particular doctorate. In the University of Cambridge both forms are used, and in the University of London the letters to signify the particular doctorate are usually given. It is, however, recommended that the letters, where known, are used to distinguish him (or her) from a medical practitioner who is known as 'Doctor', whether or not he is a doctor of medicine. (See *Medical Section.*)

> The Very Rev. John Jones, D.D.
> Lord Blank, D.Lit.
> Sir Henry Robinson, Mus.D.
> John Smith, Esq., LL.D.
> Mrs. Joan Smith, Ph.D.

See also *University Degrees* (p. 269) and *Order of Placing Degrees* (p. 270).

VERBAL ADDRESS

Dr. Smith, unless he is a peer, baronet, or knight, then by his appropriate rank.

DESCRIPTION IN CONVERSATION

As for Verbal Address.

Other Academic Appointments

The following are the usual appointments:

SCHOOLS

Boys

Headmaster, although there are certain variations, e.g.:

> High Master of St. Paul's, Manchester Grammar School, etc.
> Head Master of Westminster
> Master of Dulwich, Marlborough, Wellington, etc.

Rector of Edinburgh and Glasgow Academies, etc.
Warden of Radley, St. Edward's School, Oxford, etc.

Girls

Usually Headmistress or Principal.

Training and Technical Colleges and Schools
Usually Principal or Warden.

Teaching Hospitals, Medical Colleges, Schools and Institutes
Usually Dean.

Adult Education Centres and University Settlements
Usually Warden.

BEGINNING OF LETTER

The Head of a College, School, Educational Centre, etc., may be
addressed by his (or her) appointment if the letter concerns his
college, etc., but more usually by name.
    If the former style is adopted, then:
        Dear Headmaster,
        Dear Principal,
        Dear Warden, etc.
    Others holding staff appointments are addressed by name.

ENDING OF LETTER

Formal	Yours faithfully (see also p. 2)
Social	Yours sincerely

ENVELOPE

By appointment, i.e.:
        The Headmaster
        The Principal
        The Bursar
        The Secretary to the Principal, etc.
or by name.

VERBAL ADDRESS

        Headmaster, Principal, Warden, Dean, etc., *or* by name

DESCRIPTION IN CONVERSATION

        The Headmaster, Principal, Warden, Dean, etc., *or* by name

University Degrees

Letters which denote a particular degree often vary according to the conferring university (see below). First degrees also vary, but are often B.A. in arts and B.Sc. in science. At Oxford and Cambridge, B.A. is the first degree conferred in both, but at Oxford B.Sc. is a higher degree. At the old Scottish Universities of St. Andrews, Glasgow, Aberdeen, and Edinburgh, and at Dundee, the first arts degree is that of M.A.

In social correspondence it is generally only necessary to place letters after the name to denote a doctor's degree, and even then the term 'Dr. John Smith' is sometimes used on the envelope (see p. 267). Lesser degrees are usually omitted.

An exception is generally made for the inclusion of the degree of Bachelor of Divinity (B.D.), and in the faculty of Medicine, see *Medical Section* (p. 231).

Some graduates add their universities in parentheses after their degrees, such as in a school prospectus, e.g. Mr. John Smith, M.A. (Cantab.). The university is not included by correspondents or in lists of names, etc.

LISTS OF UNIVERSITY GRADUATES

In a formal list, such as of patrons, officers, and directors of societies and firms, *all* degrees may be placed after the name (with the exceptions mentioned below), but if a person has several Crown or other honours and awards, it is a matter of personal choice or discretion which, if any, should be included. This is particularly applicable to well-known public figures who have acquired many honorary degrees.[1]

The following rules are normally applied:

(1) The degree of B.A. is not accorded to those who have proceeded to M.A.

(2) The degree of a Bachelor or Master is not accorded to those who have proceeded to the second or final degree (e.g. one does not include 'B.Sc.' *and* M.Sc., 'M.Sc.' *and* D.Sc. or 'LL.B.' *and* LL.D.).

[1] In some lists published by the University of Cambridge (e.g. the Register of the Senate and the Roll of the Regent House), it is the custom to list the highest degree only in the case of doctors. The exception to this rule is the degree of Doctor of Philosophy, which is not a higher doctorate at the university.

(3) The degree of M.A. is not accorded to a doctor of a university where a doctor's degree is considered to include the M.A. degree.

ORDER OF PLACING DEGREES

The order of placing the appropriate letters after the name depends upon:

(a) The precedence of faculties within the conferring university.

(b) Whether a particular university places the degrees conferred in 'descending order' (i.e. in order of seniority), or in 'ascending order' (i.e. in the order by which they are taken).

The 'descending order' follows the same system applied to other honours and qualifications. Most universities, however, adopt the 'ascending order' system, which has the advantage of following the sequence of events.

Not only does the position of the appropriate letters vary according to the awarding university but also either the name of the degree or the letters to indicate it:

1.	Doctor of Civil Law	Oxford	D.C.L.
	Doctor of Law	Cambridge	LL.D.
	Doctor of Laws	Other universities	LL.D.
2.	Doctor of Literature	Cambridge Leeds Liverpool Manchester and Sheffield	Litt.D.
	Doctor of Literature	London and Belfast	D.Lit.
	Doctor of Letters	Oxford and other universities	D.Litt.
3.	Doctor of Music	Cambridge and Manchester	Mus.D.
	Doctor of Music	Oxford and other universities	D.Mus.
4.	Doctor of Philosophy	Oxford	D.Phil.
		Other universities	Ph.D.

This variance is particularly marked between degrees conferred at Oxford and Cambridge. When only a few universities existed the difference showed the conferring university.

The order of degrees conferred by four universities are given below as examples, viz:

Oxford
Cambridge
London
Birmingham

Oxford and Cambridge have both adopted the 'descending order' and are included because they are untypical.

London and Birmingham, and most other universities adopt the 'ascending order', and are included as being representative of those who have adopted this system.

UNIVERSITY OF OXFORD   UNIVERSITY OF CAMBRIDGE

(Degrees are placed in descending order)

UNIVERSITY OF OXFORD	UNIVERSITY OF CAMBRIDGE
D.D.	D.D.
D.C.L.	LL.D.
D.M.	M.D.
D.Litt. ⎤	Sc.D. and Litt.D.
D.Sc. ⎥	Mus. D.
D.Mus. ⎬ (if also M.A.)	B.D.
D.Phil. ⎥	Ph.D.
M.S. ⎦	M.Chir.
M.A.	M.A.
D.Litt. ⎤	LL.M.
D.Sc. ⎥	Mus.M.
D.Mus. ⎬ (if not also M.A.)	M.Sc. and M.Litt.
D.Phil. ⎥	M.B.
M.S. ⎦	B.Chir.
B.D.	LL.B.
B.C.L.	B.A.
B.M.	Mus.B.
B.S.	Vet. M.B.
B.Litt.	B.Ed.
B.Sc.	
B.Mus.	
B.Phil.	
B.A.	
B.Ed.	

UNIVERSITY OF LONDON

(Degrees are placed in ascending order)

First Degrees

B.D.	M.Vet.Med.
B.A.	M.Sc.
LL.B.	M.Sc.(Econ.)
B.Mus.	M.Ed.
M.B., B.S.	
B.D.S.	*Higher Master's Degrees*
B.Pharm.	M.Phil.
B.Vet.Med.	
B.Sc.	*Doctorate*
B.Sc.(Eng.)	Ph.D.
B.Sc.(Econ.)	
B.Sc.(Soc.)	*Higher Doctorates*
B.Ed.	D.D.
	D.Lit.
	LL.D.
	D.Mus.
	M.D.
	M.S.
Master's Degrees	M.D.S.
M.Th.	D.Vet.Med.
M.A.	D.Sc.
LL.M.	D.Sc.(Eng.)
M.Mus.	D.Sc.(Econ.)

UNIVERSITY OF BIRMINGHAM

(Degrees are placed in ascending order)

First Degrees	*Master's Degrees*
B.Sc.	M.Sc.
B.A.	M.A.
B.Mus.	B.D.
M.B., Ch.B.	M.Ed.[1]
B.D.S.	Ch.M.
B.Com.	M.D.S.
B.Soc.Sc.	M.Com.
LL.B.	M.Soc.Sc.
B.Ed.	LL.M.

[1] Placed here, as in faculty of Arts.

Doctorate	D.Mus.
Ph.D.	D.D.
	M.D.
Higher Doctorates	D.Soc.Sc.
D.Sc.	LL.D.
D.Litt.	

New degrees may be conferred from time to time, according to changes in faculty, e.g. Bachelor of Education is now conferred by London University, but there is provision for the degree Master of Education.

For degrees conferred by other universities, both in the United Kingdom and Commonwealth, the 'Commonwealth Universities Yearbook' should be consulted.

HONORARY DEGREES

Recipients of honorary degrees are entitled to the same letters as university graduates.

In certain universities, e.g. Essex, York, and Stirling, an honorary doctorate is conferred 'of the university', according to the system in France, instead of in a particular faculty. The appropriate letters after the name are 'D.Univ.', except Essex where 'D.U.' is used.

NON-UNIVERSITY DEGREES

The most usual of these degrees are those conferred by the Council for National Academic Awards. These are the first degrees of B.A. and B.Sc., those for post-graduate study, M.A. and M.Sc., and for research, M.Phil. and Ph.D. In addition to honorary degrees conferred, there is a proposal to award the higher doctorates of D.Sc. and D.Tech. for work of high distinction.

The Royal College of Art confers the following degrees:

Doctor	Dr. R.C.A.
Master of Design	M. Des. R.C.A.
Master of Art	M. Art. R.C.A.

These letters are placed after the name, e.g. John Smith, Esq., Dr. R.C.A.

The Council of Industrial Design also confers degrees.

Part V

OFFICIAL AND SOCIAL OCCASIONS

Royal Invitations

Invitations to Official Functions

Invitations to Private Functions

Wedding Invitations

Applications for the Royal Enclosure, Ascot

List of Names on Programmes, Brochures, etc.

Joint Forms of Address

Christmas Cards

Visiting, Professional and Business Cards

Table Plans

Specimen Table Plans

Guests Lists

OFFICIAL AND SOCIAL OCCASIONS

Royal Invitations

THE SOVEREIGN

Her Majesty's invitations are sent by:
The Lord Steward of the Household
> to a State Banquet.

The Lord Chamberlain
> to all major Court functions, such as a Garden Party, Wedding, Funeral or Memorial Service.

The Master of the Household
> to all domestic functions given by The Queen at Buckingham Palace, or where The Queen is resident.

All invitations from The Queen are *commands*, and a reply should be so worded, addressed to the member of Her Majesty's Household who has issued the invitation.

An invitation to a Garden Party is accompanied by a notice which states that there is no need to acknowledge receipt, unless the guest is unable to attend.

The Master of the Household

is Commanded by Her Majesty to invite

Mr. and Mrs. John Brown

to an Afternoon Party at Sandringham House

on Thursday, January 10th from 4 to 6.30 o'clock

ACCEPTANCE

Colonel Sir Henry and Lady Smith present their compliments to the Master of the Household, and have the honour to obey Her Majesty's Command to luncheon on May 10th at 12.30 o'clock.

NON-ACCEPTANCE

The reason for non-acceptance should be stated. 'A prior engagement' is not considered to be a sufficient reason for not obeying The Queen's Command.

> Colonel and Mrs. John Brown present their compliments to the Master of the Household, and much regret that they will be unable to obey Her Majesty's Command to........
> ....on.............................owing to the illness of Mrs. John Brown.

A LETTER OF THANKS

This is addressed to the member of the Household who forwarded the invitation, in which the writer asks him to convey his thanks to Her Majesty.

QUEEN ELIZABETH THE QUEEN MOTHER

Invitations are sent by The Comptroller of the Household to Queen Elizabeth The Queen Mother, except on very formal occasions, such as the wedding of The Princess Margaret, when

---

The Comptroller of the Household of
Queen Elizabeth The Queen Mother
is Commanded by Her Majesty
to invite
Sir Henry and Lady White

to............................ at............... on............

---

they were sent by The Lord Chamberlain to Queen Elizabeth The Queen Mother.

Invitations from The Queen Mother are *commands*, and should be so answered.

ACCEPTANCE AND NON-ACCEPTANCE

As for The Sovereign.

OTHER MEMBERS OF THE ROYAL FAMILY

Invitations from other Members of the Royal Family are not 'commands' and will usually be forwarded by a Member of their Household to whom a reply should be addressed.

In other respects, as for The Sovereign.

INVITATIONS TO MEMBERS OF THE ROYAL FAMILY

(See also *Official Functions*, p. 282.)

An invitation to a member of the Royal Family, i.e. those with the titles of 'His (*or* Her) Royal Highness', is extended by letter usually through the Private Secretary. An invitation for an official function outside London is usually extended through the Lord Lieutenant of the county concerned. The title of a Royal guest is shown in full, e.g.

> Her Majesty The Queen
> His Royal Highness The Prince Philip, Duke of Edinburgh
> Their Royal Highnesses The Duke and Duchess of Kent

A Member of a branch of the Royal Family, apart from a Royal Peer or Peeress, is given the appropriate description in all written communications, e.g.

> His Royal Highness Prince Michael *of Kent*

A married Princess is shown with her husband's title or name on an invitation and the envelope, e.g.

> Her Royal Highness The Princess Margaret, Countess of Snowdon

If the invitation includes her husband she is still described as above, e.g.

> Her Royal Highness The Princess Margaret, Countess of Snowdon, and The Earl of Snowdon

In these cases the Princess appears *before* her husband.

The word 'The' before 'Prince' (*or* 'Princess') is restricted to The Prince Philip, Duke of Edinburgh and the children of a Sovereign. Other members of the Royal Family without peerages are described as His (*or* Her) Royal Highness Prince (*or* Princess).

OTHER ARRANGEMENTS FOR ROYAL GUESTS AT FUNCTIONS

(See *Official Functions*, p. 282.)

Invitations to Official Functions

For a function given by an organization, society, etc., the invitation is usually issued on a card, which may be engraved in script from a copper plate, or printed (in script or Roman type). This should make clear the following:

(a) *The nature of the function*, e.g. For the Opening of . . . by . . .; To mark the Centenary of . . .; For a Dinner, etc.

(b) *Where the function is to be held*, e.g. at The Splendide, Park Lane, W.1. Ballroom entrance.

(c) *The date of the function.*

(d) *The time of the function*, e.g. 12.45 for 1.0 p.m. (for a luncheon); 6.0–8.0 p.m. (for a reception); 7.30 for 8.0 p.m. (for a dinner). When it is desired to indicate the time at which a function will end, there are two alternatives: '8.0 p.m.–Midnight', or '8.0 p.m. Cars (or carriages) at Midnight'. For a formal ceremony, such as the laying of a foundation stone, unveiling a statue, etc., for which an invitation gives only the starting time, e.g. at 3.0 p.m., the card should also bear some such phrase as: 'Guests are requested to be seated by 2.45 p.m.'.

(e) *The dress.* For a day function (including a cocktail hour reception) this need only be specified if it is to be other than lounge suit, e.g. morning dress, academic robes, etc. For an evening function it should always be specified, e.g. evening dress (which means tailcoat with white tie), dinner jacket, lounge suit, uniform, etc. The word 'decorations' is added if these are to be worn with either evening dress or dinner jacket.

To indicate that a member of the Royal Family will be present, one of the following is engraved or printed at the top of the card:

In the gracious presence of Her Majesty The Queen

In the gracious presence of Her Majesty Queen Elizabeth The Queen Mother

In the presence of His (or Her) Royal Highness The Prince (or The Princess) . . .

Note. The word 'gracious' is included only for The Queen and The Queen Mother.

If it is particularly desired to indicate that an important non-royal guest will be present, this may be done in the form: 'To meet (or in honour of) the Right Honourable the Lord Mayor of London and the Lady Mayoress'.

Examples :

> *The President, Sir John Blank, K.B.E., and Council of*
> *The National Society of . . .*
> *request the pleasure of the company of*
>
> ....
>
> *at their Twenty-First Annual Banquet*
> *to be held at the Hotel Magnificent, Manchester, (Oak Suite)*
> *on Saturday 27th February, 1971,*
> *at 7.30 for 8.0 p.m.*
>
> *Evening Dress* *R.S.V.P.*
> *or Dinner Jacket* *The Secretary,*
> *123, Piccadilly,*
> *Decorations* *Manchester, 1.*

> *The Chairman and Governors of*
> *The Royal College of . . .*
> *have the honour to invite*
>
> ....
>
> *to the College Hall*
> *at 3.0 p.m. on Saturday 29th February, 1971,*
> *for the Presentation of Awards by*
> *Her Royal Highness the Duchess of . . .*
>
> *Guests should be* *An answer is*
> *seated by* *requested to the*
> *2.45 p.m.* *Bursar before*
> *20th February.*

To assist the Toastmaster (announcer), or to prevent gate-crashers, 'Please bring this card with you', may be added at the bottom of the card. Alternatively (and preferably for an evening function, since a large card cannot be carried easily in a pocket or handbag), the following wording may be added: 'An admission card will be sent on receipt of your acceptance'.

The following is an example of an admission card, which should be printed in Roman type and should not exceed $4\frac{1}{2} \times 3\frac{1}{2}$ inches in size:

Please admit

....

to The Dorchester, Park Lane (Ballroom entrance)
for the Lord Mayor of Westminster's Reception
on Saturday 29th February, 1971,
from 8.0–11.0 p.m.

To be handed
to the announcer.

Note 1.—An admission card may also be used to indicate a seat number.

Note 2.—Separate admission cards should be sent for a husband and his wife, even though they have both been included on the same invitation card.

Additional information or instructions, e.g. about car parking, are best given on a separate sheet sent with the invitation, or with the admission card.

MEMBERS OF THE ROYAL FAMILY

An invitation to a member of the Royal Family is always extended by letter, either through the Lord Lieutenant of the County or to the Private Secretary, the latter being the general rule in London, the former elsewhere. A printed invitation is not sent except that a specimen may be forwarded to the Private Secretary, if desired.

NAMES ON INVITATIONS

Invitations to official functions give the host by his office and/or name. The latter is engraved, or printed, with his full title, rank, etc., and followed by his decorations, etc. (Note, invitations to private functions are treated differently, see p. 287). Prefixes such as His Grace, His Excellency, The Right Worshipful, are, however, omitted. Exceptions are:

(a) The prefix The Right Honourable is included for a Privy Counsellor who is not a peer.
(b) The prefix The Honourable (Hon.) and the suffix Esquire (Esq.) are never used. In both cases a gentleman is shown as Mr. John Smith.

Examples are:

The Duke of Loamshire, K.G., M.C., P.C.
The Lord Mayor and the Lady Mayoress of Blanktown
The President of the Royal Academy, Sir John Brown, K.B.E. (and Lady Brown)
Rear-Admiral the Earl of Blank, C.B., D.S.O. (and the Countess of Blank)
Colonel Sir John Blank, Bt., M.V.O. (and Lady Blank)
The Master of the Worshipful Company of Holeborers (and Mrs. White)
The Right Honourable William Black, LL.D., Q.C., M.P.

The guest is written on the card, either in the form of his office or by name. The latter should include his prefix as well as his title, rank and decorations, etc., but exceptions (a) and (b) above apply. The younger sons of a Duke or a Marquess are shown as, e.g. Lord John Russell, and the daughters of a Duke, Marquess or Earl, as, e.g. Lady Jane Gilbert.

The form 'and Lady' may be used when it is not practicable to ascertain whether a gentleman is married, if it is desired to allow a gentleman to bring, say, his daughter instead of his wife, and if it is desired to allow a bachelor to bring a partner. For ladies invited in their own right, etc., the comparable form is 'and Escort'.

Examples are:

The Right Honourable the Prime Minister (and Mrs. Philip Head)
The Right Honourable the Lord Mayor of London (and the Lady Mayoress)
The President of The Royal Society
His Excellency the Swedish Ambassador (and Madame Blank)
His Grace the Duke of Loamshire, K.G. (and Her Grace the Duchess of Loamshire)

His Eminence the Cardinal Archbishop of Westminster

The Right Honourable the Earl of Wessex (and the Countess of Wessex)

General Sir John Cannon, K.C.B., D.S.O., M.C. (and Lady Cannon)

The Dean of Westminster, the Very Reverend James D. Brown, K.C.V.O., M.A., D.D. (and Mrs. Brown)

Professor Albert Blossom, F.R.S., M.A. (and Mrs. Blossom)

Lord and Lady John Russell

Captain and Mrs. George Rifle (*but* Captain George Foremast, R.N. and Mrs. Foremast)

His Honour Judge Mace (and Lady)

Mr. and Mrs. Paul Neville

Dr. and Mrs. Henry James

Miss Dorothy Trubshaw and Escort

Note 1.—An invitation to a clergyman with the rank of The Reverend, and his wife, should be in the form: the Reverend John and Mrs. Henderson.

Note 2.—A retired officer who has taken Holy Orders is addressed by his ecclesiastical rank only.

Note 3.—An invitation to a pair of guests of some relationship other than husband and wife takes one of the following forms:

A brother and sister: Mr. John Brown and Miss Elizabeth Brown

A mother and son: Mrs. George Curruthers and Mr. William Curruthers

Unmarried sisters: The Misses Smith

Note 4.—An invitation to an adult son is usually sent separately from that to his parents.

THE NAME ON ADMISSION CARDS

The guest is shown on an admission card by office *or* by name, in the form in which he is to be announced to the host and hostess. If by name, this is limited to his title, rank and name, except that the following prefixes should be included:

His Grace—for the Archbishops of Canterbury and York

His Excellency—for Ambassadors and High Commissioners

The Right Honourable, The Right Worshipful, The Worshipful, etc.—for Civic Heads

A husband and wife should each be issued with a separate admission card.

Examples are :

The Right Honourable the Prime Minister	Mrs. Head
The Right Honourable the Lord Mayor (of London)	The Lady Mayoress (of London)
The President of The Royal Society	
His Excellency[1] the Swedish Ambassador	Madame Blank
The Duke of Loamshire	The Duchess of Loamshire
His Grace the Archbishop of Canterbury	Mrs. Blank
The Cardinal Archbishop of Westminster	
The Earl of Wessex	The Countess of Wessex
General Sir John Cannon	Lady Cannon
The Dean of Westminster	Mrs. Brown
Professor Albert Blossom	Mrs. Blossom
Lord Russell	Lady Russell
Captain Rifle	Mrs. Rifle
His Honour Judge Mace	Miss Single
Mr. Neville	Mrs. Neville
Dr. James	Mrs. James
Miss Trubshaw	Mr. Johnson

THE ENVELOPE

An invitation to an official function should normally be addressed only to the husband, even though his wife is also invited. He is given his full prefix, title, rank, decorations, etc. as for a formal letter. See the appropriate section.

REPLIES

These, which should be on headed paper to show the sender's address, are best illustrated by examples:

(a) Mr. and Mrs. William Brown thank the President and Council of the National Society of . . . for their invitation[2] for Saturday, 29th February, which they accept with much pleasure (*or* which they have the honour to accept).

---

[1] May be abbreviated to H.E.—but *not* by the announcer.
[2] *Or* kind invitation

(b) Lord and Lady White thank the Master of the Worshipful Company of Holeborers for his invitation[1] for Saturday, 29th February, which they much regret being unable to accept. (A reason may be given, e.g. owing to a previous engagement; because of absence abroad, etc.).

(c) The Reverend John and Mrs. White thank the Dean and Chapter of . . . for their invitation[1] for Saturday, 29th February. They accept with much pleasure for the service in the Abbey but regret that they are unable to accept for the subsequent reception.

The date is placed underneath.

REPLY CARDS

The organization of a large function is greatly facilitated by the use of reply cards (printed in Roman type) which are sent out with the invitations. These should be of small postcard size and may be numbered serially for ready reference to the invitation list, which it is seldom practicable to draw up in alphabetical order.

An example is:

Serial No.

The Lord Mayor of Birmingham's Civic Banquet
Tuesday 29th February, 1971

Name(s) ....
(Block letters, please.)

*Has/have much pleasure in accepting the invitation
of the Lord Mayor and Lady Mayoress
*Regret(s) being unable to accept the invitation of the
Lord Mayor and Lady Mayoress

*Please delete whichever is not applicable.

A reply card may also be used to obtain other information, e.g. 'I shall/I shall not* require car parking facilities'.

A guest should *always* use the printed card for his reply. Should

[1] *Or* kind invitation.

he wish to add anything, such as an explanation for his inability to accept, this should be done by a separate letter.

The reply to an invitation which takes the form '. . . and Lady', or '. . . and Escort', should always give the name of the chosen lady or escort.

Invitations to Private Functions

There are two kinds of invitations to formal functions, which (unless time is short) are prepared on cards engraved in script from a copper plate, viz.

(a) For very formal luncheon and dinner parties.
(b) 'At Home' invitations for all other parties, e.g. dances, receptions, garden parties, luncheons, dinners and suppers.

Invitations to more informal functions may be extended by letter, telephone, etc.

(a) *Invitations to very formal luncheon and dinner parties.*

Major and Mrs. John Brown

Sir John and Lady Brent

request the pleasure of * *your company*
at Dinner
on Tuesday, 29th February
at 8 for 8.30 o'clock

R.S.V.P.
   2300, *Cadogan Square,*   *Black tie*
   *S.W.*1.

---

* *or* 'honour of'
Example 1

These are engraved on a thick card of good texture, usually about $6 \times 4\frac{1}{2}$ inches in size (or slightly larger if necessary), and are prepared in the name of both the host and hostess, see Example 1. If time is short, they may be printed. They contain some of the information as for an official function (p. 280) but with certain important exceptions, which are given on pages 291–294.

Alternatively, the more old-fashioned style of 'request the pleasure of the company of', may be adopted. In this case the guests' names are added on the next line, in place of the top left-hand corner.

If the luncheon or dinner takes place at an address other than that to which the replies are to be sent, e.g. at an hotel, this is

---

Dr. and Mrs. Edward Shaw

Lady White

requests the pleasure of * *your company*

for Dinner

on Wednesday, 18th May

at Claridge's

R.S.V.P.
6004 *Berkeley Street,*
*W.*1.

8 for 8.30 p.m.
Black tie †

---

* *or* 'honour of'   † if desired to include dress

Example 2

---

stated on a line after the date. The time may be placed either after the date, or at the bottom right hand corner before, or in place of, the form of dress.

It often happens that a host or hostess keeps a stock of invitation cards engraved in script from a copper plate. The occasion, date, time, and also place (if away from home) are then added. See

Example 2. This card may also be prepared with the wording 'request the pleasure of the company of ', and the guests' names are then added.

If the luncheon or dinner is not a very formal one, an 'at Home' card may be used. See Example 5. The time, e.g. '12.45 for 1.15 o'clock' (*or* p.m.) or '8 for 8.30 o'clock' (*or* p.m.) is usually sufficient indication of the occasion.

(b) *'At Home' Invitations.*

These invitations, which for formal occasions are usually engraved on a thick card of good texture about $6 \times 4\frac{1}{2}$ inches in

---

Mr. and Mrs. Crispin Ashburnham

Mrs. Hugh Harrington

at Home

Wednesday, 30th June

R.S.V.P.   6.45 p.m.
   2555 *Cumberland*   *Mercers' Hall,*
      Terrace,   *Ironmonger Lane,*
         N.W.1.   E.C.2.

Please bring this card with you.

Example 3

size (or slightly larger if necessary), are prepared in the name of the hostess only, in the case of married couples. If the time of the function is not a sufficient indication as to its nature, the latter may be stated on the card, e.g. 'Dancing 10 o'clock'. If the invitation extends from say 6 o'clock to 8.30, the description 'cocktails', 'wine', or 'sherry' etc. is unnecessary, though it is often included. See Examples 3 and 4.

For many 'at Home' functions *except balls*, a smaller card may be used, usually $4\frac{1}{2} \times 3\frac{1}{2}$ inches, on which is engraved (or printed) the hostess's name, 'at Home', R.S.V.P. and her address. A stock of these cards is purchased for various functions. Other details are completed by the hostess. See Example 5.

Commander and Mrs John Eyre-Butler

Lady Elizabeth Berkeley

at Home

Monday, June 1st

R.S.V.P.
    Faversham Hall,
    Tinbury,   *Dancing*
    Essex.   *10.30 p.m.*

Example 4

For small informal parties a basic stock of 'at Home' cards may be purchased, which merely have 'at Home' and 'R.S.V.P.'

Miss Barbara Worth

Mrs. Richard Greene

at Home

Monday, May 12th

R.S.V.P.
    16, Argyll Lane, *Cocktails*
    W.8.   *6. 30 o'clock*

Example 5

engraved (or printed) on them. They are usually of the identical size of the above cards, $4\frac{1}{2} \times 3\frac{1}{2}$ inches. The hostess then adds her name, address, date, time, name of guests, and other necessary information.

HOST AND HOSTESS

The exact rank in the peerage of the host and/or hostess is given on all types of invitation. The word 'The' before a title is usually omitted for the ranks of Marquess and Earl, and invariably so for those of Viscount and Baron (e.g. Marchioness of Flintshire, Viscountess Longhurst).

No prefixes appear before the name, such as 'The Right Honourable', 'The Honourable' 'His Excellency', 'The Worshipful'.

No letters are placed after the name, such as those which signify decorations or degrees, or the letters 'Bt.'.

JOINT HOSTESSES

If there is more than one hostess, their names are placed one under the other. The first name corresponds to the address to

---

Miss Davina Firebrace and Partner

Mrs. Henry Waterhouse

Lady Black

Mrs. Sebastian Jones

at Home

for * Elizabeth, Henrietta and Fiona

Wednesday, June 6th

The Hyde Park Hotel

R.S.V.P.   *Dancing*
 757, *Bedford Square*,   10 *o'clock*
 W.C.1.
              Please bring this card with you.

---

* 'for their daughters', if applicable, may be inserted.

Example 6

which the replies are to be sent. See Example 6. If a joint party is to be held at a hostess's house and the replies are to be sent to her, her name is placed first on the invitation, irrespective of any title held.

If the hostesses are to deal with replies separately, their addresses are placed from left to right at the foot of the card, in the same order as their names.

OTHER INFORMATION ON THE INVITATION

'Decorations' on a *private* invitation implies that a member of the Royal Family is expected to be present. *Note*, the word does not have this meaning on an official invitation.

For functions where the hostess considers it to be necessary to indicate the dress expected to be worn, 'White tie' may be added for evening dress, 'Black tie' for dinner jackets, or 'Informal' for lounge suits. Otherwise she is content to leave this to the discretion of her guests.

If it is necessary to keep out gatecrashers, 'Please bring this card with you' may be added at the foot of the card.

If there is no information to the contrary, it is understood that the function is to be held at the address to which a reply is requested.

If the function takes place in the country, a map is often placed on the back of the card, or on a separate sheet.

ENCLOSURES

A separate slip is often sent, with times of trains, and such requests as 'Are you coming by road or rail?' or 'Do you want to be included in a dinner party, or a dinner party and house party?'

SENDING OUT INVITATIONS

If an invitation is extended and accepted verbally, e.g. by telephone, it should be confirmed by an invitation card on which 'R.S.V.P.' has been deleted, and 'To remind' substituted. This is not required to be acknowledged.

NAMES OF GUESTS

They are written in the top left corner, except for formal luncheon/dinner invitations designed to include them in the middle of the card. See also Official Invitations (p. 280), but the following should be noted.

(a) No prefixes, such as 'The Right Honourable', 'The Honourable', 'His Excellency', 'The Worshipful' are given.

(b) No letters after the name, such as those which signify decorations or degrees, or the letters 'Bt.' are given.

(c) All peers and peeresses, apart from Dukes and Duchesses, who are referred to by these titles, are given in the form of 'Lord and Lady Blank'. This is the established custom for all functions except the very important, when the exact rank in the peerage may be given.

(d) Grown-up sons and daughters are usually sent separate invitations, even when they live at home, but when their exact names, or their availability, are not known, it is permissible to add 'and family' after their parents' names.

(e) The addition 'and partner' (*not* 'and friend') may be added to allow a guest to bring an unspecified escort or partner with her/him.

(f) During Ascot week and other similar occasions and festivals for which house parties are given, invitations may show after the names of the guests 'and house party'.

Examples of showing guests are:

The Lord Mayor (and Lady Mayoress) of London
The Swedish Ambassador (and Madame Blank)
The Duke (and Duchess) of Loamshire
The Archbishop of Canterbury (and Mrs. Jones)
Lord (and Lady) Wessex
General Sir John (and Lady) Cannon
Air Commodore (and Mrs.) John Plane
Professor (and Mrs.) Albert Blossom
The Dean of Rochester (and Mrs. Proudie)
The Archdeacon of Exeter (and Mrs. Pugh)
Canon (and Mrs.) John Porter
The Reverend John (and Mrs.) Henderson
Dr. (and Mrs.) John Homer
Mr. (and Mrs.) John Brown
Miss Dorothy Brown

For other relationships, see p. 284, note 3. The ranks of officers in the Services should not be abbreviated. Sub-Lieutenants, Royal Navy, Lieutenants and 2nd Lieutenants in the Army and Royal Marines, and Flying Officers and Pilot Officers, Royal Air Force, are all shown as 'Mr. John Blank'.

ENVELOPE

An invitation to both husband and wife is addressed to the wife only. A guest is given his (*or* her) full prefix, title, rank, decorations, etc., as for a formal letter.

REPLIES

These are sent on writing paper with the address, as for Official Functions (p. 285). They are addressed to the hostess even when the invitation is a joint one from the host and hostess.

When invitations are extended to unnamed guests such as 'and partner', 'and family', the reply should contain the names of those who will attend. The substitution of a named guest is only allowed by permission of the hostess.

Wedding invitations

Wedding invitations by custom are engraved and consist of four pages, the size being usually standardized at $5\frac{1}{2} \times 7$ inches.

The wording, which depends upon who is the host and/or hostess, and their relationship to the bride, is given below. If desired, 'honour' can be used in place of 'pleasure' in all the examples.

If the church is too small to accommodate all the guests, the invitation should be worded to read 'at the Reception to be held after the marriage of their daughter Caroline to Mr. Christopher Henry Herbert, at The Old Manor House, Little Wotton, Gloucestershire, on Wednesday, 14th March 1971'. In this case a leaflet should be placed inside the invitation to give the reason, e.g.:

> 'Owing to the small size of Little Wotton Church it is only possible to ask a very few guests to the Service. We hope you will forgive this invitation being to the Reception only'.

In no circumstances is a guest invited to the wedding but not to the reception.

If the bridegroom is an officer in the Services, his rank must not be abbreviated. Lieutenants and Sub-Lieutenants, Royal Navy, retain their ranks, with 'Royal Navy' added after the name. Lieutenants and 2nd Lieutenants are described as 'Mr.' with their Regiment or Corps placed after their name. Flying Officers and Pilot Officers are described as 'Mr.', followed by 'Royal Air Force'. The words 'Royal Navy', the appropriate Regiment and 'Royal Air Force' are usually placed in slightly smaller lettering on the next line, under the surname. Alternatively, the bridegroom may prefer to be shown merely as 'Mr. John Blank'.

The names of guests are written on the top left-hand of the invitation, as for other invitations.

1. *The following is a specimen invitation where both parents of the bride are the host and hostess:*

Miss Rosemary Wallop

Lieutenant-Colonel and Mrs. John Standish

request the pleasure of

your company at the marriage

of their daughter

Caroline

to

Mr. Christopher Henry Herbert

at St. Paul's Church, Knightsbridge,

on Wednesday, 14th March, 1971

at 3 o'clock

and afterwards at

The Hyde Park Hotel

R.S.V.P.

Charlford Manor,

Washington,

Sussex.

---

2. The bride's mother is the only hostess

>Mrs. John Standish
>requests the pleasure of
>your company at the marriage
>of her daughter
>Caroline, etc.

3. The bride's father is the only host

>Mr. John Standish
>requests the pleasure of
>your company at the marriage
>of his daughter
>Caroline, etc.

4. The bride's mother and stepfather are the host and hostess

The bride's surname may be included if desired if she has not adopted her stepfather's.

>Mr. and Mrs. John Forsyte
>request the pleasure of
>your company at the marriage
>of her daughter
>Caroline, etc.

5. The bride's father and stepmother are the host and hostess

>Mr. and Mrs. John Standish
>request the pleasure of
>your company at the marriage
>of his daughter
>Caroline, etc.

6. The bride's stepmother is the hostess

>Mrs. John Standish
>requests the pleasure of
>your company at the marriage
>of her stepdaughter
>Caroline, etc.

7. The bride's parents have been divorced, but they are the joint host and hostess

If the bride's parents have married again, the subsequent husband and wife do not play a prominent part at the wedding.

Mr. John King
and
Mrs. George Tremayne*
request the pleasure of
your company at the marriage
of their daughter
Sybil, etc.

8. *The bride's relatives, guardians or god-parent(s) are the host and hostess*

The bride's surname may be added if it is different from the host's and hostess's.

Admiral Sir John and Lady Fortescue
request the pleasure of
your company at the marriage
of their niece/ward/his (her) god-daughter
Alexandra, etc.

9. *The bride's relatives who are not a husband and wife are the host and hostess or joint hostesses (e.g. brother and sister, brother and sister-in-law, or sisters)*

As in Example 8, but the surname should be repeated (except for unmarried sisters), e.g.

Captain John Buckfast and Lady Buckfast
Mr. John Buckfast and Mrs. Henry Lowndes
Mr. John Buckfast and Mrs. Edward Buckfast
The Misses Buckfast
Miss Maria Buckfast and Mrs. William Bagshot

10. *The bride is the hostess*

Miss Emily Grattan
requests the pleasure of your company
at her marriage to Mr. John FitzGerald.

This style is preferred to the following alternatives:

(a) The pleasure of your company is requested at the marriage of Miss Emily Grattan and Mr. John Fitz-Gerald . . .
    or
(b) Mr. John FitzGerald and Miss Emily Grattan request the pleasure of your company at their marriage . . .

* 'Mrs. Frances King', if she has not remarried.

11. *Second and subsequent marriages*

As in Examples 1 to 9, as applicable, but when the bride is a widow she is described as 'Fleur, widow of Mr. Michael Mont', or if her marriage has been dissolved as 'Mrs. Fleur Mont'. If she has reverted to her maiden name, only her christian name is necessary.

If the bride is hostess, then as in Example 10, with her name as Mrs. John Smith or Mrs. Mary Smith, as applicable.

12. *Invitation to the reception only*

The wording is amended to read:

> request(s) the pleasure of your company
> at the reception following the marriage
> of their daughter Ann to .... at .... on ....

If the bride is hostess, the wording should read:

> . . . at the reception following her marriage, etc.
> to .... at .... on ....

POSTPONEMENTS AND CANCELLATIONS

A card, generally, $4\frac{1}{2} \times 3$ inches, is usually sent, with the wording printed on the following lines:

1. *Indefinite postponement*

'Owing to the recent death of Colonel Samuel Braithwaite, Mr. and Mrs. John Blank deeply regret that they are obliged to cancel the invitations to the marriage of their daughter Elizabeth to Mr. Mark Braithwaite on . . .'

Invitations are sent out again when the new date is fixed.

2. *Postponement to a later date*

'Owing to the illness of Mrs. Victor Scott, Mr. and Mrs. John Blank deeply regret that they are obliged to postpone the invitations to the marriage of their daughter Anne to Mr. John Scott at St. Margaret's Church, Westminster, from Thursday, 14th December 1970 to Wednesday, 2nd February 1971'.

3. *Cancellation of invitations because the wedding is to take place quietly*

'Owing to the recent death of her husband, Mrs. John Black much regrets that she is obliged to cancel the invitations to the marriage of her daughter Elizabeth to Captain Jonathan Trelawny, which will now take place very quietly on Wednesday 10th October, 1971'.

Invitations are then sent out by letter to near relations and close friends only.

4. *Cancellation of the wedding*

'Sir John and Lady Hopley announce that the marriage of their daughter Emma to Mr. Christopher Camberley, which was arranged on Wednesday 4th June, 1971, will not now take place'.

ENVELOPES AND REPLIES

These are as for invitations to private functions (p. 293).

Applications for the Royal Enclosure, Ascot

Admittance to the Royal Enclosure, Ascot, lies within the juris-diction of Her Majesty's Representative, The Duke of Norfolk. The number of those to whom the privilege of receiving vouchers is accorded is not disclosed; nor are the reasons why vouchers have been given, or withheld, explained.

Applications are submitted to Her Majesty's Representative *after* a notice has appeared in the press usually in the middle of March (not before). This gives a final date before the end of April, after which no further applications are considered.

It does not matter whether the wife or her husband applies for vouchers, but each application should include only members of a family; friends should make a separate application.

If vouchers are required by young people between the ages of seventeen and twenty-five inclusive at the date of the Royal Meeting, the age should be stated in brackets after the name, because their vouchers are issued at a reduction in price. Children below the age of seventeen are not admitted to the Royal Enclosure.

Visitors with overseas passports should apply for vouchers for the Royal Enclosure to their respective Ambassadors or High Commissioners and not to Her Majesty's Representative.

New applicants are eventually required to be sponsored.

THE APPLICATION

Colonel John Francis presents his compliments to Her Majesty's Representative and wishes to apply for vouchers to the Royal

Enclosure for his wife Mrs. John Francis, his son Mr. William Francis (aged 22), his daughter Miss Philippa Francis (aged 19) and himself.

ENVELOPE

> Her Majesty's Representative,
> Ascot Office,
> St. James's Palace,
> London, S.W.1.

List of Names on Programmes, Brochures, etc.

Names are usually listed in order of precedence.

Members of the Royal Family are always shown with the Royal Style, usually in full (e.g. 'Her Royal Highness . . .'). Others should be treated consistently, either in the formal or social style, whichever is adopted, e.g.

Formal style	*Social style*
His Grace the Duke of Blank	The Duke of Blank
Her Grace the Duchess of Blank	The Duchess of Blank
Her Grace Mary, Duchess of Blank	Mary, Duchess of Blank
The Rt. Hon. the Earl of Blank	The Earl of Blank
The Rt. Hon. the Lord Blank	The Lord Blank
His Grace the Archbishop of Blank, *or* The Most Reverend the Lord Archbishop of Blank[1]	The Lord Archbishop of Blank
The Right Reverend the Lord Bishop of Blank	The Lord Bishop of Blank
The Very Reverend the Dean of Blank	The Dean of Blank
The Reverend John Smith	The Reverend John Smith
The Rt. Hon. John Brown	The Rt. Hon. John Brown

There is no rule for the position of 'the' in lists of peers. 'Rt. Hon. the Earl of Blank', 'the Rt. Hon. Viscount Blank', or 'Rt. Hon. Lord Blank' are not wrong, but the above usage is recommended. Similarly it is not laid down whether one should use upper or lower case for the first letter of 'the' within a sentence, but the former is usually accorded to a member of the Royal Family, and the latter to others (e.g. Major the Viscount Blank).

---

[1] An archbishop is often listed as 'His Grace the Archbishop of Blank' (*Lord* is then deemed unnecessary), though in letters he is styled 'The Most Reverend'. 'His Grace' is a simplified reference, particularly as the Archbishops of Canterbury and York are also Privy Counsellors. If 'The Most Reverend' is chosen as the prefix, the letters P.C. may be given after the name (if other letters are also listed) in place of 'the Right Honourable'. P.C. may similarly be accorded to the Bishop of London (e.g. 'The Right Reverend the Lord Bishop of London, P.C.' in place of 'The Right Reverend and Right Honourable the Lord Bishop of London').

Peers and Peeresses are only given the territorial designation if this forms an integral part of the title (e.g. Viscount Montgomery of Alamein).

Peers and Peeresses by courtesy and former wives of Peers are not accorded 'The' or the formal prefix of Most Hon. or Rt. Hon.

Untitled men are either consistently shown as 'John Smith, Esq.' *or* as 'Mr. John Smith', and doctors as 'John Smith, Esq., D.Sc.' *or* 'Dr. John Smith' (*not* 'Dr. John Smith, D.Sc.).

For the position of letters after the name, see p. 96. For other information see the appropriate section.

Joint Forms of Address

Christmas cards (and letters to close relatives, e.g. from a son to his father and mother) may have a joint address.

The use of the joint form for invitations to *public* functions is growing, although these should be addressed to the husband, and also to *private* functions, although these should be addressed to the wife.

The chief difficulty in addressing a joint envelope arises where the husband and wife are differently styled. The following is a guide. (Initials may, of course, be used instead of Christian names, if desired).

> Lieutenant-Colonel the Hon. John and Mrs. Smith
> Major John and the Hon. Mrs. Smith
> The Reverend John and Mrs. Smith
> The Hon. Guy and Lady Moira Black
> Mr. Donald Home and the Countess of Blackadder
> Mr. John and Lady Barbara Jones
> Mr. and the Hon. Mrs. John Green
> Mr. and Mrs. Thomas Brown

Christmas Cards

On a Christmas card it is customary for the husband's name to be given before his wife's, but this is a matter of personal choice.

A card should be inscribed from, 'John and Mary Smith', not from 'Mr. and Mrs. John Smith'. If the names are printed, the surname should be crossed through on cards sent to those on christian name terms. See also *Joint Forms of Address* (above).

Cards, Visiting, Professional and Business

Cards are of two kinds:

(a) Visiting cards
(b) Professional and Business cards

VISITING CARDS

These are engraved from a copper plate. A gentleman's card is now usually 3 inches long by $1\frac{1}{2}$ inches wide. The practice of having a narrower card is now seldom followed. They should give no more than a title, rank, private or Service address (two if desired), and club. In particular, telephone numbers are never included.

A lady's card is traditionally larger than a gentleman's, and is usually $3\frac{1}{4}$ by $2\frac{1}{4}$ inches, though $3\frac{1}{2}$ by $2\frac{1}{2}$ inches is sometimes used. Some ladies prefer a smaller card of the same size as a gentleman's.

Joint cards, e.g. for a husband and wife, or a mother and her unmarried daughters, are now seldom seen.

TITLES

The name of a peer or peeress is shown by his or her grade, but with no prefix, not even 'The', e.g. Duke of Norfolk, Earl of Lonsdale. Courtesy styles derived from a peerage are shown in the form Lord John Jones, Lady Emily Jones, etc., but 'Honourable' is not used: those so styled are shown as Mr., Mrs., or Miss, as applicable (Lady plus surname, if married to a baronet or knight).

BARONETS AND KNIGHTS

A baronet or knight is shown as Sir John Jones, i.e. without the suffix 'Bt.' or 'Bart.', and his wife as Lady Jones.

OTHER STYLES

The only other prefixes used on a card are ecclesiastical titles, ranks in the Armed Forces, and Doctor or Professor. Other gentlemen preceed their name with 'Mr.', followed by their christian name or initials, except that the head of a family may style himself Mr. Forsyte.

A married lady uses her husband's christian name or initials, e.g. Mrs. John Forsyte, or Mrs. J. W. Forsyte, except that the senior married lady in her family may style herself Mrs. Forsyte.

A widow uses the same style as during her husband's lifetime, e.g. Mrs. John Forsyte. She should not use her own christian name or her own initials.

A divorced lady uses either her own christian name or her own initials.

The senior lady of her family, if unmarried, is styled Miss Forsyte. Other unmarried ladies use the style Miss June Forsyte.

SUFFIXES

These are never used on a visiting card, except those which indicate membership of the Armed Forces (see below).

ECCLESIASTICAL RANK

An Archbishop, Bishop, Dean or Archdeacon shows his territorial appointment, e.g. The Archbishop of Canterbury, The Bishop of Bath and Wells, The Dean of Lichfield, *or* The Archdeacon of Lincoln.

A Canon or Prebendary is usually so styled *without* 'The Reverend', e.g. Canon John Jones *or* Prebendary J. W. H. Jones.

A retired Bishop is styled by his prefix, e.g. 'The Right Reverend John Jones'. The style 'Bishop Jones' is not normally used.

An Archdeacon Emeritus is styled Archdeacon Jones, with the personal choice of adding christian name(s) or initial(s). Alternatively, he may use the prefix 'The Venerable', in which case the use of christian name(s) or initial(s) is obligatory.

Other Clergymen are styled The Reverend John Jones *or* The Reverend J. W. Jones.

Note.—The Reverend may be abbreviated to The Revd. or The Rev., see *Churches Section*.

ARMED FORCES

Officers in the Armed Forces use their rank in full, i.e. abbreviations such as Lieut.-Col. should be avoided. Exceptions are Naval Officers below the rank of Lieutenant, Army and Royal Marine Officers below the rank of Captain, and Royal Air Force Officers below the rank of Flight Lieutenant, all of whom are styled 'Mr.'.

A Naval Officer below the rank of Rear-Admiral places 'Royal Navy' *or* 'Royal Naval Reserve' below and slightly to the right of his name.

An Army or Royal Marine Officer on the active list below the rank of Colonel, places his Regiment or Corps (or its accepted abbreviation) below his name.

A Royal Air Force Officer below the rank of Air Commodore places Royal Air Force (which may be abbreviated to R.A.F.) below and slightly to the right of his name.

Retired Officers do *not* include 'Retired' or 'Retd.' with the occasional exception of the Royal Navy, where 'Retd.' is added below and slightly to the right of the name if there is a special reason for doing so. A retired Army or Royal Marine Officer omits his former Regiment or Corps.

WOMEN'S SERVICES

Officers in the Women's Services are usually styled Mrs. or Miss, with the appropriate letters indicating their Corps or Service below and slightly to the right of their names. Officers of the rank of Major or its equivalent and above may, however, use their rank.

EXAMPLES OF CARDS

Mrs. John Berkeley

65 *Pont Lane,*   *Little Stoneley,*
        S.W.1.   *Uppingham,*
                                Rutland.

Mr. Francis Fortescue

Little Pigeons,
    Shiplake,   *Athenæum.*
      Oxon.

Captain Richard Quarterdeck
Royal Navy

H.M.S. Invincible.

Major Jack Pull-Through
Grenadier Guards

Wellington Barracks,   *Guards' Club.*
S.W.1.

Air Vice-Marshal Sir Thomas Plane

Lodge House,
Silbury,
Bedfordshire.

The Dean of Winchester

The Deanery.

Dame Katherine Carruthers,

W.R.N.S.

Ministry of Defence,   *6 Orpington Mansions,*

Whitehall, S.W.1.   *Kew, Surrey.*

Mr. John Bollard,

Royal Navy

Britannia R.N.C.,
Dartmouth.

PROFESSIONAL AND BUSINESS CARDS

These are used only for professional or business purposes. They are usually printed (using Roman type), or may be engraved (using script) if desired.

A business card being intended to show the bearer's qualifications, the appropriate letters are suffixed to his name, e.g. F.R.I.B.A. The card should indicate the firm by whom the bearer is employed or which he represents, and gives his business address and telephone number. His home address and telephone number may be added. Punctuation may be included or omitted as desired.

It is not necessary to prefix the name with any title, rank, Mr., Mrs., or Miss, but this is sometimes done, especially if the card is engraved, to be similar in appearance to a visiting card. If a retired officer from one of the Armed Forces gives his rank, 'Retd.' should be added to the right of and slightly below his name (or where applicable after Royal Navy, etc.).

EXAMPLES OF CARDS

ANTHONY BARKER
BALUCHISTAN NEWS SERVICE

LONDON BUREAU

8000, FLEET ST., E.C.4

TELEPHONE: 01-234-5678.

HOME

10, ALBANY TERRACE,

REGENTS PARK, N.W.1.

TELEPHONE 01-876-5432

01-234 5678

W. T. HAYFIELD, F.C.A.

Barrowfield & Hayfield,
Chartered Accountants,
44 Victoria Square, S.W.1.

Mr. John Halliday,
Professional Genealogist,

The Rafters,
Pewsey,

56-377-5011.   *Wiltshire.*

Captain William Mainsail,
Royal Navy (Retd.)

Rockets & Starshell Ltd.,
899 High Road,
Greenwich, S.E.10.   *01-235 1234.*

Table Plans

ROYAL GUESTS

When The Queen attends a function the host always surrenders his place to her. The host may also extend this courtesy to a visiting Head of State.

Other Members of the Royal Family (i.e. The Queen Mother and those entitled to the prefix *Royal Highness*) are given special precedence, see *Precedence* (pp. 323 and 336). The husband of a lady member of the Royal Family is accorded precedence immediately after her when both attend a function. If he attends alone, he retains his own precedence, unless he is the guest of honour, see *Guest of Honour* below.

The Suite in attendance on a Member of the Royal Family should be placed reasonably near to him or her.

No guest should leave a function before a Member of the Royal Family, except in special circumstances when prior permission should be obtained.[1]

OFFICIAL FUNCTIONS

Guest of Honour and Important Guests. The principal guest is invariably placed on the host's right.

If wives are invited to accompany their husbands, the principal guest's wife is usually placed on the host's left, the host's wife being placed on the right of the principal guest. Other important guests are placed to the right and left of these persons, in order of precedence and importance,[2] subject to the following:

(a) Important members of the inviting body and their wives should be interspersed among the principal guests.

(b) As far as possible ladies and gentlemen should be seated in alternate places.

(c) Wives, except those entitled to a precedence in their own right, should be placed according to the precedence due to their husbands.

(d) Wives should not be seated next to their husbands.[3]

At a function attended only by gentlemen (and by ladies invited

[1] This rule may be honoured in the breach rather than in the observance at Charity Balls, etc. which continue after midnight.
 The organiser of an evening function may seek (through the Private Secretary) 'blanket' permission for any guest who will have transport difficulties if they do not leave by a certain hour (e.g. to catch the last train), to do so before the Member of the Royal Family leaves.
[2] Age has sometimes to be considered: placing Midshipman the Duke of Loamshire above Admiral of the Fleet Sir Horatio Hornblower is no more likely to improve the Admiral's temper than it is to advance the Duke's naval career.
[3] They see enough of each other at home except, apparently, in the City of London, which does not follow this practice.

by virtue of their office), the second most important guest is placed on the host's left.

CIVIC FUNCTIONS

In the absence of The Queen, the Lord Lieutenant is her direct representative within his county.

When the guest of honour is The Queen or other Head of State, a Member of the Royal Family, a Prime Minister, a Member of the Cabinet, or someone of comparable importance (e.g. an Archbishop), the following should be invited, and placed in this order of precedence after the above:

1. The Lord Lieutenant of the County.
2. The Lord Mayor, Lord Provost, Mayor or Provost of the City, Borough or Burgh (if the function is held within the boundaries of one).
3. The Chairman of the County Council (not applicable if the function is held within the boundaries of a County Borough or Burgh).
4. The High Sheriff of the County.

(*Note:* Should one of these be the host, he, of course, takes precedence as such).

When a function takes place within premises belonging to some organization other than the host, the senior representative of that organization should be invited and placed high among the guests.

The Lord Mayor or other First Citizen may, on special occasions and as a courtesy, yield his senior place, e.g. to an Archbishop at a Church function, to the Lord Chancellor and the Speaker of the House of Commons at a Parliamentary function, and to the Lord Chief Justice or Master of the Rolls at a legal function.

OTHER GUESTS

High Commissioners, Ambassadors, Ministers of the Crown and Privy Counsellors should always be placed at the 'top table'.

High Commissioners of Commonwealth countries rank according to dates of arrival, and Ambassadors of Foreign States according to the dates on which they presented their letters of credence. Chargés d'Affaires rank after Ambassadors: if two or more be present they rank among themselves in accordance with the seniority of their Ambassadors. Other members of the Diplomatic Corps of equal rank are usually arranged in alphabetical order of their names, but the importance of their country may be taken into consideration. With the exception of functions to which large numbers of members of the Diplomatic Corps are invited, care should be taken to avoid placing those of countries which do not enjoy diplomatic relations in the embarrassing position of having to meet each other.

Important dignitaries of the Established Church are placed in accordance with the official order of precedence. Important dignitaries of other Churches are usually accorded a like courtesy, e.g. a Roman Catholic Archbishop, should be placed immediately after any Anglican Archbishops who may be present.

FORMAL OR INFORMAL

Subject to the above, the host must decide whether the function is to be a formal one with the order of precedence strictly observed, see *Tables of Precedence* (p. 321); or whether, as tends to be the case today, the function should be a less formal one. Even so, at a function given by a society, a firm, or other organization, its members (and their wives, if invited), should be interspersed among the guests: on no account should the guests be seated in one block and the members of the organization in another.

The placing of guests also depends upon whether invitations have been issued to:

(a) Gentlemen *and* their wives, *or*
(b) Gentlemen only, *or* gentlemen and ladies by virtue of their office.

If (a) be the case, the host must decide whether or not husbands and wives are to be seated together. The former is easier to arrange, especially when the order of precedence is observed. The latter, which is always followed at private parties, gives husbands and wives a chance to meet and talk to 'new faces'.

PRIVATE FUNCTIONS

The host is customarily seated at one end of the table, the hostess at the other end. Alternatively, the host may be seated in the centre of one side of the table, and the hostess immediately opposite to him[1]. The latter follows the custom at Court and invariably on the Continent.

The principal male guest is placed on the right of the hostess, and his wife on the right of the host. The other seating is largely

---

[1] Exceptionally, if the party numbers *eight*, the hostess may give up her place to the chief male guest: otherwise it is impracticable to preserve the rule of seating the sexes alternately. If a party numbers six or ten (i.e. in multiples of four in addition to the host and hostess), the table is easier to arrange, by alternately placing men and women, but today this custom is not too rigidly applied.

a matter for the hostess to decide according to the mutual interests of the guests. Strict order of precedence need not be observed, but should not be ignored. The latter is especially true of High Commissioners and Ambassadors whose diplomatic precedence must be respected, see *Other Guests* (p. 309).

SPECIMEN TABLE PLANS

The following examples show possible, but not necessarily the only, ways of seating the principal guests at typical functions.

(a) *A County function* at which the President of a County organization is the host, accompanied by his wife, using both sides of the top table.

Principal guests: The Queen[1]
The Queen's Suite
(normally a Private Secretary, Lady-in-Waiting, and Equerry)
The Lord Lieutenant of the County, and his wife
The Lord Mayor/Mayor and Lady Mayoress/Mayoress of the Borough in which the function is being held
The High Sheriff of the County and his wife
The Home Secretary and his wife

	Home Secretary
Lady Mayoress/Mayoress	Wife of Lord Lieutenant
High Sheriff	President of County Organization (*Host*)
Wife of President of County Organization (*Hostess*)	The Queen
Lord Mayor/Mayor	Lord Lieutenant
Wife of Home Secretary	Wife of High Sheriff

CENTRE ←——→

Note.—The Queen's Suite should be seated as is convenient in the vicinity of, but not close to, the Queen.

[1] The table plan for any function attended by The Queen must be submitted to her Private Secretary for prior approval.

(b) *A non-County function* at which the President of a Society is the host, accompanied by his wife, using both sides of the top table.

Principal guests: The Queen[1]
The Queen's Suite
(normally a Private Secretary, Lady-in-Waiting, and Equerry)
The Lord Lieutenant of the County and his wife
The Lord Mayor/Mayor and Lady Mayoress/Mayoress
High Sheriff of the County and his wife
The Home Secretary and his wife

	CENTRE	High Sheriff
Lady Mayoress/Mayoress		Wife of Home Secretary
Home Secretary		President of the Society (*Host*)
Wife of President of Society (*Hostess*)	← CENTRE →	The Queen
Lord Lieutenant		Lord Mayor/Mayor
		Wife of High Sheriff

Note.—The Queen's Suite should be seated as is convenient in the vicinity of, but not close to, the Queen.

(c) *A Company function* at which the Chairman is the host, using only one side of the top table.

Principal guests: The Lord Mayor/Mayor of the Borough in which the function is being held
The Prime Minister
The Minister of Transport
The Chairman of the Parent Company
The Anglican Bishop of the Diocese

[1] The table plan for any function attended by The Queen must be submitted to her Private Secretary for prior approval.

Chairman of Parent
  Company

Minister of Transport

Lord Mayor/Mayor

CENTRE

Chairman of Company
  (*Host*)

Prime Minister

Bishop

(d) *A Company function*, as for (c), but including ladies, and
using both sides of the top table.

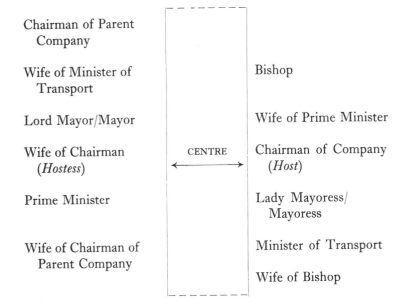

Chairman of Parent
  Company

Wife of Minister of
  Transport

Lord Mayor/Mayor

Wife of Chairman
  (*Hostess*)

Prime Minister

Wife of Chairman of
  Parent Company

Bishop

Wife of Prime Minister

CENTRE

Chairman of Company
  (*Host*)

Lady Mayoress/
  Mayoress

Minister of Transport

Wife of Bishop

(e) *A function given by a Society* at which the President is the host, accompanied by his wife, using both sides of the top table.

Principal guests: Their Royal Highnesses The Duke and Duchess of Kent[1]

Equerry and Lady-in-Waiting to the Duke and Duchess

The Lord Lieutenant of the County and his wife

The Lord Mayor/Mayor and Lady Mayoress/Mayoress of the Borough in which the function is being held

The Vice-Chancellor of the local University and his wife

The Naval Flag Officer of the area and his wife

A Roman Catholic Bishop

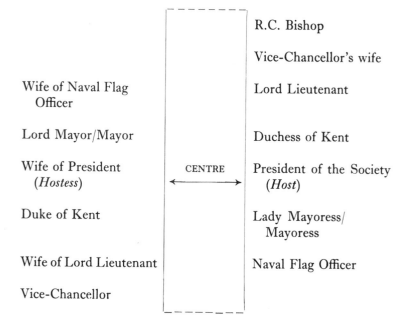

	CENTRE	
		R.C. Bishop
		Vice-Chancellor's wife
Wife of Naval Flag Officer		Lord Lieutenant
Lord Mayor/Mayor		Duchess of Kent
Wife of President (*Hostess*)	←——→	President of the Society (*Host*)
Duke of Kent		Lady Mayoress/ Mayoress
Wife of Lord Lieutenant		Naval Flag Officer
Vice-Chancellor		

Note.—The Equerry and Lady-in-Waiting should be seated as convenient in the vicinity of, but not close to, the Duke and Duchess of Kent.

[1] The table plan for any function attended by a Member of the Royal Family should be submitted to his/her Private Secretary for prior approval.

(f) *A function given by a Society*, as for (e), using only one
side of the top table:

CENTRE

Roman Catholic Bishop

Wife of Vice-Chancellor

Naval Flag Officer

Wife of Lord Lieutenant

Lord Mayor/Mayor

Wife of President (*Hostess*)

Duke of Kent[1]

President of Society (*Host*)

Duchess of Kent[1]

Lord Lieutenant

Lady Mayoress/Mayor

Vice-Chancellor

Wife of Naval Flag Officer

Note.—The Equerry and Lady-in-Waiting should be seated as is
convenient in the vicinity of, but not close to, the Duke and
Duchess of Kent.

GUEST LISTS

Guests may be shown where they are placed at table in various
ways:

(a) For a party not exceeding, say, 30, a seating plan may be
displayed on a table or board.

---

[1] The table plan for any function attended by a Member of the Royal Family should be submitted to his/her Private Secretary for prior approval.

(b) For a larger party, up to, say, 100, a numbered drawing of the table may be displayed with a list of the guests alongside it in alphabetical order, each with his seat number.

(c) For larger parties than (b), each guest should be provided with a printed table plan, with the names listed in alphabetical order, or with a table diagram with his seat ringed or arrowed.

The following rules are customarily observed: where an alternative is shown, this is at the host's discretion, subject to observing consistency throughout the list.

Any guest invited by virtue of office should be so indicated, e.g. Fenchurch, Sir William, K.B.E., President of the Society of . . .

Peers and Peeresses are shown by their exact rank in the peerage, e.g. Middlesex, The Earl of, K.B.E.; Flintshire, The Countess of, etc. The word 'The' is optional for Viscounts, Barons, their wives and widows. They must all be treated identically, except for peers by courtesy who do not have the prefix 'The (see below). The prefix appropriate to the grade of peer may be shown if desired, viz:

His or Her Grace	Duke or Duchess
The Most Hon.	Marquess or Marchioness
The Right Hon.	Other Peers and Peeresses

Again, a decision has to be taken whether this prefix is to be used. If it is, all peers and peeresses, apart from those by courtesy (see below), should be treated similarly.

Peers and Peeresses by Courtesy, and former wives of Peers have no peerage prefix, i.e. neither 'The Right Hon.', etc., nor 'The'. (See p. 42.)

Courtesy Styles, those with the prefix 'Lord' or 'Lady' before their christian names do not have the prefix 'The'.

The Courtesy Style of 'The Hon.' is shown.

Privy Counsellors are given the prefix 'The Right Hon.', but not the suffix 'P.C.' (except for peers and peeresses, when these letters *are* shown) (see p. 78).

Baronets are shown with the suffix of 'Bt.' or 'Bart.'.

Honours, Decorations and Degrees, should be included; also the principal other awards, such as Fellowships of learned societies.

Esquire or Mr. Guests without title or rank should be styled as 'Mr.'. This is especially true when both husbands and wives are invited: the solecism of mixing the styles, e.g. John Brown, Esq., and Mrs. John Brown, must be avoided.[1]

PLACE CARDS

These should be brief, honours, decorations, degrees, etc. being omitted. So too is the formal prefix for peers, who are shown as, e.g. 'The Earl of Blank' or 'Lord Blank', but 'The Right Hon.' is retained for Privy Counsellors who are not peers, and the suffixes R.N., Q.C. and M.P. for those so entitled.

Any office held should be omitted, except that important guests should be indicated by their office instead of their name, e.g. The Swiss Ambassador, The Lord Mayor, etc.

'The Hon.' is usually shown before the name at a public function, but omitted at a private party.

'Mr.' invariably takes the place of 'Esq.'

Other rules are as for *Guest Lists* (p. 315).

GRACE

Grace is usually said before a meal, and sometimes afterwards, in which case it precedes the Loyal Toast(s).

There is no Preamble to Grace. The Toastmaster announces only: 'Pray silence for Grace by your President', or 'by Canon John Jones', 'The Reverend John Jones', etc. (The description of his living, etc. should not be mentioned).

A Bishop may be asked to say Grace except that, if his Chaplain is present, it is customary for him to do so.

THE LOYAL TOASTS

The first and principal Loyal Toast, as approved by The Queen, is: 'The Queen'. It is incorrect to use such forms as: 'I give you the Loyal Toast of Her Majesty The Queen'. To obtain the necessary silence, the Toastmaster may say, without Preamble, e.g.: 'Pray silence for your President'.

The second Loyal Toast, which, if given, immediately follows the first, is likewise limited to: 'Queen Elizabeth The Queen Mother, The Prince Philip, Duke of Edinburgh, The Prince of Wales, and other Members of the Royal Family'.

---

[1] The City of London uses the style 'Esq.' for gentlemen who have served the office of Sheriff and 'Mr.' for all others without rank or title.

It is an established custom that guests do not smoke until after the Loyal Toast(s). The announcement 'Ladies and Gentlemen, you may now smoke' is unnecessary except that, if The Queen or The Queen Mother be present, it is necessary to announce: 'Ladies and Gentlemen, you have Her Majesty's permission to smoke'.

Speeches

THE PREAMBLE

It is impossible to give a list of those who should be mentioned in the Preamble of a speech, since this depends so much on those present at a particular function. In general, however, the list should be kept as short as possible, subject to avoiding an omission which would cause justifiable offence.

The speaker does not, of course, include himself in his preamble.

THE QUEEN AND QUEEN ELIZABETH THE QUEEN MOTHER

Should The Queen or Queen Elizabeth The Queen Mother be present, a Preamble begins: 'May it please Your Majesty'.

THE HOST

With the above exception, a Preamble begins with the host, who is referred to by his office, e.g.:

    Mr. President
    Mr. Chairman
    Mr. Vice-Chancellor
    Master
    Mr. Prime Warden, etc.

PRESIDENT

If a Member of the Royal Family, he or she is referred to as: 'Your Royal Highness and President'.

If a non-Royal Duke or Duchess, as: 'Your Grace and President'.

If a peer other than a Duke, as: 'My Lord and President'. ('My Lord President' is incorrect, except for the Lord President of the Council).

If a lady, either titled or untitled, with the exception of a Member of the Royal Family or a Duchess, as: 'Madam President'.

If a gentleman below the rank of peer, as: 'Mr. President'.

VICE-PRESIDENT

When a Vice-President takes the Chair, he or she may be referred to as 'Mr. Vice-President' or, 'Madam Vice-President' (with the relevant prefix mentioned under *President*), but he or she is more usually referred to as 'Mr. Chairman', or 'Madam Chairman'.

CHAIRMAN

A Chairman is called 'Mr. Chairman', or 'Madam Chairman', irrespective of his or her rank, with the exception of a Member of the Royal Family, who is referred to as 'Your Royal Highness'. A peer should *not* be called 'My Lord Chairman'.

If a Vice-Chairman, Managing Director, or other officer of the organization takes the Chair, he or she is still referred to as 'Mr. Chairman' or 'Madam Chairman', i.e. the use of these expressions is not restricted to the actual Chairman of the organization.

OTHER IMPORTANT GUESTS

The following list gives the form in which various persons should be included in a Preamble, in order of precedence, after those already mentioned above:

> Your Royal Highness
> My Lord Mayor (or My Lord Provost, Mr. Mayor, Mr. Provost) (see Note 1).
> Mr. Chairman of the Greater London Council (within Greater London), or,
> Mr. Chairman of the . . . County Council (outside Greater London)
> My Lord Chancellor
> Prime Minister (or more formally 'Mr. Prime Minister') (see Note 2).
> Your Excellency(ies) (see Note 3).
> Your Grace(s) (see Note 4)
> My Lord(s) (see Note 5)
> Ladies and Gentlemen

Note 1.—This applies only to the First Citizen of the City, Borough or Burgh in which the function takes place. If desired to mention a First Citizen from elsewhere who may be present, this should be done after 'My Lords', and before 'Ladies and Gentlemen'. More than one Lord Mayor should be covered by 'My Lords'. The form 'Your Worship' for a Mayor is archaic, but 'Your Worships' is used because there is no plural for Mr. Mayor.

Note 2.—Also:

My Lord President (i.e. of the Privy Council)
My Lord Privy Seal
Mr. Chancellor (of the Exchequer or of the Duchy of Lancaster)
Mr. President (of the Board of Trade)
Minister(s) (more formally Mr. Minister). (This covers a Secretary of State. The terms 'Mr. Secretary of State' and 'Mr. Secretary' are archaic. Other Ministers are not mentioned in a Preamble when the Prime Minister attends a function.)

Note 3.—High Commissioners and Ambassadors.

Note 4.—This covers Dukes and Duchesses. Should the Archbishop of Canterbury be present, 'Your Grace' (or 'Your Graces' if a Duke or Duchess is also attending) should be mentioned before 'My Lord Chancellor'. Similarly, the Archbishop of York is covered by including 'Your Grace' immediately after 'My Lord Chancellor', i.e. both Archbishops rank before 'Your Excellencies'.

Note 5.—For peers, other than Dukes, peers by courtesy, for diocesan Bishops by right, and for other Bishops by courtesy. In the absence of any Peers, the form 'My Lord Bishop' may be used.

GENERAL NOTES

Roman Catholic Archbishops and Bishops

A Cardinal Archbishop may be included in the form 'Your Eminence', placed by courtesy after 'Your Graces'. Other Archbishops and Bishops are by courtesy mentioned in the same way as those of the Anglican Church.

Clergy

Clergy, other than Archbishops and Bishops, should not be included. In particular the form, 'Reverend Sir', is archaic.

Guest of Honour

When the guest of honour is not covered by one of the above terms, he is included in the Preamble by his office, e.g. 'Mr. President', 'Mr. Chairman', etc. immediately before 'Ladies and Gentlemen'. This specific mention also applies when a President, Vice-Chancellor, etc. is providing the building in which the function takes place.

Aldermen and Sheriffs

Within the City of London it is customary to refer to these as 'Mr. Alderman' or 'Aldermen', and 'Mr. Sheriff' or 'Sheriffs' immediately before 'Ladies and Gentlemen'. Elsewhere, 'Aldermen and Councillors' may be included at civic functions immediately before 'Ladies and Gentlemen'.

The Ending

A speaker proposing a toast should make this entirely clear at the end of his speech in some such form as, 'I give you the toast of your guest', or, 'I ask you to rise and drink to the toast of your President'. This obviates any need for the Toastmaster to say, 'The Toast is . . .'.

Toastmaster

The Toastmaster should be given the form in which he is to make all announcements in writing, and not left to devise his own often exaggerated forms.

For the first speaker the announcement should have a Preamble, as for his speech, followed by, 'Pray silence for . . .'. For subsequent announcements the Preamble is omitted.

A speaker is announced by his name, followed by his office where applicable, e.g. 'The Right Honourable John Smith, Her Majesty's Secretary of State for . . .'. Suffixes such as 'Member of the Distinguished Service Order', 'One of Her Majesty's Justices of the Peace', etc. should not be used.

Tables of Precedence

Peers and peeresses (in each degree) rank among themselves in the following order: those created (1) of England, (2) of Scotland, (3) of Great Britain, (4) of Ireland, and (5) of the United Kingdom and of Ireland created since the Union, according to the dates of their respective patents. Baronets rank among themselves according to the dates of their respective patents *only*. Precedence of ladies is always derived from the father, or husband, except in the case of a peeress in her own right.

Official precedence, such as that of the Great Officers of State, confers no corresponding precedence on their wives or daughters. The wives and issue of Archbishops and Bishops have no special precedence as such.

A dowager peeress, or widow of a baronet, takes precedence of the wife of the incumbent of the title only while remaining a widow.

The children of a living peer, or baronet, have precedence above the children of the previous possessor, or possessors, of the title. If the daughter of a peer marries a peer she takes her husband's rank and precedence, but if she marry the eldest or younger son of a peer she ranks *either* according to her own inherent precedence (i.e., as the daughter of her father), *or* according to that of her husband (i.e., as the wife of the eldest or younger son of a Duke, Marquess, Earl, etc.), whichever happens to be the higher, no matter what the courtesy title may be. Daughters rank immediately after the wives of their eldest brothers.

The Order of Merit and the Order of the Companions of Honour do not confer precedence upon recipients.

Esquires and Gentlemen. Though these ranks appear on the Tables, their definition is now only of academic interest. Sir Charles Young, Garter King of Arms, in his *Order of Precedence,* 1851, stated under *Esquires,* 'it is extremely difficult to define accurately or satisfactorily the persons included by, or entitled to, this designation. Lord Coke, in his exposition of the Statute 1 Hen. V, cap. 5, of *Additions,* said—"The Sons of all the Peers and Lords of Parliament in the life of their Fathers are in law Esquires, and so to be named." By this Statute the Eldest Son of a Knight is an *Esquire.* (2 Inst. 667).' Young proceeded to refer to Sir William Blackstone's opinions in his *Commentaries on the Laws of England.* Camden categorised them into four sorts: '1. The Eldest Sons of Knights, and their Eldest Sons in perpetual succession. 2. The Eldest Sons of Younger Sons of Peers, and their Elder Sons in like perpetual succession. 3. Esquires created by the King's letters patent, or other investiture, and their Eldest Sons. 4. Esquires by virtue of their offices; as Justices of the Peace, and others who bear any office of trust under the Crown.' For *Gentleman,* Young wrote, 'there is no defined priority. Littleton says, "every son is as great a gentleman as the eldest".' Sir Anthony Wagner, now Garter King of Arms, writes on the history of Esquires and Gentlemen in his *English Geneaology,* 1960.

Foreign titles of nobility borne by British subjects afford their holders no official precedence in this country.

See also Notes on p. 335.

PRECEDENCE IN ENGLAND AND WALES

GENTLEMEN

  THE SOVEREIGN
  The Heir Apparent[1]
  The Sovereign's Younger Sons
  [The Sovereign's Grandsons]
  [The Sovereign's Brothers]
  The Sovereign's Uncles
  The Sovereign's Nephews
  [The Sovereign's Great Uncles]
  Archbishop of Canterbury
  Lord High Chancellor
  Archbishop of York
  Prime Minister
  Lord High Treasurer (when existing)
  Lord President of the Council
  Speaker of the House of Commons
  Lord Privy Seal
  Ambassadors and High Commissioners (i.e. from overseas)
  Lord Great Chamberlain[2]
  Lord High Constable (when existing) ⎫
  Earl Marshal   ⎪ Above all Peers
  Lord Steward of the Household   ⎬ of their own
  Lord Chamberlain of the Household   ⎪ degree
  Master of the Horse   ⎭
  Dukes of England
  Dukes of Scotland
  Dukes of Great Britain
  Dukes of Ireland
  Dukes of United Kingdom and Ireland since the Union[3]
  Eldest Sons of Dukes of the Blood Royal
  Marquesses of England
  Marquesses of Scotland
  Marquesses of Great Britain
  Marquesses of Ireland
  Marquesses of United Kingdom and Ireland since the Union[3]
  Eldest Sons of Dukes
  Earls of England
  Earls of Scotland

[1] By Royal Warrant dated 18th September, 1952, it was declared that H.R.H. the Duke of Edinburgh was henceforth to have precedence next to H.M. The Queen, thus having place before the Heir Apparent.
[2] When in actual performance of official duty.
[3] See p. 23.

Earls of Great Britain
Earls of Ireland
Earls of United Kingdom and Ireland since the Union[1]
Younger Sons of Dukes of the Blood Royal
Marquesses' Eldest Sons
Dukes' Younger Sons
Viscounts of England
Viscounts of Scotland
Viscounts of Great Britain
Viscounts of Ireland
Viscounts of United Kingdom and Ireland since the Union[1]
Earls' Eldest Sons
Marquesses' Younger Sons
Bishop of London
Bishop of Durham
Bishop of Winchester
English Diocesan Bishops according to seniority of consecration

Suffragan Bishops according to seniority of consecration
Secretaries of State, if of Baronial rank.
Barons of England
Lords of Parliament, Scotland
Barons of Great Britain
Barons of Ireland
Barons of United Kingdom and Ireland since the Union[1] (including Life Barons)

Lords Commissioners of the Great Seal (when existing)
Treasurer of the Household
Comptroller of the Household
Vice-Chamberlain of the Household
Secretaries of State, under Baronial rank
[High Commissioner for Rhodesia]
Viscounts' Eldest Sons
Earls' Younger Sons
Barons' Eldest Sons
Knights of the Garter
Privy Counsellors
Chancellor of the Exchequer
Chancellor of the Duchy of Lancaster
Lord Chief Justice of England
Master of the Rolls

[1] See p. 23.

President of the Probate, Divorce, and Admiralty Division
Lord Justices of Appeal, according to seniority of appointment
Judges of the High Court of Justice, according to seniority of appointment
Vice-Chancellor of County Palatine of Lancaster
Viscounts' Younger Sons
Barons' Younger Sons
Baronets, according to date of Patent
Knights of the Thistle[1]
Knights Grand Cross of the Bath
Knights Grand Commanders of the Star of India
Knights Grand Cross of the Order St. Michael and St. George
Knights Grand Commanders of the Indian Empire
Knights Grand Cross of Royal Victorian Order
Knights Grand Cross of the British Empire Order
Knights Commanders of the Bath
Knights Commanders of the Star of India
Knights Commanders of St. Michael and St. George
Knights Commanders of the Indian Empire
Knights Commanders of the Royal Victorian Order
Knights Commanders of the British Empire Order
Knights Bachelor
Official Referees of Supreme Court of Judicature
Judges of County Courts of England and Wales (including Judges of City of London Court) according to seniority of appointment
Masters in Chancery
Master of Court of Protection
Companions of the Order of the Bath
Companions of the Order of the Star of India
Companions of Order of the St. Michael and St. George
Companions of the Order of the Indian Empire
Commanders of the Royal Victorian Order
Commanders of the British Empire Order
Companions of Distinguished Service Order
Members of the Royal Victorian Order (4th class)
Officers of the British Empire Order
Companions of Imperial Service Order
Eldest Sons of the Younger Sons of Peers

[1] See p. 326 for Notes.

Eldest Sons of Baronets
Eldest Sons of Knights of the Garter
Eldest Sons of Eldest sons of Knights of the Thistle[1]
Eldest Sons of Knights of the Bath[2]
Eldest Sons of Knights of the Star of India[2]
Eldest Sons of Knights of the Order of St. Michael and St. George[2]
Eldest Sons of Knights of the Indian Empire[2]
Eldest Sons of Knights of the Royal Victorian Order[2]
Eldest Sons of Knights of the British Empire Order[2]
Eldest Sons of Knights Bachelor
Members of the Royal Victorian Order (5th class)
Members of the British Empire Order (viz. M.B.E.)
Younger Sons of Baronets
Younger Sons of Knights
Esquires
Gentlemen

Note 1.—Lord Lieutenants and High Sheriffs of Counties have the first places in their own Counties during office, the Lord Lieutenant taking precedence of the High Sheriff, but neither is assigned any place on the official Table of Precedence. The Lord Lieutenant has precedence within his jurisdiction over a Lord Mayor or Mayor, even within his own Borough, when present officially as the representative of the Sovereign. On all Civic occasions, however, whether of business or entertainment, the Mayor should preside, or act as host.

Note 2.—Certain Clergy, also Naval, Military and Air Force Officers, Members of the Legal and Medical Professions, Graduates of Universities, and Citizens and Burgesses have no precedence assigned to them.

LADIES

THE QUEEN
The Queen Mother
[The Princess of Wales]
The Sovereign's Daughters
[Wives of the Sovereign's Younger Sons]
[The Sovereign's Granddaughters (with style of H.R.H.)]

---

[1] Knights of the Thistle have no relative precedence accorded to them by Statute, but are customarily placed here. In Scotland they follow Knights of the Garter. (See Scottish Table.)
[2] Eldest sons of Knights Grand Cross take precedence of eldest sons of Knights of the 2nd degree.

[Wives of the Sovereign's Grandsons]
The Sovereign's Sisters
[Wives of the Sovereign's Brothers]
[The Sovereign's Aunts]
Wives of the Sovereign's Uncles
The Sovereign's Nieces
[Wives of the Sovereign's Nephews]
The Sovereign's Great Aunts]
Duchesses of England
Duchesses of Scotland
Duchesses of Great Britain
Duchesses of Ireland
Duchess of United Kingdom and Ireland since the Union[1]
Wives of the Eldest Sons of Dukes of the Blood Royal
Marchionesses of England
Marchionesses of Scotland
Marchionesses of Great Britain
Marchionesses of Ireland
Marchionesses of United Kingdom and Ireland since the Union[1]
Wives of the Eldest Sons of Dukes
Daughters of Dukes
Countesses of England
Countesses of Scotland
Countesses of Great Britain
Countesses of Ireland
Countess of United Kingdom and Ireland since the Union[1]
Wives of the Younger Sons of Dukes of the Blood Royal
Wives of the Eldest Sons of Marquesses
Daughters of Marquesses
Wives of the Younger Sons of Dukes
Viscountesses of England
Viscountesses of Scotland
Viscountesses of Great Britain
Viscountesses of Ireland
Viscountesses of United Kingdom and Ireland since the Union[1]
Wives of the Eldest Sons of Earls
Daughters of Earls
Wives of the Younger Sons of Marquesses
Baronesses of England
Ladies of Parliament Scotland

[1] See p. 23.

Baronesses of Great Britain

Baronesses of Ireland

Baronesses of United Kingdom and Ireland since the Union, including Life Baronesses and Wives of Life Barons

Wives of the Eldest Sons of Viscounts

Daughters of Viscounts

Wives of the Younger Sons of Earls

Wives of the Eldest Sons of Barons

Daughters of Barons

Wives of Knights of the Garter

Privy Counsellors (Women)

Wives of the Younger Sons of Viscounts

Wives of the Younger Sons of Barons

Wives of Baronets, according to the date of their husband's Patents

Wives of Knights of the Thistle (see note on Gentlemen's Table)

Dames Grand Cross of the Order of St. Michael and St. George

Dames Grand Cross of the Royal Victorian Order

Dames Grand Cross of the British Empire Order

Wives of Knights Grand Cross of the Bath

Wives of Knights Grand Commanders of the Star of India

Wives of Knights Grand Cross of St. Michael and St. George

Wives of Knights Grand Commanders of the Indian Empire

Wives of Knights Grand Cross of the Royal Victorian Order

Wives of Knights Grand Cross of the British Empire Order

Dames Commanders of the Order of St. Michael and St. George

Dames Commanders of the Royal Victorian Order

Dames Commanders of the British Empire Order

Wives of Knights Commanders of the Bath

Wives of Knights Commanders of the Star of India

Wives of Knights Commanders of St. Michael and St. George.

Wives of Knights Commanders of the Indian Empire

Wives of Knights Commanders of the Royal Victorian Order

Wives of Knights Commanders of the British Empire Order

Wives of Knights Bachelor

Commanders of the Order of St. Michael and St. George

Commanders of the Royal Victorian Order

Commanders of the British Empire Order

Wives of Companions of the Bath
Wives of Companions of the Star of India
Wives of Companions of the Order of St. Michael and St. George
Wives of Companions of the Indian Empire
Wives of Commanders of Royal Victorian Order
Wives of Commanders of the British Empire Order
Wives of Companions of the Distinguished Service Order
Members of the Royal Victorian Order (4th class)
Officer of the British Empire Order
Wives of Members of the Royal Victorian Order (4th class)
Wives of Officers of the British Empire Order
Companions of the Imperial Service Order
Wives of Companions of the Imperial Service Order
Wives of the Eldest Sons of the Younger Sons of Peers
Daughters of the Younger Sons of Peers
Wives of the Eldest Sons of Baronets
Daughters of Baronets
Wives of the Eldest Sons of Knights of the Garter
Wives of the Eldest Sons of Knights
Daughters of Knights
Members of the Royal Victorian Order (5th class)
Members of the British Empire Order
Wives of Members of Royal Victorian Order (5th class)
Wives of Members of the British Empire Order
Wives of the Younger Sons of Baronets
Wives of the Younger Sons of Knights
Wives of Esquires
Wives of Gentlemen

Note 1.—Wives of the Clergy, Naval, Military and Air Force Officers, Members of the Legal and Medical Professions, Graduates of Universities, and Citizens and Burgesses have no precedence assigned to them,

PRECEDENCE IN SCOTLAND

GENTLEMEN

[THE SOVEREIGN]
Lord High Commissioner to the General Assembly of the Church of Scotland (during sitting of General Assembly)[1]

---

[1] By Royal Warrant dated 18th September, 1952, it was declared that H.R.H. the Duke of Edinburgh was henceforth to have precedence next to H.M. The Queen, thus having place before the Lord High Commissioner.

Duke of Rothesay[1]
The Sovereign's Younger Sons
[The Sovereign's Grandsons]
[The Sovereign's Brothers]
The Sovereign's Uncles
The Sovereign's Nephews
The [Sovereign's Great-Uncles]
Lord Lieutenants of Counties[2]
Lord Provosts of Cities being *ex-officio* Lord Lieutenants of Counties of Cities[1]
Sheriffs Principal[1]
Lord Chancellor of Great Britain
Moderator of the General Assembly of Church of Scotland (during office)
The Prime Minister
Keeper of the Great Seal of Scotland (Secretary of State for Scotland) (if a Peer)
Keeper of the Privy Seal of Scotland (if a Peer)
Hereditary High Constable of Scotland
Hereditary Master of the Household in Scotland
Dukes (as in English Table)
Eldest Sons of Dukes of the Blood Royal
Marquesses (as in English Table)
Eldest Sons of Dukes
Earls (as in English Table)
Younger Sons of Dukes of the Blood Royal
Eldest Sons of Marquesses
Younger Sons of Dukes
Keeper of the Great Seal (Secretary of State for Scotland) (if not a Peer)
Keeper of the Privy Seal (if not a Peer)
Lord Justice-General
Lord Clerk Register
Lord Advocate
Lord Justice-Clerk
Viscounts (as in English Table)
Eldest Sons of Earls
Younger Sons of Marquesses
Barons or Lords of Parliament (Scotland) (as in English Table)

[1] The eldest son of The Sovereign in the Peerage of Scotland (i.e. The Prince of Wales).
[2] During term of office, and within their respective Counties, Cities, and Sheriffdoms. Lord Lieutenants of Counties and of Counties of Cities during their term of office and within the limits of their jurisdiction have precedence before the Sheriffs Principal having concurrent jurisdiction.

Eldest Sons of Viscounts
Younger Sons of Earls
Eldest Sons of Barons or Lords of Parliament (Scotland)
Knights of the Garter
Knights of the Thistle
Privy Counsellors
Senators of the College of Justice (Lords of Session), includ-
ing Chairman of Scottish Land Court
Younger Sons of Viscounts
Younger Sons of Barons or Lords of Parliament (Scotland)
Baronets
Knights Grand Cross and Knights Grand Commanders of
Orders (as in English Table)
Knights Commanders of Orders (as in English Table)
Solicitor-General for Scotland
Lyon King of Arms
Sheriffs Principal (when not within own County)[1]
Knights Bachelor
Sheriffs Substitute
Companions of the Order of the Bath
Thence as in English Table

LADIES

THE QUEEN
The Queen Mother
[Duchess of Rothesay] (see Duke of Rothesay)
The Sovereign's Daughters
[Wives of Sovereign's Younger Sons]
[The Sovereign's Granddaughters]
[Wives of Sovereign's Grandsons]
The Sovereign's Sisters
[Wives of Sovereign's Brothers]
[The Sovereign's Aunts]
Wives of Sovereign's Uncles
The Sovereign's Nieces
[Wives of Sovereign's Nephews]
[The Sovereign's Great-Aunts]
Duchesses (as in English Table)
Wives of the Eldest Sons of Dukes of Blood Royal
Marchionesses (as in English Table)
Wives of Eldest Sons of Dukes

---

[1] In Scotland Sheriffs exercise judicial functions.

Daughters of Dukes
Wives of Younger Sons of Dukes of Blood Royal
Wives of Eldest Sons of Marquesses
Daughters of Marquesses
Wives of Younger Sons of Dukes
Countesses (as in English Table)
Viscountesses (as in English Table)
Wives of Eldest Sons of Earls
Daughters of Earls
Wives of Younger Sons of Marquesses
Baronesses, or Ladies of Parliament (Scotland) (as in English Table)
Wives of Eldest Sons of Viscounts
Daughters of Viscounts
Wives of Younger Sons of Earls
Wives of Eldest Sons of Barons or Lords of Parliament (Scotland)
Daughters of Barons or Lords of Parliament (Scotland)
Wives of Knights of the Garter
Privy Counsellors (Women)
Wives of Younger Sons of Viscounts
Wives of Younger Sons of Barons
Wives of Baronets
Wives of Knights of the Thistle
Dames Grand Cross of Orders (as in English Table)
Wives of Knights Grand Cross and Knights Grand Commanders of Orders (as in English Table)
Dames Commanders of Orders (as in English Table)
Wives of Knights Commanders of Orders (as in English Table)
Wives of Knights Bachelor and Wives of Senators of the College of Justice (Lords of Session) including the wife of the Chairman of the Scottish Land Court[1]
Commanders of the Order of St. Michael and St. George
Thence as in English Tables

PRECEDENCE IN NORTHERN IRELAND

Noblemen and Gentlemen who have personal precedence above that of their Official rank will take the higher precedence. Officials

---

[1] Taking precedence among themselves according to the dates of their husbands' creation as Knights or appointment as Senators of the College of Justice, respectively.

of the United Kingdom not mentioned in this Table will take rank according to the Table of Precedence when in Northern Ireland.

The wife of the Governor of Northern Ireland will, unless she is entitled to higher precedence in her own right, have precedence next after the wives of the nephews of the Sovereign. Any other lady whose husband's precedence is governed by his official rank will be granted that precedence, unless she is entitled to higher precedence in her own right. In all other cases the Table of Precedence in England is followed.

THE SOVEREIGN

Governor of Northern Ireland in the absence of The Sovereign

Heir Apparent (The Prince of Wales)[1]

Relatives of The Sovereign (as in English Table)

Lieutenants of Counties at large, the Lieutenants of Belfast and Londonderry, and the High Sheriffs of Counties at large within the bounds of their respective jurisdictions, and in order above stated, shall have precedence next after the Royal Family and the Governor of Northern Ireland.

Primates of Ireland and other Archbishops according to the dates of their consecration or translation; and the Moderator of the General Assembly of the Presbyterian Church in Ireland according to the date of election.

Prime Minister of Northern Ireland

Lord Mayor of Belfast and the Mayors of Boroughs in Northern Ireland within the bounds of their Cities; but if within the precincts of their City Halls they shall be granted precedence next after the Royal Family and the Governor of Northern Ireland

Recorders of Boroughs in Northern Ireland at civic functions within the bounds of their Boroughs

High Sheriffs of Belfast and Londonderry at civic functions within the bounds of their Boroughs

Peers and their Sons (as in English Table, except the Sons mentioned below), but after Younger Sons of Marquesses and before Barons of England appear all Bishops of the Church of Ireland and all Roman Catholic Bishops in Ireland, according to the date of consecration

---

[1] By Royal Warrant dated 18th September, 1952, it was declared that H.R.H. the Duke of Edinburgh was henceforth to have precedence next to H.M. The Queen, but in the absence of Her Majesty, the Governor, as her representative, would take first place.

Lord Chief Justice of Northern Ireland
Speaker of the Senate of Northern Ireland
Speaker of the House of Commons of Northern Ireland
Minister of Finance of Northern Ireland
Minister of Home Affairs of Northern Ireland
Minister of Health and Social Services of Northern Ireland
Minister of Education of Northern Ireland
Minister of Agriculture of Northern Ireland
Minister of Commerce of Northern Ireland
Minister of Development of Northern Ireland
Minister of Community Relations of Northern Ireland
Eldest Sons of Viscounts
Younger Sons of Earls
Eldest Sons of Barons
Knights of the Garter
Knights of the Thistle[1]
Privy Counsellors
Senior Naval Officer In Charge in Northern Ireland waters, the General Officer Commanding Northern Ireland, and the Air Officer Commanding Northern Ireland, their relative rank and precedence being determined by the Queen's Regulations on the subject

Attorney General of Northern Ireland
Lord Justices of Appeal in Northern Ireland
Judges of the High Court of Justice in Northern Ireland
Recorders of Boroughs in Northern Ireland within the bounds of their Boroughs other than at civic functions

High Sheriffs of Belfast and Londonderry within the bounds of their Boroughs otherwise than at civic functions

Younger Sons of Viscounts
Younger Sons of Barons
Baronets
Knights Grand Cross and Commanders, Knights Commanders, and Knights Bachelor (as in English Table)

Town Clerks and the City Chamberlain of Belfast and Boroughs in Northern Ireland within the precincts of their Cities

Judges of County Courts in Northern Ireland (including Recorders of Boroughs outside the bounds of their Boroughs)

[1] Then follow the Knights of St. Patrick of whom only two survive, the Dukes of Gloucester and Windsor, who are accorded earlier places as the Sovereign's uncles.

Companions, Commanders and Officers of Orders of Chivalry, Eldest Sons of Younger Sons of Peers, Eldest Sons of Baronets, Knights of the Garter and Knights, Members of the Royal Victorian Order, Members of the Order of the British Empire, Younger sons of Baronets and Knights (as in English Table)

Permanent Secretary to the Ministry of Finance of Northern Ireland

Permanent Secretary to the Cabinet of Northern Ireland

Permanent Secretary to the Ministry of Home Affairs of Northern Ireland

Permanent Secretary to the Ministry of Health and Social Services of Northern Ireland

Permanent Secretary to the Ministry of Education of Northern Ireland

Permanent Secretary to the Ministry of Agriculture of Northern Ireland

Permanent Secretary to the Ministry of Commerce of Northern Ireland

Permanent Secretary to the Ministry of Development of Northern Ireland

Clerk of the Parliaments of Northern Ireland

Comptroller and Auditor-General of Northern Ireland

Parliamentary Draughtsman of Northern Ireland

Chief Crown Solicitor of Northern Ireland

Clerk of the Privy Council of Northern Ireland

Queen's Counsel of Northern Ireland

Inspector-General of the Royal Ulster Constabulary

Esquires

Gentlemen

NOTES ON ORDER OF PRECEDENCE

The Tables of Precedence for use in England and Wales and in Scotland, which appear on pages 323–332, are arranged in two lists, one for gentlemen, the other for ladies. Wives of the holders of certain offices do not derive a title from their husbands (e.g. Bishops, Ministers of the Crown, etc.) and so do not appear in the ladies table: they are nonetheless accorded the same precedence as their husbands when both attend a function. It may also be desirable to accord them their husband's precedence even when he is not present.

The Table for England and Wales does not include the following:

(a) The direct representative of the Queen in the County under his jurisdiction i.e. The Lord Lieutenant.
(b) Lord Mayors and Mayors (England and Wales): Lord Provosts and Provosts (Scotland).
(c) The High Sheriff of the County.
(d) Officers of the Armed Forces.

The Tables of Precedence are particularly valuable for placing the holders of various offices in their correct order, e.g. The Speaker of the House of Commons ranks above the Bishop of London.

ROYAL FAMILY

Certain Members of the Royal Family are assigned places in the Tables according to their relationship to The Queen, viz.:

Gentlemen	*Ladies*
The Duke of Edinburgh	Queen Elizabeth The Queen Mother
The Prince of Wales	The Princess Anne
The Duke of Gloucester	The Princess Margaret, Countess of Snowdon
	The Duchess of Gloucester

Those not specifically mentioned by their relationship to the Queen are:

The Duke of Kent	The Princess Alexandra, The Hon. Mrs. Angus Ogilvy
Prince William of Gloucester	The Duchess of Kent
Prince Richard of Gloucester	Princess Alice, Countess of Athlone
Prince Michael of Kent	

These are customarily placed before all non-Royal guests.

PEERS, PEERESSES AND THEIR CHILDREN

Commonsense must be used in deciding the precedence to be accorded to peers, peeresses, and their children. It is often necessary to take age and other factors into account. For example, it is usually unwise to seat the younger son of a Marquess above a Baron, simply because this is how he ranks in the Table of Precedence, when the former is a youth of 20 and the latter an old gentleman of 80. Again, it may be best to sit a high ranking officer in one of the Armed Forces, or the Chairman and Managing Director of a firm, with a low place in the Table, above a peer who, although he has a much higher place in the Table is only a junior officer or employee.

OFFICERS OF THE ARMED FORCES, OF THE FOREIGN AND
COMMONWEALTH SERVICE, AND THE CIVIL SERVICE

Senior members can be placed according to the Tables of Precedence as peers, knights or members of an Order of Chivalry. Where an officer of senior rank has not received an honour covered by the Tables, he is usually placed before an officer of junior rank who is, nonetheless, senior to him in the Tables, e.g. a Major-General with no more than an O.B.E. should be placed before a Brigadier with a C.B.E.

IMPORTANT PEOPLE IN INDUSTRY, THE PROFESSIONS, IN THE
ACADEMIC AND ARTISTIC FIELDS

Except for the few who have received the honours mentioned in the Tables of Precedence, discretion must be used in placing these so that relative importance in their respective fields is adequately recognized.

PRECEDENCE OF CIVIC HEADS IN GREATER LONDON

These have the following precedence among themselves:

(a) The Lord Mayor or Mayor in whose City or Borough the function takes place.
(b) The Lord Mayor of London.
(c) The Chairman of the Greater London Council.
(d) The Lord Mayor of Westminster.
(e) The Mayor of the Royal Borough of Kensington and Chelsea.
(f) The Mayor of the Royal Borough of Kingston upon Thames.
(g) The Mayor of other London Boroughs, in alphabetical order of their Boroughs.

Rules for Hoisting Flags on Government Buildings

The following regulations are circulated by Her Majesty's Command.

DATES ON WHICH FLAGS ARE TO BE FLOWN

The dates named on the Schedule below.

The only additions will be those which are notified to the Ministry of Housing and Construction by Her Majesty's Command.

PROVINCIAL BUILDINGS

This Schedule applies to Provincial as well as to London Buildings (but see Notes 1 and 3). Where it has been the practice—as in the case of some Custom Houses—to fly the flag daily, this may continue.

OCCASIONS ON WHICH FLAGS ARE TO BE FLOWN AT HALF MAST

(a) From the announcement of the death up to the funeral of the Sovereign, except on Proclamation Day, when they are hoisted right up from 11 a.m. to sunset.

(b) The funerals of members of the Royal Family, subject to special commands from Her Majesty in each case.

(c) The funerals of Heads of States, subject to special commands from Her Majesty in each case.

(d) The funerals of Prime Ministers and former Prime Ministers of the United Kingdom.

(e) Other occasions by special command of Her Majesty, which will be communicated by the Ministry of Housing and Construction to other Departments.

RULES WHEN DAYS FOR FLYING FLAGS COINCIDE WITH DAYS FOR FLYING FLAGS AT HALF MAST

To be flown—

(a) although a member of the Royal Family, or a near relative of the Royal Family, may be lying dead, unless special commands be received from Her Majesty to the contrary:

(b) although it may be the day of the funeral of a Head of State.

If the body of a very distinguished subject is lying at a Government Office the flag may fly at half-mast on that office until the body has left (provided it is a day on which the flag would fly) and then the flag is to be hoisted right up. On all other Public Buildings the flag will fly as usual.

DAYS FOR HOISTING FLAGS ON GOVERNMENT BUILDINGS

From 8 a.m. till sunset

6th February—Her Majesty's Accession
19th February—Birthday of The Prince Andrew
1st March—St. David's Day (See Note 1(a))
10th March—Birthday of The Prince Edward
31st March—Birthday of The Duke of Gloucester
21st April—Birthday of Her Majesty The Queen
23rd April—St. George's Day (See Note 1(b))
2nd June—Coronation Day
. . . June (as appointed)—Official Celebration of Her Majesty's Birthday, which is also Commonwealth Day
10th June—Birthday of The Duke of Edinburgh
4th August—Birthday of Her Majesty Queen Elizabeth The Queen Mother
15th August—Birthday of The Princess Anne
21st August—Birthday of The Princess Margaret
November—Remembrance Day (See Note 2)
14th November—Birthday of The Prince of Wales
20th November—Her Majesty's Wedding Day
30th November—St. Andrew's Day (See Note 1(c)

Also : The day of the opening of a Session of the Houses of Parliament by Her Majesty. (See Note 3)

The day of the prorogation of a Session of the Houses of Parliament by Her Majesty. (See Note 3)

Note 1.—(a) Flags should be flown on this day in Wales only.
(b) Flags should be flown on this day in England only.
(c) Flags should be flown on this day in Scotland only.

Where a building has two or more flagstaffs the appropriate National flag may be flown in addition to the Union Jack (properly the Union Flag), but not in a superior position.[1]

Note 2.—Remembrance Day is the second Sunday in November. Flags should be flown right up all day.

[1] When two or more flagstaffs are available, the superior position is the flagstaff furthest to the left, as seen by an observer looking at the front of the building from outside it.

Note 3.—Flags should be flown on this day irrespective of whether or not Her Majesty performs the ceremony in person, but only from buildings in the Greater London area.

Note 4.—The Royal Standard is never hoisted when Her Majesty is passing in procession; if The Queen is to be present in a building, instructions should be sought through the Ministry of Housing and Construction.

PRONUNCIATION OF TITLES AND SURNAMES

'Ch' in Scottish, Welsh and Irish names is pronounced as in 'loch'. Mac is not normally stressed so the 'a' is hardly pronounced at all. In Scots the letter 'z' stood for a gutteral 'y', which explains why Menzies was originally Meyners; also Elizabeth (English) is spelt Elisabeth in Scotland.

The Scots 'l' in such prefixes as Col, Fal, Bal, and Dal was usually not pronounced, and 'quh' was the Scots way of writing. 'wh' (e.g. 'what' was spelt 'quhat'). This explains the pronunciation of Colquhoun.

Names ending in intrusive forms for s (e.g. ys, yss and is), the vowel should not be pronounced, such as in Wemyss, Inglis and Spottiswoode.

Abercrombie	Aber-crum-by
Abergavenny	Aber-*genny* (title) (hard 'g'); town as spelt
Abinger	Abin-jer
Alleyne	Alleen
Alnwick	Annick
Althorp	*All*-trup
Altrincham	Altringham
Alvingham	All-ving-am
Aman	Amman
Ampthill	Ampt-hill
Annesley	*Anns*-li
Apethorpe	App-thorp
Arbuthnot(t)	Ar-*buth*-not
Ardee	Ar-*dee*
Arundel	*Arun*-del
Ashburnham	Ash-*burn*-am
Assheton	*Ash*-ton

Atholl	*Uh*-thol or *Ah*-thol
Auchinleck	Affleck or as spelt
Audley	*Awd*-li
Ava	Ah-va
Ayscough	Askew
Baden-Powell	Bayden-Poell
Bagot	*Bag*-ot
Balcarres	Bal-*carris*
Balogh	Balog (Bal as in Hal)
Bampfylde	*Bam*-field
Baring	*Bear*-ing
Barnardiston	*Bar*-nar-*dis*-ton
Barttelot	Bartlot
Basing	Bayzing
Bathurst	*Bath*-urst (a as in cat)
Beauchamp	Beecham
Beauclerk	Bo-clare
Beaudesert	Bodezair
Beaufort	*Bo*-foot
Beaulieu	*Bew*-ly
Beaumont	Bo-mont
Becher	Beacher
Bedingfeld	Beddingfield
Bellew	*Bell*-ew
Bellingham	Bellingjam
Belvoir	Beevor
Beresford	*Berris*-fud
Berkeley	Barkli
Bertie	Barti
Bethune	Beaton
Bicester	Bister
Blakiston	Blackiston
Bledisloe	Bledslow
Blenheim	*Blen*-im
Bligh	Bly
Blois	Bloyss
Blomefield	Bloomfield
Blount	Blunt
Blyth	Bly
Boevey	Boovey
Bolingbroke	*Bulling*-brook

Boord	Board
Boreel	Borale
Borrowes	Burrows
Borwick	Borrick
Bosanquet	*Bozen*-ket
Boscawen	Bos-*cowen*
Botetourt	Botti-tort
Boughey	Boey
Boughton	Bought-on (family)
	Bough-ton (N'hamptonshire)
Bourchier	*Bough*-cher
Bourke	Burke
Bowden (Aylestone)	Bowden (as in now)
Bowden (Baron)	Bowden (as in no)
Bowes	Bose (to rhyme with rose)
Bowman	Boman
Bowyer	Bo-yer (as in no)
Brabazon	*Brab*-azon
Brabourne	*Bray*-burn
Breadalbane	Bread-*au*burn
Brereton	Breer-ton
Brocas	Brockas
Broke	Brook (but H.M.S. Broke as spelt)
Bromhead	Brumhead
Brougham	Broom
Broughton	Brawton
Broun	Brune
Bruntisfield	Bruntsfield
Buccleuch	Buck-*cloo*
Bulkeley	Buckley
Burgh	Borough
Burghersh	Burg-ish
Burghley	Ber-li
Bury	Berry (England)
	Bure-y (Ireland)
Caccia	Catch-a
Cadogan	Ka-*dugan*
Caius	Keys (College)
Caldecote	Call-di-cot
Calderon	*Call*-dron
Callaghan	*Calla*-han

Calverley	*Car*-verly
Camoys	Cam-oyz
Capell	*Cay*ple
Carew	As spelt—Cary has generally become archaic[1]
Calthorpe	*Call*-thorpe—Cal-trop has become archaic
Carnegie	Car-*neggie*
Carteret	*Carter*-et
Cavanagh	*Cava*-na
Cassilis	Cassels
Castlereagh	*Castle*-ray
Cavan	*Cav*-en (a as in cat)
Cecil	Cecil (Salisbury line)
	Cicil (Exeter lines)
Chandos	Shandos
Charlemont	Shar-le-mont
Charteris	As spelt—Charters is becoming archaic[2]
Chattan	Hattan
Chernocke	Char-nock
Chetwode	Chetwood
Chetwynd	Chetwind
Cheylesmore	*Chyles*-more
Cheyne	Chain
Chisholm	*Chis*-um
Cholmeley ⎫	
Cholmondeley ⎭	*Chum*-li
Claverhouse	Clayvers
Clerk	Clark
Clough	Cluff
Clwyd	*Cloo*-id
Cochrane	*Coch*-ran
Cockburn	*Co*-bun
Coke	Cook (Earl of Leicester) and others, but sometimes as spelt
Colquhoun	Ca-hoon
Combermere	*Cumber*-mere
Compton	Cumpton (usually)
Conesford	*Connis*-ford
Conolly	*Con*-olly

[1] Sometimes Pool-Carey, but usually Carew Pole.
[2] The old pronunciation of Charters is correct, for it is the French place name of Chartres in origin.

Conyngham(e)	Cunningham
Cottesloe	*Cots*-low
Cowper	Cooper
Cozens	Cuzzens
Craigavon	Craig-*avv*-on
Creagh	Cray
Creighton	Cryton
Crombie	Crumbie
Crespigny	See De Crespigny
Crichton	Cryton
Cromartie	*Crum*-aty
Culme	Cullum
Cuming	Cumming
Cunynghame	Cunningham
Dacre	Dayker
Dalhousie	Dal-*howsi*
Dalmeny	Dul-*menny*
Dalyell ⎫	
Dalzell ⎭	Dee-el
Darcy de Knaith	Darcy de Nayth
Daresbury	Darsbury
Daventry	As spelt—Daintry now archaic
De Blacquiere	De Black-yer
De Burgh	De Burg
Decies	Desshies
De Courcy	De Kursey
De Crespigny	De *Crepp*-ni
De Freyne	De Frain
De Hoghton	De Horton
De la Warr	Della-ware
Delamere	Della-mare
De la Rue	Della-rue
De L'Isle	De Lyle
De Moleyns	*Demo*-lins
Dering	*Deer*-ing
De Ros	De Roos
Derwent	Darwent
De Salis	De *Saals*
De Saumarez ⎫	De *Summer*-ez
De Sausmarez ⎭	De *Summer*-ez
Devereux	Dev-rooks (Viscount Hereford)
	or Dever-oo

De Vesci	De *Vessy*
De Villiers	De Villers
Dilhorne	*Dill'*n
Doneraile	Dunnaral
Donoughmore	Duno-more
Doune	Doun
Douro	*Dur*-o
Drogheda	*Droye*-da
Drumalbyn	Drum-*albin*
Duchesnes	Du *Karns*, but sometimes as spelt
Ducie	*Dew*-si
Du Cros	Du *Crow*
Dumaresq	Du-*merrick*
Dunally	Dun-*alley*
Dundas	Dun-*das*
Dungarvan	Dun-*gar*-van
Dunglass	Dun-*glass*
Dunsany	Dun-*saney*
Duntze	Dunts
Du Plat	Du-Pla
Dupplin	*Dupp*-lin
Durand	*Du*-rand
Dymoke	Dimmock
Dynevor	*Dinny*-ver
Dysart	*Dy*-z't
Ebury	*Ee*-bri
Echlin	Eck-lin
Edwardes	Edwards
Egan	*Ee*-gan
Egerton	*Edger*-ton
Elcho	Elco
Elgin	El-gin (hard g)
Elibank	Elli-bank
Elveden	*Elve*-den (place Elden)
Elwes	*El*-wes
Ernle	Earnley
Eveleigh	*Eve*-ley
Every	As spelt
Eyton	*I*-tun
Falconer	Fawkner
Falkiner	Fawkner

Faringdon	Farringdon
Farquhar	Farkwar
Farquharson	Farkwerson
Fayrer	Fair-er
Featherstonhaugh	Fetherston-haugh or occasionally Fetherston[1]
Feilding	*Field*ing
Fenwick	*Fenn*ick
Fergusson	Ferguson
Fermor	Farmer
Feversham	Fevver-sham (place Favversham)
Ffolliott	*Foll*-y-ot
ffolkes	Foaks
Fiennes	Fines
Fingall	Fin-*gawl*
Fitzhardinge	Fitzharding
Foljambe	Full-jum
Forestier	Forest-tier
Foulis	Fowls
Fowke	Foke
Fremantle	*Free*-mantle
Freyberg	*Fry*-burg
Furneaux	*Fur*-no
Gairdner	Gardner
Galway	Gaulway
Garioch	Garey
Garvagh	*Gar*-va
Gathorne	Gaythorn
Geoghegan	*Gay*-gan
Gerrard	Jerrard
Gervis	Jervis
Giffard	Jiffard
Gifford	Jifford
Gill	As spelt (hard g)
Gillespie	Gill-*es*-py
Gilmour	Gillmoor
Glamis	Glahms
Glasgow	*Glass*-go
Glenavy	Glen-*avy* (as in day)
Glerawly	Gler-*awly*

[1] I can find no record that this name was even pronounced Fanshaw or Feeston as is popularly believed.

Gorges	Gorjes
Gormanstown	*Gor*-mans-ton
Goschen	*Go*-shen
Gough	Goff
Goulding	Goolding
Gower	Gore
	(Gower Peninsula and Gower St., London, as spelt)
Graeme	*Gray*-um
Greaves	Graves
Grosvenor	*Grove*-nor
Guise	Gyze
Haden-Guest	Hayden-Gest (hard 'g')
Haldane	*Hall*-dane
Halsey	*Hall*-sey
Halsbury	*Halls*-bry
Hamond	Hammond
Harcourt	*Har*-cut
Hardinge	Harding
Harewood	*Har*-wood (title)
	Hare-wood (village)
Harington	Harrington
Hawarden	*Hay*-warden
	Harden for the title has become archaic
Heathcoat ⎫ Heathcote ⎭	Hethcut
Heneage	Hennidge
Hepburn	*Heb*-b'n
Herschell	*Her*-shell
Hertford	*Har*-ford
Hervey	Harvey
Hever	Heaver
Heytesbury	*Hetts*-b'ry
Heywood	Haywood
Hindlip	*Hynd*-lip
Hobart	Hubbard
Hogan	*Ho*-gan
Holbech	*Hole*-beech
Home	Hume
Honywood	Honeywood
Hopetoun	Hopeton
Horsbrugh	Horsbro'

Hotham	*Huth*-am
Howick	Hoyck
Hugessen	*Hu*-ges-*son* (hard 'g')
Hylton	Hilton
Iddesleigh	*Idd*-sli
Ikerrin	I-kerrin
Iliffe	I-liffe
Inchiquin	Inch-quin
Inchrye	Inch-rye
Inchyra	Inch-*eye-ra*
Ingestre	Ingustry (like industry)
Inglis	Ingles
Inigo	*Inni*-go
Innes	Inniss
Inveraray	Inver-*air*-a
Isham	I-sham
Iveagh	I-va
Jervis	as spelt
Jervoise	Jervis
Jocelyn	Josslin
Joliffe	*Joll*-if
Kavenagh	*Kavan*-a
Keighley	*Keith*-li
Kemeys	Kemmis
Kennard	Ken-*ard*
Kenyon	*Ken*-yon
Ker ⎫ Kerr ⎭	Carr
Keynes	Kaynes
Killanin	Kil-*lah*-nin
Kilmorey	Kil-*murray*
Kingsale	King-*sale*
Kinnoull	Kin-*ool*
Kirkcudbright	Cuc-*coo*-bri
Knollys	Nowles
Kylsant	Kill-*sant*
Knyvett	Nivett
Lacon	*Lay*-kon
Laffan	Laf-*fan*
Lascelles	*Lass*-ells
Lathom	*Lay*-thom
LaTouche	La *Toosh*

Latymer	Latimer
Laurie	Lorry
Layard	Laird
Lechmere	Letchmere
Le Fanu	*Leff*-new
Lefevre	Le-*fever*
Legard	Le-jard
Legh	Lee
Leighton	Layton
Leinster	Linster
Leitrim	Leetrim
Le Mesurier	Le *Mezz*-erer
Leven	*Lee*-ven
Leverhulme	*Leaver*-hume
Leveson-Gower	Loosun-Gore
Levinge	As spelt
Levy	Levvy or Leevi
Ley	Ley
Leycester	Lester
Lisle	Lyle
Listowel	Lis-*toe*-ell
Londesborough	Londs-bro'
Londonderry	*London*d'ry (title)
	London-*Derry* (City)
Loudon	*Loud*-on
Loughborough	*Luff*-bro
Louth	(England) *th* as in mouth
	(Ireland) *th* as in breathe
Lovat	Luv-at
Lowson	*Lo*-son (low as in go)
Lowther	*Low*-ther (as in now)
Lygon	Liggon
Lyon	Lion
Lysaght	Ly-set
Lyveden	*Live*-den (as in give)
Macara	Mac-*ara*
Macbean	Mac-*bain*
McCorquodale	M'*cork*-o-dale
McCulloch	M'*cull*-och
McEvoy	*Mac*-evoy
McEwan } Ewen }	Mac-*ewen*

McFadzean	Mac *fadd*-yen
McGillycuddy	*Mac*-li-*cuddy*
Machell	*May*-chel
McIvor	Mac-*Ivor*
McKay	M'*Kye* (as in eye)
McKie	*Mack*-ie
Maclean	Mac-*layne*
Macleay	Mac-*lay*
Macleod	Mac-*loud*
Macnaghten	Mac-*nawton*
Macmahon	Mac-*mahn*
Maelor	Myla
Magdala	Mag-*dahla*
Magdalen ⎫ Magdalene ⎭	Maudlin
Magrath	Ma-*grah*
Mahon	Mahn or Ma-*han*
Mahony	*Mah*-ni
Mainwaring	*Manner*-ing
Mais	Mayz
Majendie	Maj-*endy*
Makgill	Mc*Gill*
Malpas	*Mawl*-pas
Malet	Mallet
Malmsbury	*Marms*-bri
Mandeville	Mande-ville (first 'e' slightly inflected)
Mansergh	Manser
Margesson	*Mar*-jesson
Marjoribanks	Marchbanks
Marlborough	*Maul*-bro
Masham	*Mass*-ham
Masserene	Mazereen
Maunsell	*Man*-sol
Meath	Meeth (th as in breathe)
Meiklejohn	*Mickel*-john
Melhuish	*Mell*-ish
Menteth	Men-*teeth*
Menzies	Ming-iz (Scotland)
Merioneth	Merry-*on*-eth
Mereworth	*Merry*-worth
Metcalfe	Met-calf

Methuen	Meth-wen
Meux	Mews
Meynell	*Men*-el
Meyrick	Merr-ick
Michelham	*Mitch*-lam
Michie	Micky
Midleton	*Middle*-ton
Millais	*Mill*-ay
Molyneux	{ *Mully*-neux { *Mully*-nu
Monck	Munk
Monckton	Munkton
Moncreiffe } Moncrieff }	Mun-*creef*
Monro	Mun-*roe*
Monson	Munsun
Montagu	*Mon*-tagu
Montgomery } Montgomerie }	Mun-*gum*-eri
Monzie	M'*nee*
Moran	Moor-*an*
Moray	Murray
Mordaunt	*Mor*-dant
Mosley	Mozeley
Mostyn	*Moss*-tin
Moulton	*Mole*-ton
Mountmorres	Mount-morris
Mowbray	*Mo*-bray
Moynihan	*Moyni*-han
Munro	Mun-*roe*
Myddelton	Middle-ton
Naas	Nace
Naesmyth	*Nay*-smith
Nall	Nawl
Napier	*Nay*-pier
Nathan	Naythan
Nepean	Ne-*peen*
Newburgh	*New*-bro'
Niven	Nivven
Northcote	*North*-cut
Nunburnholme	Nun-burnham
Ochterlony	Ochter-*lony*

Ogilvie ⎫ Ogilvy ⎭	*Ogle*-vi
O'Hagan	O'*Hay*-gan
Olivier	⎧O-livier ⎩O-liviay
O'Loghlen	O'*Loch*-len
Ormonde	*Or*-mund
O'Shaughnessy	O'*shaw*-nessy
Outram	*Oot*-ram
Pakington	Packington
Paget	*Paj*-it
Pakenham	*Pack*-en'um
Pasley	*Pais*-ly
Paton	Payton
Paulet	*Paul*-et
Paunceforte	*Pawns*-fort
Pauncefote	*Pawns*-foot
Pechell	*Peach*-ell
Pennefather	*Penn*-ifither
Pennycuick	*Penny*-cook
Pepys	Peppis (Peeps has become archaic, except for the Diarist)
Perceval	Percival
Pery	Pairy
Peto	*Peet*-o
Petre	Peter
Petrie	*Peet*-rie
Phayre	Fair
Pierpoint	Pierpont
Pleydell	Pleddel
Plowden	Ploughden
Plumtre	*Plum*-tri
Pole	Pole (see also Carew)
Poltimore	Pole-ti-more
Polwarth	*Pol*-worth
Ponsonby	Punsunby
Poulett	*Paul*-et
Powell	Powell (as in now) usually, or Poell
Powerscourt	*Poers*-caut
Powis	Po-iss (Earl)
Powlett	*Paul*-et

Powys	Po-iss (name)
	Powiss (place) (as in now)
Praed	Praid
Prevost	*Prev*-o
Puleston	*Pill*-ston
Pytchley	*Pietch*-li
Quibell	Quy-bel (as in high)
Raleigh	*Raw*-li
Ranfurly	*Ran*-fully
Rankeillour	Rank-illour
Ratendone	Ratten-dun
Rathdonnel	Rath-*donnell*
Rea	Ree
Rearsby	*Rears*-bi
Reay	Ray
Redesdale	*Reads*-dale
Renwick	*Renn*-ick
Reresby	*Rears*-bi[1]
Reuter	*Roy*-ter
Rhys	Rees (usually), or Rice
Riddell	*Rid*dle
Roborough	*Roe*-bro'
Roche	Roach, *or* sometimes Rosh
Roden	Roe-den
Rolleston	*Roll*-ston
Romilly	*Rum*-illy
Romney	Rumney
Ronaldshay	*Ron*-ald-shay
Rotherwick	as spelt
Rothes	*Roth*-is
Rous ⎫	
Rouse ⎭	Rowse (as in grouse)
Rowley	*Roe*-li
Roxburghe	Rox-bro'
Ruthin	Ruth-in (as the girl's name)
Ruthven	Rivven
Sacheverall	Sash-*ever*-al
Sacheverell	Sash-*ev*-rell
St. Aubyn	St. *Aw*-bin
St. Clair	Correctly Sinclair, but sometimes as spelt

[1] Roars-by has become archaic.

St. Cyres	Sin-cere
St. John	Sin-jun
St. Leger	Correctly *Sill*-inger but sometimes St. Leger
St. Levan	S'nt Leaven (as in leaven for bread)
St. Maur	*Sea*-mer
Salisbury	*Sawls*-bri
Saltoun	*Salt*-on
Salusbury	*Sawls*-bri
Sandbach	Sandbatch
Sandys	Sands
Sanquhar	Sanker (Sanwer is historically correct)
Saumarez ⎫ Sausmarez ⎭	Summer-ez
Savernake	Savver-nack
Savile	Saville
Saye and Sele	Say and Seal
Schuster	*Shoo*-ster
Sclater	Slater
Scone	Scoon
Scrymgeour	*Scrim*-jer
Segal	Seagal
Segrave	Sea-grave
Sempill	Semple
Seton	Seaton
Seymour	Seamer
Shakerley	As spelt
Shaughnessy	Shawnessy
Shrewsbury	*Shrows*-b'ry
Shuckburgh	*Shuck*-bro'
Sieff	Seef
Simey	Symey
Smijthe	Smythe
Smyth	Smith or Smythe
Smythe	Smythe[1]
Somers	Summers
Somerset	Summerset
Soulbury	*Sool*-bri
Southwark	*Suth*-erk

[1] The family of Smyth of Methven, Scotland, is pronounced 'Smith of Meffane'.

Southwell	*Suth*-ell (surname and city)
Spottiswoode	Spotswood
Stanhope	Stannup
Stavordale	*Stav*-erdale
Stonor	Stone-er
Stourton	Sturton
Strabane	Stra-*bann*
Strabolgi	Stra-*bogie* (hard 'g')
Strachan	
Straghan	Strawn
Strahan	
Strachie	*Stray*-chie
Stratheden	Strath-*eden*
Strathspey	Strath-*spay*
Stucley	*Stewke*-li
Suirdale	Sure-dale
Synge	Sing
Talbot	Tallbot
Tangye	Tang-y
Taylour	Taylor
Teignmouth	*Tin*-muth
Teynham	*Ten*-'am
Thame	Tame
Thellusson	*Tellus*-son
Thesiger	*Thesi*-jer
Thorold	Thurrald
Thynne	Thin
Tighe	Tie
Tollemache	*Tol*-mash[1]
Torphichen	Tor-*fikken*
Touchet	*Touch*-et
Tgvey	Tuvvy
Trafalgar	Traffle-*gar* (title)
Traquair	Tra-*quare*
Trefusis	Tre-*fusis*
Trevelyan	Tre-*villian*
Trimlestown	Trimmels-ton
Trowbridge	Troobridge
Tuchet	*Touch*-et
Tuite	Tute
Tullibardine	Tulli-*bard*-in

[1] The old pronunciation Tall-mash has become archaic.

Turnour	Turner
Tuvey	Tuvvy
Twysden	Twis-den
Tynte	Tint
Tyrrell	Tirrell
Tyrwhit	Tirrit
Urquhart	*Urk*-ut
Uvedale	*Youv*-dale
Valentia	Val-*en*-shia
Vaughan	Vawn
Vaux	Vokes
Vesey	Veezy
Vigor	Vygor
Villiers	Villers
Vyvyan	Vivian
Waechter	Vechter (guttural ch)
Wagner	As spelt (English families)
Waldegrave	Wall-grave
Waleran	*Wall*-ran
Walrond	*Wall*-rond
Wauchope	*Walk*-up (ch as in loch)
Waugh	As spelt, to rhyme with flaw
Wellesley	*Wells*-li
Wemyss	Weems
Wernher	Werner
Westenra	*Westen*-ra
Westmeath	West-*meath* (th as in breathe)
Wharton	*Whor*-ton
Wigram	*Wigg*-ram
Wilbraham	*Will*-bram
Willoughby de Eresby	*Willow*-by *deersby*
Willoughby de Broke	*Willow*-by de *Brook*
Woburn	*Woo*-burn
Wodehouse	*Wood*-house
Wollaston	*Wool*-aston
Wolmer	*Wool*-mer
Wolseley	*Wool*-sli
Wombwell	*Woom*-well
Worsley	*Wers*-li
Wortley	*Wert*-li
Wriothesley	Rottisli[1]

[1] The pronunciation Risely is archaic.

Wrottesley	*Rotts*-li
Wykeham	*Wick*-ham
Wyllie	*Wy*-lie
Wyndham	*Wind*-'am
Wynford	*Win*-fud
Wythenshaw	*With*-in-shaw
Yerburgh	*Yar*-bro'
Yonge	Young
Zouche	Zooch

SPELLING OF PEERAGE TITLES

Note, the following spellings differ from those now adopted for placenames.

England :   Ailesbury, Guilford, Scarbrough, Winchilsea.

Wales :   Carnarvon.

Ireland :   Donegall, Downe, Kingsale, Rosse.

INDEX